To Paul. Leone.
With Love for a happy Xmas 74.
and a good New Year.
from Harry. Sven.

VELÁZQUEZ' WORK
AND WORLD

I. Velázquez, Philip IV in brown and silver. 1631–2.
London, National Gallery

VELÁZQUEZ' WORK AND WORLD

by

JOSÉ LÓPEZ-REY

FABER AND FABER

24 Russell Square

London

First published in 1968
by Faber & Faber Limited
24 Russell Square, London W.C.1
This book incorporates some
material from 'Velázquez:
A Catalogue Raisonné of his Oeuvre'
by José López-Rey
published by Faber and Faber in 1963
Printed in Great Britain by
R. MacLehose and Company Limited
The University Press Glasgow

FOR JUSTA

Viva vida viva

CONTENTS

CONTENTS

ILLUSTRATIONS

COLOUR PLATES

MONOCHROME PLATES

The list of the monochrome plates will be found at the end of the book,
on pages 165–72, immediately preceding the plates themselves.

The publishers and the author are grateful to those whose generosity,
courtesy and effort have facilitated the reproduction of the paintings and
drawings which illustrate this book.

The radiographs of paintings at the Prado Museum (plates 42, 46, 49,
56, 61, 86, 115, 116, 129, and 155) were taken by the technical staff of the
National Gallery of Stockholm and have been made available for reproduction by the Prado. Dr. Enriqueta Harris, of the Warburg Institute,
has lent the photograph for plate 144, and Professor Ellis Waterhouse, of
the Barber Institute, that for plate 139.

The photographs for plates 6, 20, and 91 are respectively from Más,
A. C. Cooper, and Hauser y Menet. Those used for the rest of the plates
have been supplied by private or public collections, or are the author's
property.

FOREWORD

In the pages that follow, I offer an interpretation of Velázquez as a creator and, as such, a historical individual. In pursuit of my aim, I have delved into the artistic traditions, trends and usages and the way of life and thought of the world into which he was born and in which he lived. I have also taken into account the personal, national and world events which were part of his experience. I have, nevertheless, mainly drawn the substance of my interpretation from what Velázquez created out of his own mind, feeling and work: his paintings, every extant one of which I have fortunately been able to study in the original, unhurriedly, with leisure enough to answer my own questions, and even to verify the validity of my answers before the very works that provoked them.

This study was originally conceived as introductory to my *catalogue raisonné* of Velázquez's *oeuvre*, and it appeared as such, in a shorter form, in 1963.[1] As I then explained, connoisseurship cannot be, and has never been, divorced from the interpretative approach to the history of art. Even the matter-of-fact collector, the *valet de culture* or, for that matter, the cataloguer who stolidly believes that the stylistic elements of a work of art are tangible and can be pigeonholed in a ready-made system of art-trends or period-classification, postulates some sort of historical understanding, however crude or stale.

Nor can connoisseurship be based on what some call a painter's handwriting, meaning the sameness of his handiwork. There may perhaps be something comparable to penmanship in a painter's handiwork, but it is dangerous, as oversimplifications always are, to assume an identity between the two. Obviously, a painter's brushstrokes respond to his creative intent, and their structure, texture, sweep and hue are one with his images and compositions. Such, of course, is not the case with the penstrokes that the writer, whether of a letter or a literary work, puts on paper.

If it is possible to establish an analogy between the painter's brushstrokes and any phase of the writer's creative act, one must think of the latter's use of words, which he handles with a feeling for their direct signification, shades of meaning, associations of sound, and literary or colloquial connotations, harmonizing, contrasting, emphasizing or subduing them according to his creative intent.

It is a fact that creative painters develop a manner of their own more readily and more often than do their uncreative fellows. Indeed, great masters, whether of the past or of the present, modify the quality of their brushwork, refining or roughening it, momentarily or lastingly, in response to their own expressive needs. It is also true that pupils, followers, imitators, restorers, and even forgers are sometimes able to acquire or counterfeit a great master's manner, but not his sentience of touch, and hence of image, on which we depend for enjoyment and understanding of his art, as well as for recognition of his hand.

[1] *Velázquez: A Catalogue Raisonné of his Oeuvre, with an Introductory Study*, London, Faber & Faber, 1963.

11

Attributions, whether of works of philosophy, literature or the other arts, must, of course, be consistent with the available historical data concerning both the subject depicted or referred to in the work at issue and the author or artist to whom it is attributed. Likewise, the composition and execution of the work under consideration must tally with what we know from works which are undoubtedly by the artist or writer in question, be it train of thought, syntactic usage, choice of colours or words, handling of pigment, or the like. Ultimately, though, the validity of an attribution rests on whether or not we can discern in the work under study a riveting analogy with the quality of expression, inseparable from actual meaning, exclusively found in works executed by the man whom we claim as its maker. Thus, attributions require an empathic study of the documented authentic works by the master we are concerned with. This is true whether the issue is the *Seventh letter* attributed to Plato, Jonathan Swift's authorship of 'The History of Martin' added to the 1720 edition of *a Tale of A Tub*, or, to refer to Velázquez's Spain, the momentous poem, *Católica, sacra y real majestad*, addressed to Philip IV, held by some to have been written by Quevedo. Coming to Velázquez himself, such is the case, for instance, with the latest addition to the galleries devoted to him at the Prado, a *Christ on the Cross*, which, according to the Museum's catalogue, is a signed and authentic painting by the Master, while I have rather catalogued it as a 'derivative picture, most likely from Velázquez's workshop'.[1]

Early in our century, in 1911, Aureliano de Beruete, author of a monograph on Velázquez which is still rewarding to read, brought to 94 the number of paintings which he held to have been totally or partly executed by Velázquez.[2] During the following fifty years, the main points of Beruete's interpretation of Velázquez's art were adhered to by most scholars, even though some of his attributions were questioned and many new ones were made. The documents bearing on the matter discovered during that time were also more often than not interpreted in the light of Beruete's ideas, even when the newly found data ran counter to his assumptions or conclusions.

In 1925, Juan Allende-Salazar compiled a catalogue which was appended to a perfunctory account of Velázquez's life and art written by Walter Gensel; it included 115 paintings, to which Allende-Salazar himself later added one more, as being totally or in part by the Master.[3] Since then the number and quality of the paintings so regarded has varied considerably, not only from author to author, but even from year to year in the case of some cataloguers. August L. Mayer, author of several valuable studies on Velázquez, including a thorough monograph, brought out in 1936 a comprehensive and well-illustrated *catalogue raisonné* in which he collected a wealth of data on 556 paintings; he regarded 164 of them as having been totally

[1] Op. cit., p. 127, no. 15; Museo del Prado, *Catálogo de las Pinturas*, Madrid, 1963, p. 749, no. 2903.

[2] Beruete's monograph on *Velázquez*, never published in Spanish, appeared first in French (Paris, 1898), then in English (London, 1906), and finally in German (Berlin, 1909). His latest contribution to the subject was *El Velázquez de Parma*, Madrid, 1911. Unless otherwise stated, my subsequent references are to the English edition.

[3] *Velázquez, Des Meisters Gemälde*, vol. VI of *Klassiker der Kunst*, 4th ed., Berlin and Leipzig, n. d. (1925). See also Allende-Salazar's *expertise* of a portrait of *Philip IV* published in the catalogue of the exhibition held at the gallery Tomás Harris Ltd., *From Greco to Goya*, London, 1938, p. 40.

or partly painted by the Master, and the rest as by his assistants, imitators or forgers.[1] In 1943, Enrique Lafuente Ferrari catalogued 122 paintings as by Velázquez, but the following year he produced a new catalogue, omitting six works included in that of 1943 and adding twelve more, thus bringing the total up to 128, which an addition that he made in 1961 increased to 129.[2] Bernardino de Pantorba, borrowing freely from the data collected by Mayer, to the point of appropriating even misprints, assembled a catalogue, printed in 1955, ascribing 123 paintings to Velázquez; in 1960-1, he added six more, and in 1964 he cut down to 115 the total of 129 which he had reached three years earlier.[3] José Camón Aznar, in a catalogue that he does not consider exhaustive, also published in 1964, has included 144 paintings as executed wholly or in part by Velázquez.[4]

The exhibition *Velázquez y lo velazqueño*, held at Madrid in 1960-1 by the Spanish Dirección General de Bellas Artes to commemorate the third centenary of Velázquez's death, brought into the open the widespread confusion that beclouded the understanding of his art. Of the 84 paintings shown under his name, hardly a third were actually by his hand or could reasonably, even if not convincingly, be attributed to him.[5] In fact, the exhibition effectively illustrated the difference between the connoisseur's and what may be called the attributionist's viewpoint. It ought to be noted that, during the period 1936-1960, scholars, experts and museum curators had published in the aggregate no fewer than 194 paintings as having been totally or partly executed by Velázquez.

The interpretation of his art and, as a result, the catalogue of his *oeuvre* had, indeed, become a hit-or-miss patchwork. To cite one example, the suggestion had earnestly been made that the well known fragment of a painting showing the right hand of an ecclesiastic emerging from a black sleeve and holding a paper with Velázquez's signature might be part of a half-length portrait of *Cardinal Borja*, attributed to the Master, in which only the sitter's left arm, in a red sleeve, is visible.[6]

[1] *Velázquez, A Catalogue Raisonné of the Pictures and Drawings*, London, 1936. There are blanks in the numeration of the entries which reaches up to 610, though there are actually only 575. This number includes nineteen drawings, ten of which are catalogued as by Velázquez. Mayer's earlier books on the subject were *Kleine Velázquez-studien*, Munich, 1913, and *Diego Velázquez*, Berlin 1924. Later he published a brief monograph *Velázquez*, Paris, 1940.

[2] *Velázquez*, London, 1943 (it includes ten drawings as by Velázquez in addition to the paintings); *Velázquez*, Barcelona, 1944, and 'Velázquez y Felipe IV' in *Mundo Hispánico*, Madrid, February, 1961, pp. 21-5.

[3] *La vida y la obra de Velázquez*, Madrid, 1955; *Sobre un retrato de la Reina Isabel de Borbón*, Madrid, 1960; *Sobre un retrato perdido de Velázquez*, Madrid, 1960; *Chiens par Don Diego Velázquez*, Paris, 1960; *Velázquez en este momento*, Madrid, 1961, and *Tutta la pittura del Velázquez*, Milan, 1964. In the publications of 1960, Pantorba attributed to Velázquez three formerly unknown paintings, and in that of 1961 he endorsed the attribution to the Master of three other paintings which he had not included in his 1955 catalogue. None of the three paintings which Bernardino de Pantorba published as by the hand of Velázquez in 1960, and only one of the three whose attribution to the Master he endorsed in 1961, was included in the catalogue of Velázquez 'autograph' works which Pantorba himself brought out in 1964. 'Bernardino de Pantorba' is a pseudonym of Mr. José López Jiménez, of Madrid.

[4] *Velázquez*, Madrid, 1964.

[5] Ministerio de Educación Nacional, Dirección General de Bellas Artes, *Velázquez y lo velazqueño, Catálogo de la exposición homenaje a Diego de Silva Velázquez en el III centenario de su muerte*, Madrid, 1960.

[6] Enrique Lafuente Ferrari, *Velázquez*, 1943, nos. LXXIX and LXXX. The fragment, *Hand of an ecclesiastic*, is at the Madrid Royal Palace, where Lafuente was then keeper of the art collection. The portrait of *Cardinal Borja* had just been acquired by the Metropolitan Museum of Art, New York; it is now at the Museo de Arte, Ponce, Puerto Rico; it surely is not by Velázquez. (See López-Rey, *Velázquez: A Catalogue Raisonné*, nos. 462-7 and 480.)

FOREWORD

In the *catalogue raisonné* of Velázquez's *oeuvre* which I published in 1963, I ascribed to the Master only one painting not previously attributed to him, the *Portrait of a young lady* in the Duke of Devonshire collection which, probably because few, if any, earlier scholars had actually seen it, had habitually been referred to as a copy of Velázquez's portrait of an obviously older lady at the Wallace Collection.[1] I should like to make it clear that I do not share the smug belief that denying the authenticity of a genuine work by a creative master is a lesser error than attributing to him a work by one of his imitators. As I see it, to conclude that the authentic is false is a more grievous error than to mistake contrived appearances for the real thing.

My count of Velázquez's extant paintings comes to 111 oils on canvas and one miniature on copper by his hand, plus nine more oils only partly executed by him. Included in the 111 canvases originally painted by the Master are seventeen that I have described as more than slightly damaged by time, accident, unsound cleaning or opinionative restoration, several of which I reproduced in both their former and their present condition in my catalogue. A few are tantalizing wrecks; like other such remains, they still ought to be preserved and recorded under their artist's name, but bearing in mind that their relevance to our understanding of his art is likely to be in inverse proportion to the extent of their restoration. There are even instances in which the very reality of a work of art has been overwhelmed by a restorer's misguided efforts. The number of Velázquez's paintings marred by unwise cleaning or restoration has unfortunately increased since 1963, when I published my *catalogue raisonné* of his *oeuvre*.

Several of my conclusions concerning Velázquez have been confirmed by factual evidence discovered after I formulated them. For instance, the date 1618 which I, at variance with other scholars, suggested in 1963 for *Christ at the house of Martha and Mary* (London, National Gallery) was found on the painting itself during its recent cleaning.[2]

When I was compiling my catalogue of Velázquez works, every scholar who had actually seen the portrait of *Calabazas holding a portrait and a pinwheel*, now at the Cleveland Museum, had concluded that it had been painted by the Master. However, other scholars, whose approach to the subject was rather literal, had rejected that conclusion on the ground that this portrait could not be the one in which, as stated in an inventory of 1701, Velázquez had represented *Calabazas* holding a letter, not a pinwheel, in one hand. The direct study of the painting led me to agree with the connoisseurs who held it to be a work by Velázquez, whatever its relation might have been to the 1701 inventory. As the reader will see, I have now found several documents that reveal that the 1701 description of the painting was wrong, due to an error made by the clerk who recorded the inventory entries; misunderstanding the appraiser who dictated the description of the painting, he wrote *villete* (letter) instead of *reguilete* (pinwheel).[3]

The excellent radiographs, made by the technical staff of the Stockholm National Gallery,

---

[1] *Velázquez: A Catalogue Raisonné of his Oeuvre*, no. 600. My catalogue includes nine drawings ascribed to Velázquez, and 51 paintings which, according to documentary data, were painted by him and are no longer extant. The total number of my catalogue entries is 651; most of them refer, of course, to works by Velázquez's assistants followers, imitators or forgers.

[2] See page 28 following.

[3] See pages 87–9 following.

of works by Velázquez or his followers at the Prado Museum have been particularly valuable.[1] They were shown for the first time in 1961 at the Prado, to which the Swedish National Gallery had donated them. The radiographs of *A dwarf with a dog* rendered unmistakable the superficiality of execution of this picture which I had for years held to be a seventeenth-century pastiche after Mazo rather than a work by Velázquez as the Prado catalogue has it (no. 1203).[2]

Of greater import was the evidence provided by the radiographs of the Prado full-length portrait of *Philip IV in black*: it corroborated a conclusion which I had expressed some time earlier as essential for the understanding of Velázquez's art. I had taken exception to the view expounded by Beruete and shared by all succeeding scholars that the dissimilarities in the quality of light, shade and brushwork noticeable in Velázquez's works ought to be understood in terms of a chronological development of his art. I pointed out that such dissimilarities are noticeable not only between paintings of different periods, but also between companion pieces of exactly the same date, and even within a single painting.

I also pointed out that Velázquez expressed the polarity of the human and the divine by means of certain dissimilarities in the quality of light, shade and brushwork, and that he did so rather consistently throughout his career. As part of my argument, I called attention to the fact that, though young Velázquez won his appointment as Court painter with a portrait of Philip IV, painted in August 1623, known to us only from a contemporary account that describes it as of striking naturalism, all the extant portraits of the monarch unquestionably by Velázquez's hand are truer to an idea of the quasi-divine nature of the person of the King than to Philip's physical appearance.[3] The radiographs of the full-length *Philip IV* mentioned above revealed in their own tantalizing way that, lying underneath, there is another image of the King which corresponds to the contemporary description of the portrait with which young Velázquez won his astounding success in August 1623. It is a true-to-life likeness of Philip, different in that respect from all the others by Velázquez's hand which have come down to us in visible pigment, slightly so from those executed late in 1623 or in 1624, quite markedly from those painted later, including the one that the Master himself brushed over it sometime in 1626–8. Obviously, young Velázquez soon became dissatisfied with the physical verisimilitude achieved in his first portrait of *Philip IV* as the idea came into his mind of portraying the quasi-divine nature of the King rather than the reality of his appearance.

Added support of this kind for conclusions drawn from what is visible to the naked eye is

[1] They were shown in February–March, 1961, at the Prado Museum. Unfortunately, no catalogue or handlist was published. The radiographs were of the following twenty-four paintings, listed according to their number in my above-mentioned catalogue of Velázquez's oeuvre: Velázquez: no. 14, *Christ on the Cross*; no. 56, *The fable of Arachne*; no. 57, *Bacchus*; no. 61, *Mars*; no. 62, *Mercury and Argus*; no. 68, *The forge of Vulcan*; no. 80, *The surrender of Breda*; nos. 157 and 158, *Villa Medici*; no. 229, *The royal family*; no. 239, *Philip IV*, bust; no. 241, *Philip IV*, full-length; no. 304, *Prince Baltasar Carlos as a hunter*; no. 355, *Queen Mariana*; no. 420, *Don Diego de Acedo, 'el Primo'*; no. 424, *Calabazas*; no. 503, *Martínez Montañés*; no. 549, *Man with a goatee*; and no. 580, *Doña Antonia de Ipeñarrieta*. Mazo: no. 152, *View of Saragossa*, and no. 409, *The Infanta Margarita*. Unknown painters: no. 15, *Christ on the Cross*; no. 372, *Queen Mariana at prayer*, and no. 437, *A dwarf with a dog*.

[2] 'A Pseudo Velázquez: The Picture of a Dwarf with a Dog', in *Gazette des Beaux-Arts*, Paris, October–December, 1950 (actually printed in 1959), pp. 275–84. See also: *Velázquez: A Catalogue Raisonné*, pp. 269–70, no. 437.

[3] 'Pincelada e imagen en Velázquez', in *Varia velazqueña*, Madrid, 1960, vol. I, pp. 200–6.

naturally gratifying. However, I should like to emphasize at this point that technological devices, such as photography, radiography, and chemical analysis, helpful though they are to the historian of art, cannot be for him more than a tool, and that there is no substitute for the toil of the mind's eye. It is for the historian to evaluate the data at hand and to build data into history by dint of thought, which for the historian of art ought to mean making individual human creations stand out cogently in the continuum of historical time.

Technology is constantly giving us new means for the gathering of data in nearly every humanistic field. We ought to be grateful for that and, of course, for the scientific thought in whose wake technology rides. We also ought to guard against letting the ever increasing flow of information flood rather than challenge our minds. There are today efficient research centres for the classification and publication of data, archival, bibliographical, iconographical, technical or the like. The scholar's task is thus unquestionably, and duly, eased. For instance, nowadays there is seldom need for him to embark on a time-consuming search for bibliography on a particular subject since he can usually quickly find it up-to-date in bibliographical indexes or in specialized libraries; conversely, he should not ordinarily feel compelled to include in his publications an exhaustive, or near exhaustive, bibliography, a practice which has long become a substanceless ritual. The need now is not for blanket bibliographies, but for selective ones which test the author's live knowledge of the subject, his critical acumen and his intellectual integrity. Indeed, the line ought to be drawn a little tighter between the true scholar and the parascholar, to use a term which has been refreshingly applied to today's practitioner of an old trade.

In our day, the danger to true inquiry in the history of art or, for that matter, in older humanistic fields is that scholars may be stunted by the expanding institutional means at their disposal and may mislead themselves into substituting some sort of corporate thinking for individual thought, dismissing as 'subjective' any idea which does not conform to their stock views or routines. The growing number of practitioners of art-historical scholarship who are plainly weary of intellectual ways, sometimes to the point of seeming to claim freedom from thought, is cause for some concern.

Since I have departed from views shared and regarded as central by other scholars from whom I have nevertheless learned, I have dwelt on matters which, to my mind, are essential for a historical understanding of Velázquez's art, such as the traditional values and the tenets of modernity which he encountered early in life, the challenge of his journeys to Madrid and to Italy, his own discernment of artistic tradition, his sense of individual creation, the stuff of which his images are made, the sentience of his brushwork, and the polarity of the divine and the human that gives meaning to his naturalism and is at the core of his art. As I have underlined in my discussion of these matters, no true artist works to a fixed programme. Nevertheless, a creative artist achieves in his works a living sequence, the overall meaning of which we can only grasp by discerning the sentiments or ideas, whether consistent or contradictory, which underlie his *oeuvre*.

The time sequence that I propose for Velázquez's *oeuvre* is based on a study of his works and of available documentary data. It differs substantially from the time sequence that, generally speaking, has been accepted for the last sixty years by art-historians who assume that any and every great master changes his means of expression step by step in a straight chronological sequence which lends itself to a clear-cut division into periods, to each of which ought exclusively to be assigned works that are closely similar in both composition and execution, even against the evidence provided by documentary data. It seems odd that art-historians who have, or should have, witnessed the variety, overlapping and recurrence of Picasso's modes of expression should abide by such assumptions. Lest I be misunderstood as intending to substitute one fixed scheme for another, I should like to explain that I simply hold that the art-historian should try to follow, as closely as stylistic and documentary data permit, the sequence, whether straight or tangled, of the artist's expressive means, without forcing a pattern on it.

Some of the dates that I suggest for Velázquez's works are not as specific as I wish I could have made them. I feel, however, that nothing would have been gained by substituting surface tidiness for unresolved doubt.

I have brought into focus Velázquez's position vis-à-vis other painters of his time, including members of his generation as well as some of his elders and followers, Mazo in particular. I have also outlined the make-up of his workshop in the light of available data. However, I have not indulged in speculation about those of his pupils of whom we hardly know more than their names, perhaps because they did not have the root of the matter in them and, whatever incidental recognition they attained in their day, their paintings were so soon forgotten that they are at present deservedly lost or in the penumbra of unidentified works. I willingly open myself to the criticism of those blood brothers of Unamuno's character, that fictional Antolín S. Paparrigópulos, who today appears quite real, whose most ambitious scholarly projects were a literary history of authors whose works had all been lost, and another of those who, having thought of writing, had never come to the point of doing so.[1]

In the Selected Bibliography I have listed the publications which, to my mind, have made a substantial contribution to the knowledge of Velázquez's art, or which represent the main diverging approaches to the subject that have been held throughout the years. I have consistently mentioned in the text the books and articles which I have found helpful or illuminating on specific points, as well as those to whose views I have taken exception; all of them are listed in the Bibliographic Register. On the other hand I have mentioned only occasionally the kind of hollow scholarly endeavours to which Moliére alone could have done justice.

The composition of this book is essentially the same as that of my 1963 study, slightly redesigned to interpolate five new sections and to enlarge a few in the light of my further thought on certain points and of new data which I have uncovered. A re-examination of the inventories preserved in the Archive of the Madrid Royal Palace has enabled me to correct a few inaccuracies, luckily none of them of consequence, into which I had fallen. Naturally, I have also taken into account, and benefited from, other scholars' recent publications bearing on the matter. Several of my fellow art-historians, in the role of reviewers, have obligingly praised my earlier treatment of the subject, which they have found succinct and pithy. I hope that they will

---

[1] Miguel de Unamuno, *Niebla*, first ed., Madrid, 1914, chapter XXIII (English translation by Warner Fite: *Mist*, New York, 1928).

FOREWORD

not now feel that their praise has been unheeded, for I hold with them that conciseness is of the essence to the history of art, as it has, indeed, always been to humanistic studies.

With very few exceptions, the full text of every document concerning Velázquez's family, life or works to which I refer in this book can be found, in chronological sequence, in *Varia velazqueña*, published by the Spanish Dirección General de Bellas Artes at Madrid in 1960 (vol. II, pp. 211–413). The compilers of this publication have recorded the name of the scholar who first published each document, together with the pertinent archival and bibliographical information. I have consequently chosen to dispense with specific references to such sources. In all other cases, however, I have provided the necessary information. I am grateful to Mr. José Valverde Madrid, of Cordoba, and Mr. Volker Schierk, of Madrid, both of whom have generously communicated to me data relevant to my subject. I also wish to thank my friend, William J. Park, Professor of English literature at Sarah Lawrence College for his advice on a literary point. I am deeply grateful to another friend, Mrs. Adaline P. Potter, of the Department of English, Mount Holyoke College, who has read the manuscript and made many helpful suggestions. A word of appreciation is also due to Mrs. Patricia Herrmann, of Faber & Faber, for her valuable assistance.

Though, as I have already noted, my interpretation of Velázquez's art is based on a study *de visu* of every one of his extant works, I have not found it necessary to discuss or reproduce all of them here, particularly since I did so in the *catalogue raisonné* of the Master's *oeuvre* published five years ago. I have mainly, though not exclusively, left out those works which are in an unsatisfactory state of conservation, except when doing so would have resulted in some kind of historical distortion or incompleteness. In these exceptional cases, I have called attention to the present condition of the works in question to the best of my ability.

For over a decade, I have travelled wide and long, back and forth, in Europe and in America, in pursuit of my research on Velázquez. I certainly could not have accomplished my purpose without help from others, individuals as well as institutions, to whom I take pleasure in renewing here the expression of my gratitude.

I had long before felt the challenge of Velázquez's art, especially at the Prado, where I have since my school days spent many hours, swerving from leisure into work and veering round to a deeper sense of leisure. I shall be happy if my readers, whether laymen or scholars, do not feel that I have encroached upon their leisure time.

Institute of Fine Arts
New York University

José López-Rey
New Year's Day, 1968

FAMILY AND NAME

On Sunday, 6 June 1599, Diego, the child of Juan Rodríguez de Silva and Jerónima Velázquez, was baptized at the church of St. Peter, in Seville, with Pablo de Ojeda as godfather. The christening must have followed the baby's birth by no more than a few weeks, or perhaps only a few days.[1]

The boy's grandparents, Diego Rodríguez de Silva and María Rodríguez, had moved to Seville from their native Porto, probably within the previous two decades, at a time when the political boundaries between Spain and Portugal had been removed by the expansion of the Spanish monarchy. The Portuguese crown was then held by the Spanish king, who would lose it, together with much of his power over the world, within Velázquez's lifetime.

As for Juan Rodríguez de Silva and his wife, both were born in Seville, where they were married, also at the church of St. Peter, on 28 December 1597. They were held to come from the lesser nobility — which he, at least, certainly did — and were accorded the privileges generally enjoyed by the gentry. Diego was their first child; he was followed by three brothers Juan, Fernando, and Silvestre; then, by a sister, Juana, and finally by two more brothers, Roque and Francisco. The last was born on 28 May 1617, when Diego had just passed the guild's examination and was starting on his own as a painter. Of Velázquez's brothers and sister we know little more than their names and the dates of their christenings.

With the freedom in the adoption of family names then prevailing, it was as Diego Velázquez that the lad was apprenticed at twelve to the painter Francisco Pacheco by his father, who signed himself Juan Rodríguez. Some five years later, when the young man was admitted to the painter's guild, he gave and signed his name as Diego Velázquez de Silva. Whether he did this out of affection for his father or simply to assert his gentle birth, the fact is that he immediately went back to the name of his apprenticeship, plain Diego Velázquez, as his signatures on paintings and documents up to the late 1640's show. Even the church registries where his marriage and the baptisms of his two daughters were entered, consistently record his name as just Diego Velázquez, while that of his brother, godfather to his second daughter, is given as Juan Velázquez de Silva.

[1] Unless otherwise indicated, the text of every document bearing on Velázquez's family, life and works referred to in this book can be found, in chronological sequence, in *Varia velazqueña*, Madrid, 1960, vol. II, pp. 211–413. For further data concerning the provenance and state of preservation of works by Velázquez or from his circle, as well as for a fuller disussion of matters of dating and attribution, see the corresponding entries in José López-Rey, *Velázquez: A Catalogue Raisonné of his Oeuvre*, London, 1963.

Obviously, though, he remained sensible of his gentle birth, and later in life, when his renown as a painter and his steady advancement at the Court underscored each other, Velázquez, moving as he did in an aristocratic society, sought to be known by the more genteel name of Diego de Silva Velázquez. This wish of his, which several documents and the one painting that he signed after 1647 make obvious, was on occasion complied with at the royal offices.

Pacheco, in the manuscript of his *Arte de la Pintura*, finished in January 1638, mentioned five times the man who was then his son-in-law as Diego Velázquez de Silva; three of the references occur in the narrative of the artist's life, and the other two elsewhere in the text. Eleven years later, when the book was published posthumously, the painter's name had been changed to Diego de Silva Velázquez in all three passages on his life, though not in the other two. The changes may well have been made in deference to Velázquez's own preference, rather marked at the time. In any event, even though one of the corrections was entered in the manuscript, it seems unlikely that the change originated with Pacheco who, in his testament, drawn one and a half years after the completion of the manuscript of *Arte de la Pintura*, still repeatedly gave his son-in-law's name as Diego Velázquez de Silva.[1]

Plain Velázquez, however, remained the name by which the artist was readily known in the Royal Palace and elsewhere, except to those of his friends and colleagues at Madrid who called him just 'the Sevillian',[2] and when in 1627 he signed the painting, now lost, by which his superiority over the other painters to the King was conclusively acknowledged at the Court, he added *Hispalensis*, Latin for Sevillian, to his name.

EDUCATION AND APPRENTICESHIP

The boy's early education was, in the fashion of the time, grounded on the study of the humanities, in which he did very well, revealing a knack for languages — which must have included Latin — and philosophy, the taste for which he kept throughout the years as the books he gathered in his library show.[3] Nevertheless, his vocation for painting led him to enter a painter's workshop at the then not unusual age of eleven.

His own statement when he petitioned in 1617 for admission to the guild of St. Luke, that he had 'learned the painter's art' in Seville from 'qualified teachers', clearly indicates that he owed his training to more than one. According to Palomino — whose life of Velázquez is largely based on one written by a pupil of the artist — Francisco de Herrera, the Elder (c. 1590–1656),

---

[1] Francisco Pacheco, *Arte de la Pintura*, ed. F. J. Sánchez Cantón, Madrid, 1956, vol. I, pp. 155, 162, 166; vol. II. pp. 146, 154. Pacheco completed the manuscript on 24 January 1638, but it was not published till 1649, at Seville. All my references are to Sánchez Cantón's edition of the original manuscript.

[2] We owe, in fact, this information to three of the witnesses who in 1658, when Velázquez's ancestry was being scrutinized to decide whether he could be admitted into the Order of Santiago, testified that he was descended from the nobility and had always behaved accordingly. For a fuller discussion of the matter, see José López-Rey 'Nombres y nombradía de Velázquez', *Goya*, Madrid, July–October, 1960, pp. 4–5.

[3] See F. J. Sánchez Cantón, 'La librería de Velázquez', *Homenaje a Don Ramón Menéndez Pidal*, vol. III, Madrid, 1925, pp. 379–406.

and Francisco Pacheco (1564–1644) were those teachers.[1] As the story has been developed by other writers, the lad seems to have entered Herrera's workshop only to be soon frightened away by the unbearable temper of the master, whom he left for Pacheco.

We know from Pacheco himself that he gave 'five years of education and training' to Velázquez. This statement coincides with another contained in the contract by which the boy's father apprenticed him to Pacheco, on 17 September 1611.[2] Like similar agreements entered into by Pacheco and other masters of the time, it called for a six-year apprenticeship; it was, however, stated that the agreed period of time had 'begun to run on 1st December, of the past year, 1610'. Consequently, the contract was actually binding for little more than five years from the date of signature — which happens to be the length of time that Pacheco remembered Velázquez had spent with him as an apprentice.

Pacheco was away from home on an extended journey during a good part of 1611, and it is possible that he had left Seville before 1 December 1610, when Velázquez began his apprenticeship. Indeed, for all we know, Pacheco may have started on his journey any time after 7 October 1610, when he signed a document as security for a fellow artist in Seville;[3] the following year, according to his own testimony, he was in Madrid, the Escorial and Toledo, at times that he did not specify,[4] and the earliest reference to his being back in Seville is provided by the contract for Velázquez's apprenticeship, which he signed on 27 September, ten days after the boy's father had done so.

This absence of Pacheco from Seville explains the exact coincidence between the terms of the contract and Pacheco's specific recollection of the length of Velázquez's apprenticeship with him. It is possible that the lad came to Pacheco's workshop on 1 December 1610, as the master was about to leave, or had already left, on his journey, and was tentatively entrusted to, or accepted by, an assistant, leaving the final decision for Pacheco to make on his return. On the other hand, it might also be that, on that date, the boy entered Herrera's or some other master's workshop and quit it within ten months to study with Pacheco, who would then have given him credit, as it were, for the time he had served his apprenticeship elsewhere.

Pacheco in his *Arte de la Pintura* found it necessary to denounce the 'audacity' of someone — whom he chose to leave unnamed — who claimed to have been Velázquez's teacher. Whether this 'someone' was Herrera, one of Pacheco's former assistants, or some other painter, he may have had some basis for his claim, which would make all the more understandable both Pacheco's indignation and his factual statement as to the 'five years of education and training' that he had given to Velázquez.

In formally accepting Velázquez as an apprentice, Pacheco undertook to teach him the art of

[1] Antonio Palomino Velasco, *El Museo Pictórico*, Madrid, 1947, pt. III, p. 892 (1st ed., Madrid, 1724).

[2] For this and all other quotations from Pacheco's narrative of Velázquez's life see *Arte de la Pintura*, vol. I, pp. 155–62. Whenever the references to Velázquez are from other sections of this work, the corresponding page number has been indicated.

[3] For the document, see Celestino López Martínez, *Desde Jerónimo Hernández hasta Martínez Montañés*, Seville, 1929, pp. 127–8.

[4] Pacheco, *Arte de la Pintura*, vol. I, p. 370; vol. II, pp. 8, 165.

painting as well and as thoroughly as he knew how — this was the 'training' that he imparted to the boy during those five years of apprenticeship. As for the 'education' which, though unmentioned in the contract, went with it, it must have come about in a spontaneous vital manner since both the pupil and the teacher had a penchant for humanistic studies.

PACHECO'S WORKSHOP

Pacheco's workshop was a meeting place not only for painters but for poets and scholars as well. Most of them were men of substantial attainments whose learning readily flowed from work into leisure and from leisure into work and whose various interests were held together and alive by the weight and tension of discriminating taste. As recorded in *Arte de la Pintura*, they enjoyed discussing, among other subjects, the achievements and techniques of outstanding artists, and the significance of their works. Pacheco's references to other authors show that he was well read in the humanities and up to date in the literature on art. He must have owned a sizeable library, and probably from it Velázquez derived the interest which led him to accumulate that substantial number of books listed among his possessions at the time of his death.

It would be idle to try to ascertain what topics young Velázquez heard discussed at Pacheco's workshop during his apprenticeship there. The evidence provided by *Arte de la Pintura* is hardly conclusive, for Pacheco did not complete the manuscript till some twenty years after Velázquez had left his workshop, a period during which he remained much alive to new experiences, including two or three more stays in Madrid, where he witnessed the early success of his former apprentice, and the correspondence which, *Arte de la Pintura* makes plain, he had with him throughout the years.

Certainly Velázquez must have heard Pacheco expound the importance of copying from antique sculptures, and Michelangelo's or Raphael's works, in order to achieve mastery in painting.[1] Pacheco, who confessed to having always striven to imitate Raphael, owned for many years what he described as an original wash drawing for *The School of Athens*, over which he very likely pored with his friends, possibly young Velázquez among them.

As we know from Pacheco himself, Velázquez during his first Italian journey, in 1629–30, made many drawings from Michelangelo's *Last Judgement* and Raphael's frescoes at the Vatican, as well as from antique sculptures at Villa Medici, in Rome. Unfortunately none of these drawings has come down to us, and we cannot even surmise the nature of his response to the two masters whom Pacheco admired above all others. We know, of course, that some twenty years later he emphatically declared that Raphael did not please him a bit, and that Venetian painting, particularly Titian's, was the thing.

Titian, who had for decades been regarded as a paragon by leading painters at the Spanish Court, must have come up for discussion at Pacheco's workshop after his return from Madrid, just at the time when he signed up Velázquez as an apprentice. Pacheco was then, of course,

---

[1] *Arte de la Pintura*, vol. I, pp. 366–71, and passim. A critical edition of *Arte de la Pintura*, which has not yet been undertaken, would help to clarify Pacheco's views on the matter.

fresh from his visits to the royal collections, rich in masterpieces by the Venetian master, whom he extols in *Arte de la Pintura* as one of the greatest colourists, even making an effort to explain the 'unfinished' nature of his works.[1]

Pacheco undoubtedly told his friends then of his astonishment a few weeks or months earlier at hearing from Dominico Greco, a great painter in spite of his blotchy brushstrokes, that Michelangelo was a good man who did not know how to paint.[2] That might have been the first time that the twelve-year-old Velázquez had heard the name of Domenikos Theotokopoulos.

If the subjects touched on in *Arte de la Pintura* are any guide, the lad most likely listened to discussions of such favourite topics of the time as, for instance, *up pictura poesis*, the superiority of painting over sculpture, the hierarchy of the different kinds of subject matter in painting, or the comparison of naturalist painting with the images of things or men reflected in full colour and motion on shining surfaces, like water or mirrors.

Out of the stream of these conversations young Velázquez must have seized for himself now and then a distinct idea of the world into which he was born. He must also have arrived soon at a divination of his own purpose in the midst of the sentiments, ideas, tastes, achievements and traditions which he encountered or which were revealed to him. As we know, it was then and there that he reached out for the world of painting that was to be his own.

Pacheco, in discussing the ideas on portraiture in which Velázquez had been raised, tells in a truly understanding manner how the lad, while still an apprentice, devised a method of his own to 'attain assurance in portraying'. He used to bribe a peasant-boy apprentice — presumably one of menial rank — to sit for him 'in different gestures and poses, now crying, now laughing, without shrinking from any difficulty', and would draw from him a good many heads and other parts of the body in charcoal with white chalk for the highlights on blue paper.[3]

Unfortunately, none of these drawings has been preserved, and the *Head of a girl*, executed, like Pacheco's portraits for his *Libro de retratos*, in red and black chalk on white, now yellowish, paper, is probably Velázquez's earliest extant drawing (plate 3).[4]

THE TEACHER AND THE PUPIL

In the 1610's nearly every painter, within and outside of Italy, had Caravaggesque naturalism at the centre or, at the least, at the edges of his attention. As Giulio Mancini, writing at the end of the decade, put it: 'our time is much indebted to Michelangelo de Caravaggio for

[1] Op. cit., vol. I, p. 478.   [2] Ibidem, vol. I, p. 370.

[3] Pacheco, *Arte de la Pintura*; vol. II, p. 146. The verb *cohechar* (to bribe) with which Pacheco refers to the agreement between Velázquez and the peasant-boy apprentice connotes an idea of mischief which can only be understood if Velázquez, too, was still an apprentice. Pacheco certainly would not have spoken of bribing if, as Miss Elisabeth du Gué Trapier believes, the peasant boy was Diego de Melgar, who was apprenticed to Velázquez in 1620 (*Velázquez*, New York, 1948, p. 57).

[4] The *Libro de retratos* was left unfinished by Pacheco, who was at work on it as early as 1599, when he dated the title-page of the manuscript. A facsimile edition of the incomplete text and drawings was brought out some eighty years ago by José María Asensio, who published at the same time a study of Pacheco's literary and artistic works: Francisco Pacheco, *Libro de descripción de verdaderos retratos de illustres y memorables varones* [Seville, n.d.], and José María Asensio, *Francisco de Pacheco: Sus obras artísticas y literarias*, Seville, 1886. Pacheco's manuscript is now at the Museo Lázaro Galdiano, Madrid.

the colouring that he has brought out and which is now followed quite generally'.[1]

Velázquez and the youths of his generation could see works by Caravaggio, or copies after them, in Seville and elsewhere in Spain.[2] Pacheco praised Caravaggio, together with Jacopo Bassano, Ribera and El Greco, as a painter whose works could be lacking in beauty or polish but not in relief. In Pacheco's view, Caravaggio effected a life-like reality by painting from nature not only the human face, limbs or nude body, but also clothing, whether of wool or silk, and everything else, as could be seen in the pictures of *The Crucifixion of St. Peter*, 'even though they are just copies'.[3] Pacheco's offhand mention of these copies, one of which at least was in Seville, indicates that they were widely known.

The *Arte de la Pintura* reveals a conflict between Pacheco's theoretical views, rooted, as his marginal notes acknowledge, in treatises of the *Cinquecento*, and the taste that, well along in his sixties, he developed for the new mode of painting, Caravaggesque naturalism. It is hard to decide whether Pacheco had acquired that taste by the time he signed up Velázquez as an apprentice or had developed it later. His praise of Caravaggio could not have been written before 1631. Indeed, the paragraph includes a mention of the pictures by Ribera in the collection of the Duke of Alcalá, who had been Viceroy of Naples till that year, when he returned to Spain, bringing with him the works that he had acquired from Ribera. It might, of course, be that Pacheco had not actually seen these paintings, even though he described them as looking 'alive' among all the others in the Duke's collection. If so, Pacheco might have echoed his son-in-law's views, for Velázquez was in Naples in December 1630, when he portrayed the *Infanta María* at the Viceregal Palace (plate 67), where he undoubtedly saw the Duke's collection. Even in that event, Pacheco could not have written the paragraph in question before 1631.

There is a distinct analogy between young Velázquez's device of drawing from his model 'in different gestures and poses, now crying, now laughing' and what, to Mancini, was the high accomplishment, as well as the limitation, of Caravaggism: the portrayal of human figures 'laughing or crying, walking or still', though lacking in the refinements of gracefulness and sentiment.[4] It is to Pacheco's credit, both as a connoisseur and as a teacher, that his knowledge, rooted in the past, did not dull him to the present, and that he came to enjoy the tang of the new naturalism, of which that bright lad, Velázquez, was so much a partisan. As for the bright lad, he had a creative outlook, and so he took hold of the modernity of his day, seeing in it not an aim, but an exhilarating point of departure, which he naturally soon left behind.

Caravaggio's vivid chiaroscuro was fundamental to his followers. He achieved it by the use of a sheer light which draws men and things out of shadow, heightening their shapes and

[1] *Considerazioni sulla Pittura*, ed. by Adriana Marucchi, Rome, 1956, vol. I, p. 223.

[2] For data on works by Caravaggio, or copies after them, in Spain early in the seventeenth century, see J. Ainaud, 'Ribalta y Caravaggio', in *Anales y Boletín de los Museos de Arte de Barcelona*, July–December 1947, pp. 345–413.

[3] *Arte de la Pintura*, vol. II, p. 13.

[4] Op. cit., vol. I, pp. 108–9. Mancini points out the unnatural character of Caravaggesque chiaroscuro: 'It is peculiar to this school to light up [the composition] with an even light, coming from above, without reflections, as if through a window into a room with the walls painted black, for by so doing, by making the lights very light and the shades very dark, they succeed in giving relief to the painting, even though in an unnatural manner.'

colours with an unvaried sheen. Neither the quality of the brushwork, nor the texture of pigment, nor the intensity of light varies significantly within any one of Caravaggio's works, not even in *The Supper at Emmaus* (London, National Gallery, plate 15), where he uses the same brushwork for the figure of Christ and for those of the Apostles, the pilgrim, the food or the tableware. In this, Caravaggio was within the tradition from which he had otherwise departed in a naturalist manner that was as creative with him as it was appealing or offensive to others. His portrayal of men and things is the more emphatic as a direct light shapes the corporeal out of shadow in an airless space.

If *Caravaggism* was the main tenet of modernism to Velázquez's generation, his early works show that he soon went beyond it. Indeed, unlike Caravaggio, young Velázquez uses a diffused light, with a greenish tinge, that sets men and things in a fluid environment, bringing out at the same time their textural differences. Much as he may have had Caravaggio at the back of his mind, Velázquez achieved from the beginning a sensuous rendering of the variety of shape, colour and texture, an atmospheric depiction of spatial depth, and a distinct expression of the polarity of the divine and the human — all of which were alien to Caravaggio's naturalism.

In achieving that, Velázquez revealed a commanding feeling for the texture of whatever he portrayed, as well as of the pigment itself. This led him to a fluid handling of light and shade and to the use of a variety of brush-strokes, rough or smooth, always vigorous, more akin to Titian's than to Caravaggio's.

Velázquez was obviously impelled by his own disposition to admire, first in Madrid and then in Italy, Titian's sketchy strokes and the chiaroscural effects which gave sensorial depth to his compositions.[1] It may well be that he imparted his enthusiasm to his father-in-law, whose praise of Titian, admittedly based on Lodovico Dolce's *L'Aretino* (1557), appears greater than his understanding of the Venetian master's works.

Pacheco, in extolling a 'famous' self-portrait, now lost, executed by Velázquez in Rome in 1630, pointed out that it 'was painted in the manner of the great Titian, and if it is permissible to say so, not inferior to his heads'. Pacheco was, of course, aware that his former pupil had attained the freedom of an individual creator, and he must have had that in mind when he proudly wrote that 'the teacher's honour is greater than the father-in-law's'.[2]

EARLY WORKS

Velázquez's youthful works lend themselves to a division into two groups. First come three compositions of the genre known at the time as *bodegones* and a head study for one of them; though undated, these four paintings betray an intentness on the portrayal of human expression quite suggestive of the time when the lad Velázquez applied himself to a depiction of primal human emotions modelled for him by that hireling apprentice. The second group includes a larger number of works and a greater variety of subjects, some of them dated, executed between

[1] Cf. Theodor Hetzer, *Tizian, Geschichte seines Farbe*, Frankfurt a/M., 1948, pp. 232 ff.
[2] *Arte de la Pintura*, vol. I, pp. 155 and 160; vol. II, p. 154.

1618 and 1622; in all of them, the portrayal of the human figure is important, and in some also the depiction of the textures of victuals and tableware, but the rendition of human expression or gesture is less emphatic. A measure of atmospheric unity is achieved in nearly every picture from either group by a greenish hue which shades slightly the space of the composition.

The three *bodegones* in the first group, *Musical trio*, *Three men at table*, and *A girl and two men at table* (plates 1, 13 and 18), portray the bustle of conviviality. In each, three half- or three-quarter figures sit or stand round a table laid with food and drink; the point of view is high, and local lights accent the shape of food and tableware and stress the grimacing faces and gesturing hands which are well built in the round, while the bodies are not quite substantially set in space; indeed, the rendering of spatial depth is mainly achieved by the multiplicity of points of distance marked off by hands, faces and inanimate objects. This is particularly true of *Musical trio*, obviously the earliest and the most tentative of the three works, the one where there is less of an atmospheric unity.

This manner of defining space, fairly common in the late *Cinquecento*, had been handed down to young Velázquez and would not serve for long his purpose of portraying the live and the transient; he achieved, nonetheless, a sort of equilibrium as the vivid rendering of the grimacing and gesturing of the figures, whose bodies do not quite occupy the space plotted by means of the table, vies with the depiction of victuals or tableware which underlying shadows make the sharper.

There are significant differences even among these very early works. For instance, the stress on the depiction of facial expressions and hand gestures has been somewhat lessened in *A girl and two men at table* (plate 18), where the diagonals on which the composition is based are not so overexplicit, and hence distracting, as in the other two works. It should be pointed out though, that this distracting effect is further emphasized in *Three men at table* by the painting's present darkened condition.

Yellows prevail in both *Musical trio* and *Three men at table* (plates 1 and 13). In the latter, however, they show a greater variety of hues; in the costume of the youth at the right, the rinds of the pomegranates, the loaf of bread, and the wine in both the glass on the table and the bottle held by the boy; in this painting, moreover, a purplish tinge on the grey sleeve of the old man enhances the purple hue of the turnip he is eating and white touches light up both the buckle on the boy's dark brown costume and the mussels and herring in the bowl in front of him.

Three men at table and *A girl and two men at table* are obviously based, to a large extent, on the same studies of men and things. The glass and the loaf of bread on the table are almost identical in both paintings and so is the figure of the old man except for his hands. As for the youth sitting at the right, his trunk and arms, though not his head, are very nearly the same in both works. In *A girl and two men at table*, the youth's head, which appears to have been reworked, derives from a study in which Velázquez had stressed somewhat more the facial expression (plate 4).

Yet, for all their similarities, the two compositions differ substantially and their differences make us realize the creative nature of young Velázquez's labours and the sentience of his naturalism. The shadow which keenly duplicates the shape of the sword hanging on the wall in *Three men at table* reveals Velázquez's gift for the depiction of aerial depth, but it is rather in *A girl and two men at table* that the rendition of aerial space appears as essential to his art. To achieve it he has underscored the width and depth of the interior by pushing the figure of the young man more to the side, thus disencumbering the foreground edge of the table, and by making the figure of the girl in the background bend over slightly. He has, moreover — and more decisively — made his palette brighter and richer in hues, loosened the brushwork, thinned the shadows, and made fewer and of greater range the diagonals on which the composition is built.

It is safe to assume that the pictures in the first group were executed around 1617, or not much later, when Velázquez was completing his apprenticeship or just after he had taken his examination for admission to the painters' guild, all the more so since the paintings which may be held to mark the dividing line between the two groups are dated 1618, when he already had his workshop (plates 5 and 14). This dividing line, like any other chosen to mark an artist's creative course, can hardly be regarded as without divergences, and it is possible that Velázquez's execution of *A girl and two men at table* overlapped that of *Old woman frying eggs* or *Christ in the house of Martha and Mary*, the works that he finished in 1618 when he was nineteen.

THE YOUNG MASTER'S SUCCESS

On 14 March 1617, Velázquez was made a member of the Guild of St. Luke, after having passed a qualifying examination. His examiners were Pacheco and Juan de Uceda, another painter. Once admitted to the guild the eighteen-year-old artist was entitled to have his own workshop, to take in apprentices and to paint for churches or public places — privileges he lost no time in availing himself of.

He advanced smoothly into comfort and recognition. On 23 April 1618 he married Juana Pacheco who was three years younger than he. Her father gave to them, as part of the dowry, 'some houses' in the city which they sold ten years later. Pacheco had favoured the marriage, induced by Velázquez's 'virtue, purity of blood, and good parts, and by the hopes of his natural and great intellect'. The Spanish word *limpieza* in this sentence has somewhat amusingly been taken to mean that Pacheco married Velázquez to his daughter, among other reasons, because of the young man's 'cleanliness'.[1] There is nothing to suggest that Velázquez was not as neat as a pin, but the word *limpieza* in the cited context unequivocally means 'purity of blood', that is, an ancestry free of any Jewish, Moorish, or heretic — i.e., non-Catholic — strain.

The wedding took place in the church of St. Michael, with the poet Francisco de Rioja (1583–1659), who was soon to become influential at the Court, among the official witnesses. At the bountiful wedding banquet, in Pacheco's house, the occasion was made the more festive by the wit of the learned guests and by the singing and dancing which followed.[2]

---

[1] Trapier, *Velázquez*, p. 34.

[2] Baltasar de Cepeda, one of the guests at the wedding banquet, wrote a poem describing it. See William L. Fichter, 'Una poesía contemporánea inédita sobre las bodas de Velázquez', *Varia velazqueña*, vol. I, pp. 636–9.

Within less than three years, two daughters were born to the young couple: Francisca, who was baptized on 18 May 1619, and Ignacia, to whom her uncle, Juan Velázquez de Silva, was godfather on 29 January 1621. Ignacia died rather soon, and Francisca remained the painter's only child.

In 1618 he dated both *Christ in the house of Martha and Mary* and *Old woman frying eggs* (plates 5 and 14),[1] and the following year *The adoration of the Magi* (colour plate II) which was most likely commissioned and, as such, encouraging to the now twenty-year-old painter. On 1 February 1620 he signed up an apprentice, Diego de Melgar, which must again have been heartening for the young master. By the spring of 1622 he felt so confident of himself that he set out for Madrid, 'desirous' — as Pacheco put it — 'of seeing the Escorial', which housed a wealth of pictures by great masters, and hoping to portray young Philip IV, recently come to the throne, and his Queen.

By the time Velázquez set out on his first journey to Madrid, he had made an impact on the Sevillian painters of his generation, and possibly on older ones too, considering the number of pictures which are evidence of a rather eager acceptance of his early manner. Some of these works betray a desire for emulation which gives them vigour, and it is not surprising that they have at times been attributed to Velázquez himself; others are without significance beyond their derivative character. As is often the case with creative people, followers pressed Velázquez's early manner into lifelessness while he went on striking new forms of expression, vitally asserting the freedom and cogency of his art.

Of the works that he executed between 1618 and 1622, twenty-odd authentic ones have come down to us, together with a large number of copies or imitations, some of which probably date back to approximately those years. Though from what we know of his early pictorial interests, young Velázquez must have enjoyed painting portraits, the larger number of his extant paintings from that period is made up of *bodegones* and religious subjects, including two, *Christ at the house of Martha and Mary* and *Christ at Emmaus*, which lend themselves to either classification (plates 5 and 20). In a replica that he painted of the latter, he turned the composition into a straight *bodegón* simply by omitting the small religious background scene (plate 21). There is actually a unifying religious undertone in all Velázquez's youthful works, and for that matter in his later paintings, which is not surprising in a sentient man of his upbringing and beliefs.

---

[1] Aureliano de Beruete listed *Christ at the house of Martha and Mary* as Velázquez's earliest extant work, datable in 1615 or 1617, and *Old woman frying eggs* as executed in 1619 or later (*Velázquez*, London [1906], p. 157, and *Velázquez*, Berlin, 1909, p. 91). It has since been discovered that *Old woman frying eggs* bears the date 1618 (David Baxandal, 'A dated Velázquez bodegón', *The Burlington Magazine*, vol. 99, 1957, pp. 156–7). As for *Christ in the house of Martha and Mary*, all other Velázquez scholars had dated it significantly later than Beruete, not earlier than 1619 and as late as 1622, till I concluded that it must have been painted about 1618 on account of its close stylistic analogies with *Old woman frying eggs* (*Velázquez: A Catalogue Raisonné of his Oeuvre*, London, 1963, pp. 32 and 125, no. 8). My conclusion has been confirmed by the partially visible date found on the painting during its recent restoration, which has been read as 1618, according to a report by a member of the staff of the London National Gallery (Allan Braham, 'A second dated bodegón by Velázquez', *The Burlington Magazine*, vol. 107, 1965, pp. 362–5).

II. Velázquez, The adoration of the Magi. 1619. *Prado*

BODEGONES

Pacheco makes it clear that Velázquez had been acknowledged early in his career as the greatest painter of *bodegones*, a genre on which older painters still living in Seville had partly built their reputation. Though all the Velázquez *bodegones* which have come down to us are from the Sevillian period, it would seem that he went on painting them for some time after moving to Madrid.

A word of clarification is perhaps necessary here. *Bodegón* originally meant a low eating place. In art terminology the term is nowadays almost interchangeable with still-life. Yet to Velázquez's generation it rather meant a figure-composition keyed to the depiction of food, drink, tableware or the like. At least, I have not seen any description of a *bodegón* painting written before 1660 which does not explicitly mention one or more human figures as part of the composition. The diminutive form, *bodegoncillo*, was, however, sometimes applied to compositions without figures, that is, to what today we would call still-lifes.

Pacheco unequivocally distinguishes *bodegones* from fish, game, hunting, or banquet pieces — that is, from what was to become generally known as still-life — as well as from the genre composition then known in Italy as *bambocciatta* and in Spain first as *bamboche* and later as *bambochada*.

So much for the subject matter. As for quality, a good *bodegón* ought to bring to the same degree of vividness the human figures and the objects with which they are grouped without letting the depiction of any one overpower the others. Such, at least, were the views expressed by Pacheco who admittedly based them on Velázquez's works, and probably too on discussions with him.[1]

Old woman frying eggs bears the date 1618, half erased but with the first and last figures clearly recognizable (plate 14). It shows a surer sense of composition than any of Velázquez's earlier works, though his hand still appears fettered under the restraint of study, as in the point of the knife which bends down, shadowlike, and in the boy's left forearm, seen distorted through the glass in too studied a manner. The figure of the old woman, with her head but not her bust in full profile, somehow makes us grasp the problem which exercised Velázquez's sense of composition when he transformed one of the figures in *Three men at table* into that of the young man whose head is in profile in *A girl and two men at table* (plates 13 and 18).

More objects are represented in *Old woman frying eggs* than in any earlier Velázquez *bodegón*. Yet gone is the fussiness of local definitions of objects which made the composition somewhat unstable; gone also is the emphasis on human expressions and motions. Now there is a subtle

[1] For this and the preceding references to Pacheco's understanding of *bodegones*, see *Arte de la Pintura*, vol. II, pp. 135–9. Antonio Palomino, writing in the first quarter of the eighteenth century, defined the term *bodegón* somewhat more broadly as a 'type of painting in which victuals are depicted' (see *Índice de los términos privativos del Arte de la Pintura* appended to the second volume of his *El Museo Pictórico*, first published in Madrid in 1724). About a century later, Juan Agustín Ceán Bermúdez, after describing several *bodegón* compositions with no reference to human figures, explained that 'to paint *bodegones* is the same as painting food and kitchenware' (*Diálogo sobre el Arte de la Pintura*, Seville, 1819, pp. 26–8).

interplay of light and shade which rounds human figures and things into a quiet atmosphere. Both the woman and the boy truly occupy space beyond and above the victuals and kitchenware which build the foreground plane. The gestures of both converge round the reddish frying pan where the eggs are seen in the very process of coalescing; yet the expressions of the two are rather unrelated, vacant of thought or aim; both are, indeed, as much earthly presences as the fully-hued things they are handling.

The young master achieved a more compelling depiction of the stillness of the earthly in *The waterseller*, circa 1619–20 (plate 22), and in *Two young men at table*, painted two or three years later (plate 33). Live but quiescent diagonals build the breadth and depth in each composition, where the figures are related to one another by their poses rather than by their vacant expressions. Though the subject of only one of them could be said to require it, both works appear to be portrayals of slumber, accented in *Two young men at table* by the lustre of the mortar, of the pieces of earthenware — some with green, some with a white glaze — and of the fully textured orange which sits in the mouth of a jug (colour plate III).

In *The waterseller* — a masterpiece which was impeccably cleaned in 1959 — the subtlest of greenish tints tinges the figures and objects, notably those in the foreground. The vender hands a glass of water, with a fig for freshening it at the bottom, to a lad as another youth — his figure just shadowed forth — drinks from a jar. The shapes and expressions of the three men are not more vivid, or less quiet, than the watery film shimmering on the stopper of the jug, or the three drops of water which trickle down its side, or the interplay of transparencies which intensely define the glass, the water and the fig within.

Velázquez's *bodegones* are a portrayal of the drowsing of the senses. This significance is perhaps keener in the two works just discussed where the narrative counts for little or nothing and men and things are depicted as much of the same clay and mortised into a pictorial whole.

THE DIVINE AND THE HUMAN

In the portraits of these years, Velázquez brings out the sitter's mettle and earthliness, that is, his human individuality. Half a dozen of the likenesses of the young and the old who sat for him then have come down to us, on canvas or paper: the *Young man*, of about 1618–19 (plate 24); the portraits of an unknown man (plate 23) and of Doña Jerónima de la Fuente (plates 29, 30, and 31), of 1620; the two drawings, each portraying a young girl, executed one or two years later (plates 25 and 26); *Don Luís de Góngora*, painted in 1622 (plate 41). In each of these portraits the sitter's expression, however quiet, accents his age and character traits. The same is true of the young master's portrait of his wife's godfather, the priest *Don Cristobal Suárez de Ribera*, painted sometime between 1618 and 1620, after the subject's death (plate 32).[1] This picture and two likenesses of *Mother Jerónima de la Fuente*, both signed and dated by Velázquez in 1620, are the only full-length portraits from his Sevillian period which have come down to us.

[1] See López-Rey, *Velázquez: A Catalogue Raisonné of his Oeuvre*, no. 475. The painting was cleaned and restored in 1910 and again in 1960.

In the portrait of *Mother Jerónima de la Fuente* at the Fernández Araoz collection, the scroll around the crucifix in the sitter's hand has an architectural, space-building quality that endows the effigy of Christ on the Cross with a fit sense of heroic monumentality (plate 31). In the version at the Prado, the scroll has been unwisely erased on the assumption that it was a later addition, and now the crucifix in the sitter's hand looks awkward and void of its former monumentality, as a comparison of the picture's original and present condition reveals (plates 29 and 30).[1]

Young Velázquez's compelling rendering of the mundane and transient, whether a light-permeated cord round the rind of a melon, a few drops of water trickling down the side of a jug, or a human face on which age and character traits are accented, exists side by side with his portrayal of the divine persons in *The adoration of the Magi*, dated 1619 (colour plate II). In this early masterpiece, light models the faces of the Virgin and the Child into unblemished shapes while the facial characteristics of the Three Kings and their young assistant, as well as St. Joseph's, are accented by a live contrast of light and shade.

The same distinction in the depiction of human and divine persons is evident in *The Immaculate Conception* and *St. John writing the Apocalypse* with the vision of the woman followed by the dragon (plates 27 and 28). These two works must also have been painted about 1619 as their composition and execution suggest. Their subjects are closely related, and they are of identical size and provenance, the Chapter Room of a Carmelite convent in Seville; yet, as the difference in the scale of the figures indicates, they were not intended to be on the same wall or altar, or at least not at the same level.

The belief that the Virgin had been conceived without taint of original sin did not become Catholic dogma till 1854. Debated for centuries, it aroused a great deal of feeling among its upholders in the mid- and late 1610's, especially in Seville. In 1615, the Carmelites of this city urged all the Spanish prelates to request from the Pope an affirmative declaration on the matter. Two learned treatises furthering the point were published in Seville that very year.[2] By 1619 the number of such books printed in Spain was at least thirty-eight.[3] On 1 January 1620, Pacheco completed a paper on the subject.[4]

Though Pacheco's paper on the sinless conception of the Virgin did not touch upon matters of iconography, such matters must have been discussed at his workshop in the late 1610's, when he was writing it, all the more so since precisely then Velázquez undertook to paint the two companion pieces on the subject, which very likely had some impact on the development of Pacheco's views.

[1] This portrait was acquired by the Prado Museum in 1944; soon after, the scroll around the crucifix was erased, and the inscription at the bottom was toned down (López-Rey, op. cit. no. 577).

[2] Alfonso Sobrino, *Tratado de la Immaculada Concepción*, Seville, 1615, and Alvaro Piçaño de Palacios, *Discurso primero en confirmación de la purissima concepción de la Virgen María*, Seville, 1615. The latter was followed by a *Discurso segundo, etc.*, published by the same author in 1616, also in Seville.

[3] See Ramón Menéndez Pidal, 'Onomástica inspirada en el culto mariánico', *Cuadernos del idioma*, Buenos Aires, 1965, vol. I, no. 1, pp. 9–16.

[4] *Apacible conversación entre un tomista y un congregado acerca del misterio de la purísima concepción de Nuestra Señora*, Seville, 1620 (reprinted in José María Asensio's *Francisco Pacheco: Sus obras artísticas y literarias*, Seville, 1886, pp. LVII–LXVIII).

In *Arte de la Pintura*, Pacheco discusses the iconography of the Immaculate Conception of the Virgin as related to the vision of the woman chased by the dragon described in the *Apocalypse*.[1] He advises the painter that, though the youth of St. John when he joined Jesus signifies his perpetual virginity, pictures of him writing the *Apocalypse* ought to represent him as the old man that he then was.

As for *The Immaculate Conception*, Pacheco says that the Virgin ought to look twelve or thirteen years old, have twelve stars round her head, and wear an imperial crown on golden hair; she must be dressed in a white tunic and blue mantle, and her feet should rest on the moon, depicted with its points downward; she must also be enclosed in the sun, represented as an oval shape in ochre and white.

Obviously Pacheco did not arrive at the final formulation of these views before 1626, a date which he mentions as significant for his argument. Nor did he, as far as we know, paint *The Immaculate Conception* before 1621, when he signed two pictures of the subject, which like another dated 1624, does not represent the Virgin wearing a crown as he later prescribed (Seville, Cathedral, formerly Ibarra collection, and San Lorenzo).

In Velázquez's *The Immaculate Conception*, painted about 1619, the Virgin wears no crown but has twelve stars round her head; her white tunic is shadowed by purplish tints as she stands against the sun, painted in ochre within luminous white clouds, with the moon under her feet, and the symbols of the litanies built into the landscape below. Her face, framed by her golden-brown hair, and her hands are flawless, limpid shapes, laved as it were by the smooth brushwork. It is a masterpiece, alive with a naturalism which is as visual as conceptual.

In the companion piece, Velázquez represented *St. John writing the Apocalypse* as a young, brown-haired man, in a white tunic and umber-rose mantle, his shape roughened by shadow and gesture which the uneven impasto makes sharper. The saint's vision of the winged woman and the three-headed dragon is seen in the upper left corner, as he, with his half-open mouth and the quill suspended over the page for live centres, embodies in his figure the wondrous experience of the Revelation and the contemplative pause needed to put it into words.

One cannot fully understand Velázquez's art unless one realizes the differentiation he makes between the portrayal of the divine and that of the human, which, as we have just seen, extends to the textural quality of the brushwork and is to be found not only between companion pieces, such as *The Immaculate Conception* and *St. John writing the Apocalypse*, but even within one single work, as in the case of *The adoration of the Magi*.

Throughout his life, Velázquez made use not only of the variety of hues but also of the variety of textures that pigments afforded to express pictorially the divine-human polarity which makes his world of painting cogent. Had he been a poet, he might likewise have coupled, balanced, aligned, opposed, reflected, contrasted, accented or subdued the various, at times diverging, connotations and shades of words. Pigments though, were the materials for his work, and he used them with a fullness of meaning which we can grasp today — provided, of course, we do not mistake the lines of our understanding for a programme to which the artist would have worked.[2]

---

[1] Vol. II, pp. 208–12, and 317–9.

[2] See José López-Rey, 'Pincelada e imagen en Velázquez', *Varia velazqueña*, vol. I, pp. 200–6.

Only two *bodegón*-like religious pictures by Velázquez are extant. Their composition stems from a sixteenth-century Flemish tradition which originated with Pieter Aertsen (1508–75).[1] Many of this master's works were destroyed by iconoclasts in his own day and there is no reason to conclude that Velázquez did see any of them or those by Joachim Beuckelaer, Aertsen's nephew and prominent follower who was born about 1535 and died in 1574. One may, however, assume that if Velázquez did not see any of those pictures, he was perhaps acquainted with their compositional scheme through derivative paintings, whether or not they were Flemish, or drawings, or engravings, or perhaps even from oral descriptions — never so infrequent a means of communication among painters as might be supposed.

Many of Aertsen's and Beuckelaer's extant works represent an interior, sometimes just a merchant's stall open on all sides, where pots, vessels and baskets with fruits, vegetables, raw or cured meats, cheese, game, fish, or the like nearly fill the foreground, their profusion underlined by bright local colours and the somewhat jerky manner in which the various planes recede; often, though not always, there are figures in the foreground, the middle distance, or both; whether or not they are handling food, they are related to the narrative, or at least to the sense, of the smallish figure-scene from the New Testament which an architectural structure frames in the far background.

A sizeable number of these paintings have *Christ in the house of Martha and Mary* for subject (plate 2). And so does the earlier of the two extant Velázquez *bodegón*-like religious pictures, dated 1618 (plate 5). Though the condition of this much restored painting is far from good, the main lines of its composition remain visible as a somewhat tantalizing suggestion of what it originally was. The foreground is taken up by the three-quarter figures of an old woman and a girl who is busy with mortar and pestle at a table where other pieces of kitchenware, some fish and other food are displayed. This young woman, identifiable as Martha, looks into the space outside the field of the composition. In the background, in what, as has been suggested, appears to be a reflection in a mirror, there is the scene of Jesus seated with Mary at His feet and another woman standing.[2] The sides of the mirror, seen in a diagonal perspective, are naturally of unequal apparent width and, for that matter, height.

[1] Cf. August L. Mayer, 'Velázquez und die niederländischen Küchenstücke', *Kunstchronic und Kunstmarkt*, 3 January 1919, pp. 236–7, and *Velázquez*, Berlin, 1924, p. 57; Kurt Gerstenberg, *Diego Velázquez*, Munich and Berlin, 1957, pp. 22 ff., and Halldor Soehner, 'Die Herkunft der Bodegones de Velázquez' [sic], *Varia velazqueña*, vol. I, pp. 233–44.

[2] This suggestion has recently been renewed by Emilio Orozco Díaz ('Un aspecto del barroquismo de Velázquez', *Varia velazqueña*, vol. I, pp. 184–99) and the present writer (*Velázquez: A Catalogue Raisonné*, pp. 32–3). To some, however, the background scene is seen through an opening into another room. Others hold it to be a picture hanging on the wall. If either were the case, Velázquez would have represented Jesus gesturing with His left hand and with the right one motionless, and Mary holding her mantle close to the chin with her high-lighted left hand, while the right, hardly noticeable, rests on her lap. Had the painter so represented both Christ and Mary, an awkward emphasis would have crept into the composition, of which he could not have been unaware since left-handed people were then, and later, regarded in Spain and elsewhere as mischievous or even devilish. This does not, of course, imply that Velázquez, or for that matter any other painter of his, earlier or later times, would have felt compelled to exclude altogether left-hand gestures from his representations of the divine persons or of the saints. I ought, however, to underline that we are here concerned with one particular painting which can only be understood in terms of its own composition.

The other Velázquez painting of this type recalls in its execution *Two young men at table* (plate 33) and is consequently datable to 1620-1. It is also a kitchen interior where a girl pensively lingers over her work; the background scene, *Christ at Emmaus*, is visible this time through an open hatch which gives upon another room (plate 20).

The analogy between either of these paintings and those by Aertsen or Beuckelaer is evident, though of limited range. The points of coincidence may be summarized as follows: in both the Flemish master's pictures and in Velázquez's the food and kitchenware take up most of the foreground, and together with the figures form the main scene which is related to the smallish one in the background. As for differences, there is in Velázquez's pictures neither the galaxy of comestibles to which the figures are rather ancillary in both Aertsen's and Beuckelaer's compositions, nor the sense of bustling activity which fills them. To begin with, in Velázquez's pictures the victuals and pieces of kitchenware are few in number, and, striking though they are, they do not dominate the composition; secondly, instead of the manifold bright local colours which make luxuriant the perspective-heavy space of the Flemish pictures, there is in Velázquez's a unifying atmospheric tint which makes the textures of food, brass and earthenware pieces glow one against the other, thus achieving a sensorial expression of disarray with just a few objects, without overpowering the three-quarter or half-length human figures, to whose pose and prominence the overall composition is keyed; indeed, the relation between the large and the small, more luminous background scene is vividly enhanced rather than lessened by the impact of the main figures.

A plainer and closer analogy is to be found between Pacheco's *St. Sebastian nursed by St. Irene* (plate 6), of 1616, and the later Velázquez's *bodegón*-like religious compositions. In Pacheco's painting — destroyed by fire in 1936 — St. Sebastian was seen in an interior, the blood-stained arrows hanging on the wall; a window framed the view of a landscape with St. Sebastian tied to a tree and the archers aiming their arrows at him.[1] Unlike Pacheco, however, Velázquez does not represent two moments of the same narrative in either *Christ in the house of Martha and Mary* or in *Christ at Emmaus*. In composition, moreover, Velázquez differs as much from Pacheco as from Aertsen or Beuckelaer. His is a different sense of space. Indeed, the stare of Martha — and, for that matter, the gaze of the kitchenmaid — suggests a diagonal leading to the outlying space from where the viewer encompasses both the foreground and the background scenes as a dynamic whole.

FIRST STAY AT THE COURT

Young Velázquez started from Seville on his first journey to Madrid in the second half of April 1622.[2] As we know, he was desirous of seeing the Escorial, a marvel of architecture in

---

[1] For Pacheco's own description of this picture, see his *Arte de la Pintura*, vol. II, pp. 327-8. Cf. Priscilla E. Muller, 'Francisco Pacheco as a Painter', *Marsyas*, vol. X, 1960-61, p. 40.

[2] Pacheco states that Velázquez 'left Seville for Madrid sometime in April of the year 1622'. On the 14th, Velázquez was still in Seville and signed a document empowering Pacheco to collect in his behalf any and all moneys or merchandises due to him.

itself, where a great many masterpieces, mainly paintings, were displayed. Another of his ambitions was to portray the new sovereigns, a venture which might have sped his success.

Philip IV, now seventeen, had come to the throne just one year earlier and had from the beginning left the cares of state to the Count of Olivares, who had been in his service ever since, as a Prince, he had had a household of his own. He retained as Court painters Rodrigo de Villandrando, Bartolomé González, Eugenio Caxés, and Vincencio Carducho, all of whom had served his father, the late Philip III.

It is likely that Velázquez's work was known to Olivares, who in 1619, as he was moodily toying with the idea of withdrawing from the Court, had spent several months at Seville, where he liked to surround himself with scholars and poets. One of them was Francisco de Rioja, whom he held in high esteem. Rioja, who was a close friend of Pacheco and had the year before acted as a witness at Velázquez's wedding, might well have mentioned the promising young painter to the Count whose keen sense of power sharpened his interest in art and made him find pleasure in patronizing creative artists — a diversion which was not uncommon at the time among those of high social rank. Pacheco also knew the Count, whose portrait he had painted as early as 1610, and from what we know of him he would surely have endeavoured not to let the young master of such pictures as *Old woman frying eggs* or *The adoration of the Magi* go unnoticed by so important a Maecenas as Olivares.

Those whom Pacheco mentioned as having taken care of his son-in-'aw in Madrid came from Seville. Particularly obliging was Don Juan de Fonseca, a canon from the Cathedral of Seville and writer on art, who was now a chaplain to the new King; he was fond of Velázquez's paintings and decided to further his success at the Court. He failed though in his effort to secure an opportunity for his protégé to portray the sovereigns. It was instead with the portrait of the famous poet Don Luís de Góngora that Velázquez first won recognition in Madrid (plate 41). The likeness of Góngora — his eyes and hair black, clad in a black cassock and a white collar permeated by light — is quite vivid; his head, half in the light and half in the shadow, stands out against a greenish background, half of which is dark while the rest is lighted — the rose and yellowish flesh tones, the blackish shade on the shaven face, and the greenish tinge on the grey moustache resulting in a golden glow.

Besides the royal collection at the Escorial, the young painter would naturally have seen the paintings in the Royal Palace, as well as those in some of the oustanding private collections at Madrid. It is also probable that he stopped at Toledo on his way to or from Seville, for Pacheco would undoubtedly have urged him to do so. That Velázquez went there is all the more likely since admirers of El Greco were still prominent in Madrid intellectual life. Góngora (1561–1627) had written a sonnet on the occasion of his death, and the subtle poet and fashionable Trinitarian preacher, Fray Hortensio Félix Paravicino (1580–1633), then at the peak of his reputation, was the author of four sonnets exalting the meaning of El Greco's art. Young Velázquez must have admired the old master's handling of pigment, sure and free, and the naturalism of his portraits.

Since El Greco's day, Toledo had been a more vital art centre than the Escorial, where his *Martyrdom of St. Maurice* failed to please Philip II in 1580. It was at Toledo, in El Greco's circle, that Pedro de Orrente (1580–1645), sometimes referred to as the 'Spanish Bassano', acquired the mastery in the handling of light and texture that was to make of him a naturalist painter, admired and imitated at the Court and other Spanish art centres. On 10 August 1603, when Juan Sánchez Cotán (1561–1627), then in his forties, closed up his workshop at Toledo to enter monastic life, he left behind a number of still-lifes in which sheer space intensified the reality of things to a degree that no other seventeenth-century painter would surpass (plate 9). By the 1620's, Alejandro de Loarte, who, after spending some time in Madrid, had returned to Toledo, had become an outstanding master of still-lifes and *bodegones*; he signed the last one in 1626, when he died, apparently still a young man.

As for the painters influential at the Court, most of them had been brought up in the tenets of mannerism which, from the 1570's till early in the 1600's, had radiated from the Escorial. Spanish masters such as Juan Fernández de Navarrete (1526–79) and Alonso Sánchez Coello (ca. 1532–88) had executed paintings for the church, the monastery or the royal chambers there, and so had a good many Italian painters, including Luca Cambiaso (1527–1585) and Federico Zuccaro (1542–1609).

When Bartolomé Carducho (1554–1608) left his native Florence to become an assistant to Zuccaro at the Escorial, he took with him his nine-year-old brother, Vincencio (1576–1638). Zuccaro himself was less than a success at the Escorial and he returned to Italy scarcely three years later. Bartolomé Carducho, however, remained in Spain in the service of Philip II, who in 1598 appointed him Court painter, a position which at his death was granted to his brother Vincencio by the new king, Philip III. Eugenio Caxés (ca. 1577–1634), another Court painter, owed his training to his father, Patricio (ca. 1544–1611), who in his early twenties had come from Rome to Spain, where he remained in the royal service till his death.

Vincencio Carducho and Eugenio Caxés had won recognition and influence at the Court during the reign of Philip III, who came to the throne in September 1598. When Rubens visited the Spanish Court, at Valladolid in 1603, he commented that the painters there were pathetically incompetent or sloppy.

By the 1620's, the taste for naturalism was rather pronounced among painters, and even more among writers and connoisseurs at Madrid, to which the Court had been once more moved. Orazio Borgiani (1575–1616), whose naturalistic outlook was more akin to that of the Carracci's than to Caravaggio's, whom he strove to emulate, had been at Valladolid and elsewhere in Spain early in the century, and perhaps before; that he had been successful is shown by the number of paintings he left behind and by the fact that in 1605 he was entrusted, together with Eugenio Caxés, to draw up the inventory of the Marqués de Poza's collection. There is reason to surmise that his painting continued to find a market in Spain even after his return to Rome.[1]

The taste for naturalism is discernible in the works of both Eugenio Caxés and Vincencio Carducho. As early as 1605, Caxés endeavoured to give a naturalist cast to the otherwise stock Michelangelesque figures of his *Fall of the angels* (plate 8). In a like manner, Carducho, at an

[1] For Borgianni's years in Spain, see Alfonso E. Pérez Sánchez, *Borgianni, Cavarozzi y Nardi en España*, Madrid, 1964, pp. 10 ff.

unknown date, though presumably before the 1620's, had tried to achieve a striking naturalism in his *Colossal head of a man*, measuring 2·46 × 2·05 m., in which line and shading define the individual human traits without aiming at the dramatic expression of the momentary which Caravaggio's sheer light achieves (plate 10).

More spirited, though also derivative, was Antonio de Lanchares (d. 1630),[1] who at least in his *Adoration of the shepherds*, of 1612, had carried his naturalism, rooted, like Orrente's, in the Bassenesque tradition, somewhat closer to Caravaggio's use of light for overall dramatic composition (plate 16).

Other Spanish painters had seen Caravaggio's works in Italy, and paintings by him, or copies of them, had certainly arrived in Spain shortly after his death, and probably even long before. In any case, by 1622, they could be seen in churches and private collections in Seville, Madrid and elsewhere. In 1610, on retiring as Viceroy of Naples, the Count of Benavente had brought with him to his palace in Valladolid a 'very large' *Crucifixion of St. Andrew* by the hand of Caravaggio; it was still there in 1653.[2]

The popularity of Caravaggio in Spain is documented by the many references, most of them eulogistic, found in writings of that time. It is also attested to by the sarcasm with which Vincencio Carducho retold years later, in his *Diálogos de la Pintura*, the story of the success of that 'Antichrist', or 'Antimichelangelo'. Carducho's prose is weighted with images of food, gluttony, digestion, ill-digestion, and the like, as he disparagingly describes the naturalism of Caravaggio and his followers, even contriving to bring in 'natural' as a noun in an awkward effort to suggest the picture of a simpleton.[3]

Fray Juan Bautista Maino may rightly be regarded as more alert, more sensitive, and richer in accomplishment than most of the painters who were influential at the Court at the time of Velázquez's arrival. He had practised the art of painting in Toledo during El Greco's last years; there in 1613, at thirty-five, he entered the Dominican Order. Later he was appointed drawing master to Prince Philip, who, after ascending the throne, kept him on at the Court. Some of his works bring to mind those by Luis Tristán, El Greco's pupil, who died in 1624. Yet, his art as a whole appears to have been more significantly oriented to that of the Caracci.[4]

Truly creative was the Madrilenian Juan van der Hamen y León (1596–1632), whose work as a still-life painter was rooted in that of Juan Sánchez Cotán (1561–1627). Though

[1] I am indebted to Mr. Volker Schierk for having let me know the date of Lanchares's death, 14 March 1630, which he has found and plans to publish together with other new data bearing on the same painter. Jusepe Martínez, who in 1634, while at Madrid, mixed with many of his fellow painters, recorded that Lanchares, an outstanding pupil of Eugenio Caxés, had spent a long time in Rome, and had died prematurely (*Discursos practicables del nobilísimo arte de la pintura*, ed. Valentín Carderera y Solano, Madrid, 1866, p. 115).

[2] It was then inventoried in the collection of the Count of Benavente's son and heir to his title. Its whereabouts since is unknown. See J. Ainaud, *art. cit.*, pp. 380–1. There is no reason to believe that this *St. Andrew* is the painting of the same subject which belonged years ago to Emmerich and Christa Back-Vega, who published it rather unconvincingly as Caravaggio's original ('A lost masterpiece by Caravaggio', *The Art Bulletin*, March 1958, pp. 65–6).

[3] *Diálogos de la Pintura*, Madrid, 1633, fol. 89 r. and ff.

[4] For data on Maino see Fray Antonio García Figar, O.P., 'Fray Juan Bautista Maino, pintor español', *Goya*, Madrid, July–August 1958, pp. 6–12. Jusepe Martínez wrote that Maino 'had been a pupil and friend of Annibale Carracci, and a great crony of our great Guido Reni' (op. cit., pp. 120–1).

Sánchez Cotán had closed up his workshop at Toledo in 1603 to enter the Carthusian monastic order and his pictorial activity had since been limited to conventual commissions, the still lifes that he left behind in the world had a lasting impact on younger painters, for whom he seemed to have discovered the very appearance of things by depicting them against sheer space. One of his achievements was a cardoon which he cast into so compelling a pictorial entity that other painters used it time and again in their still-life compositions (plate 9).

Van der Hamen's earliest recorded work is a still-life, now lost, painted in 1619 for the Royal Palace at El Pardo, near Madrid. Though he also painted portraits and other figure-compositions, his contemporaries admired him mainly for his still-lifes, rather to his annoyance. Yet they were right for, as can be seen in the one extant portrait by his hand, *Don Francisco de la Cueva*, of 1625 (plate 34), Van der Hamen, not unlike Carducho, effected a naturalist portrayal of the human figure chiefly by the overdrawing of details, which, without the flux of light, appear stark, almost lifeless. His still-lifes, however, are unique for the architectural quality with which he endows the spaces between the various things represented — a quality which brings order into the disarray of fruits, sweetmeats, tableware and the like (plate 35).[1]

Philip IV favoured Rodrigo de Villandrando over the other Court painters.[2] In 1619 or soon after, shortly before the young sovereign came to the throne, Villandrando had portrayed him and his wife, the then Princess Isabel. Velázquez probably saw these two portraits at the Royal Palace during his first stay in Madrid. It is also likely that he saw then the portraits of the late sovereigns, Philip III and Queen Margarita, as well as those of Philip IV's brother and sister, the Infante Don Fernando and the Infanta Doña María, all by the hand of Villandrando.

Villandrando's portrait of *Philip IV* shows the sovereign resting his right hand on the head of the dwarf *Soplillo* (plate 38). As a work of art, it shows the refinement of a pictorial tradition which for some sixty years, since the time of Alonso Sánchez Coello (1531/2–88),

---

[1] José López-Rey, foreword to the catalogue of the exhibition, *The Golden Age of Spanish Still-life Painting*, The Newark Museum of Art, Newark, N. J., 1964, p. 4. See also William B. Jordan, 'Juan van der Hamen y León: A Madrilenian Still-life Painter', *Marsyas*, New York 1964–5 [actually printed in 1966], pp. 52–69.

[2] Little has been known till now about Rodrigo de Villandrando, except that he was a pupil of Pantoja de la Cruz, signed several portraits, and, according to the 1963 catalogue of the Prado Museum, 'died before 4 September 1628'. However, an examination of his personal file and related documents, preserved at the Archive of the Madrid Royal Palace, discloses that he took the oath as 'Usher of the Chamber without perquisites' on 6 July 1621, and that he died in December 1622. Moreover, the inventory of the Madrid Royal Palace drawn up in 1636 describes in some detail six portraits by his hand. The sitters were Philip III and his wife, Queen Margarita; Prince Philip, who became Philip IV on 31 March 1621, and his wife, Isabel; the Infanta Doña María, and the Infante Don Fernando. The description of the dress of Princess Isabel ends with the statement that it is the one she wore on the occasion of Philip III's entrance into Lisbon, which took place on 29 June 1619. That royal journey ended with the return of the King to Madrid on 4 December 1619. A few weeks later, on 31 December, Bartolomé González was paid 400 *reales* on account for a life-size portrait of Philip III in the stately robes that he wore when he made his formal appearance at the Portuguese Cortes (Marqués del Saltillo, 'Artistas madrileños', *Boletín de la Sociedad Española de Excursiones*, 1953, p. 167). Consequently, Villandrando's portrait of *Princess Isabel* and its companion piece, *Philip IV as Prince with the dwarf Soplillo*, neither of which is dated though both are signed, must have been painted sometime between the summer of 1619 and 31 March 1621.

had been kept alive by a few masters of succeeding generations at the Spanish Court.

Such was the world of art in which Velázquez's portrait of the baroque poet Góngora was 'much praised', as Pacheco reported. The challenges that stirred that world were not unlike those felt elsewhere in Europe, then torn by bitter religious differences, antagonistic political systems, contrasting social structures, and even diverging views on the purpose of life, whether individual or national. New schools of painting, national or local, each with characteristics of its own, had sprung up here and there as the creative painter turned his mind's eye from the idea of man and nature to the appearance of men and things, and hence to his immediate surroundings.

The young master painted the portrait of Góngora at the request of Pacheco, who probably wanted to use it to draw a likeness of the poet for his *Libro de retratos*. Eight of the portraits made by Pacheco for this book, left unfinished, represent poets or humanists crowned with laurel wreaths. And so Velázquez did depict Góngora at first, though he quickly painted over the wreath, still noticeable under X-ray examination, casting the portrait into a fully naturalistic image (plates 40 and 41). Almost forty years later when Velázquez died, either the portrait with which he had first won recognition at Madrid or, less likely, a replica of it, hung in one of his rooms at the Royal Palace.

While in Madrid, Velázquez would surely have heard that Philip IV had rewarded Rodrigo de Villandrando the year before with the appointment to the position of Usher of the Chamber. On his way back to Seville, the young painter probably mused over the high recognition and honours that an artist could attain only at the Court.

THE CALL TO THE COURT

Don Juan de Fonseca, that early, and as such presumably keen admirer of Velázquez, kept a watchful eye on the Court scene, waiting for a new opportunity for the young painter. He did not have to wait long, for within a matter of months, in December 1622, Rodrigo de Villandrando died, and in the spring of 1623 Fonseca conveyed to Velázquez the Count of Olivares' command to come to the Court.

The young painter once more set out for Madrid, this time accompanied by Pacheco. Now Fonseca left nothing to chance; he lodged Velázquez in his own home, and sat for him, and, as soon as the portrait was finished, Don Gaspar de Bracamonte, also a Sevillian, and chamberlain to the King's brother, Cardinal Infante Don Fernando, took it to the Royal Palace, where within an hour everybody, the courtiers, the Infantes, and even the King, had seen and admired it. Velázquez was directed to paint the portrait of the Cardinal Infante but 'it was thought more advisable' that he should first portray His Majesty — which gives the full measure of the painter's and Fonseca's success — even though it was necessary to wait till Philip could spare the time for the sittings.

According to Pacheco, Velázquez painted the portrait of the King on 30 August 1623. Needless to say, in one day, the painter could hardly have done more than a sketch of the head. It is, however, more likely that Pacheco meant that the portrait was finished on the mentioned date.

The King was pleased with the portrait; Olivares said that till then no one had really portrayed Philip IV and all the noblemen felt the same way. The young master's highest expectations were fulfilled as Olivares commanded him to move his home to Madrid and promised him that from then on he would be the only painter to portray the King and that such other portraits of the sovereign as existed would be withdrawn.

Those were days of both concern and festivity at the Spanish Court where the Prince of Wales, later Charles I, was still discussing his contemplated marriage to the Infanta María, Philip IV's sister. Velázquez, while busy with the portrait of the King, made a colour sketch, now lost, of the English Prince, who rewarded him with one hundred *escudos*.[1] The Prince's visit which, though unexpected, had at the beginning appeared promising for both countries, came to a dead end early in September 1623, when the Spanish King accompanied his royal visitor to El Escorial where they said their adieus.

Velázquez was formally admitted into the King's service on 6 October 1623 at a salary of twenty ducats a month with the obligation of painting such works as might be ordered; but before the month was over Philip bettered the financial terms stipulating that, in addition to his monthly salary, Velázquez was to be paid for whatever pictures he should paint as painter to the King.

PORTRAITS OF THE KING AND OF OTHERS

Neither the portrait of Fonseca, which opened the way for the success of Velázquez at the Royal Palace, nor that of the Prince of Wales, with which the young painter's name travelled for the first time to England, has been identified. As for the portrait of the King that won for Velázquez the appointment as Court painter, it has been preserved, though only underneath another likeness of the sovereign painted by Velázquez himself a few years later.

In fact, radiographs recently made show, though, of course, only in black and white, what must be the first portrait of Philip IV painted by Velázquez: the King is seen standing by a table, his right hand holding a petition while the left one rests on the sword hilt; he has a flabby face, roundish at the chin, and a short neck — which, from all we know, corresponded to his actual physique (plates 42 and 49).

Such was the portrait with which Velázquez won his decisive success at the Court, where even the King admired it. Yet, the young master very soon became dissatisfied with it, as he set

---

[1] Pacheco's report about the portrait of Philip IV finished by Velázquez on 30 August 1630 closes with the statement: '*Hizo también de camino un bosquexo del Príncipe de Gales, que le dió cien escudos*'. The expression *de camino* without reference to any destination alludes to no journey in the quoted text, and therefore cannot be understood to mean 'at the time of the trip' to the Escorial, as Miss Trapier has ventured to guess (*Velázquez*, p. 94). Nor could it mean that Velázquez represented the Prince of Wales 'in travelling dress' as a contributor to *The Connoisseur* has asserted in what can only be regarded as a display of freedom from knowledge of the Spanish language (July 1964, p. 206). What Pacheco says is that Velázquez made a colour sketch of the Prince while he was at work on the portrait of Philip IV.

out to portray the quasi-divine nature of the person of the King rather than the reality of his physique. Hence, in 1626–8, he painted out that true-to-life likeness of Philip, substituting for it another in which the royal sitter's natural characteristics were not his subject (plate 48).

The earliest portrait of Philip IV executed by Velázquez which has come down to us in visible pigment is bust-length. The young master painted it probably still within 1623, surely no later than 1624, when he used it for a full-length which was finished by 4 December.

In the bust portrait, Philip is seen clad in black with a greyish-white collar, against an olive-grey background; a quiet light bathes his countenance, thinning the shadows to the faintest veil; the face is firmly modelled in ivory and rose hues with redder touches for the ear and eyelids, the gleam in the blue-grey eyes as still as the highlights on the crimson lips. The ample outline of the broad shoulders adds to the quiet of the whole composition (plate 43). Young Velázquez achieved in this portrait a sentient image of the King which was to remain his own, as even his latest portrait of Philip, painted some thirty years later, shows (plate 151).

Two portraits executed by the young artist late in 1624 have come down to us fully documented. Though one is of Philip IV and the other of the Count of Olivares, both were commissioned, or at least paid for, by the widow of Don García Pérez de Araciel, Professor of Law at the University of Salamanca and a member of the Council of Castille. Ever since coming into power, Olivares had had Pérez de Araciel at his elbow, having appointed him to some of the most demanding positions, such as the commission of judges instituted to investigate the conduct of the former Viceroy of Naples, the Duke of Osuna.[1]

A document signed by Velázquez on 4 December 1624 shows that he had received from the widow of Pérez de Araciel a payment on account for the portraits of Philip IV, the Count of Olivares and the deceased professor.[2] Since the latter had died only a few months earlier, it might be that he rather than his widow had commissioned the three portraits, of which only those of the King and his chief minister have come down to us.

It is unlikely that Philip IV would have sat for a portrait commissioned by a royal servant or his widow. Obviously, Velázquez painted the head after the bust I have just discussed, while he used for the rest of the figure the full-length of 1623, now visible only under X-rays.

Though the portrait of *Philip IV* has been restored, particularly about the eyes, it is plain that Velázquez gave expression in it to his view of the King as a quasi-divine person, an idea shared by some of the best minds of the time (plate 45).[3] As in the earliest bust portrait, Philip is clad in black with greyish-white collar and cuffs; he stands against a light grey background, the space around him built by the floor line and shadows and the red- and

[1] See Francisco de Quevedo y Villegas, 'Grandes anales de quince días (1621)', *Obras completas, Obras en prosa* ed. Luis Astrana Marín, Madrid, 1932, p. 476.

[2] The document is not at the archive of the ducal house of Granada de Ega-Zaráuz as stated in *Varia velazqueña*, vol. II, p. 224, but at The Metropolitan Museum of Art, New York.

[3] Francisco de Quevedo drew a vivid parallel between the figure of Christ on Earth and the person of the King, in his *Politica de Dios, Gobierno de Cristo*, the first part of which was published in 1626. See the volume of *Obras completas*, pp. 302–447, cited in n. 1, above. Father Francisco de los Santos refers to the Spanish monarchs from the Hapsburg family as 'Vicegods on earth' ('*Vicedioses en la tierra*') in a context which indicates that the expression was current at the time (*Descripción breve del monasterio de S. Lorenzo el Real del Escorial*, Madrid, 1657, fol. 166 r.).

gold-covered table in the middle distance. His face, rose and ivory, with a scarlet note for the lips, is one with his self-contained pose — the quiet rhythm of his figure marked by the gold chain falling in a long curve from his right shoulder and by the badge of the Golden Fleece hanging from a black ribbon. There is no emphasis on his natural characteristics; indeed, light rounds his head and hands into smooth shapes with shading used only in the flowing contour; as for royal attributes, his divine kingly power is embodied in an effortless gesture, one hand on the sword hilt and the other holding a petition.

For a contrast, we may look at another full-length portrait, approximately of the same size, representing *Philip IV in parade armour*. As I have suggested elsewhere, it was painted by Juan Bautista Maino, certainly not before January 1623, when the King adopted the simple collar he is seen wearing, and very likely not after 30 August of that year, when Velázquez's overwhelming success with his first likeness of Philip IV led to the thought, at least, that all other portraits of the King ought to be withdrawn (plate 37).[1]

In Maino's portrait, the blond Philip is seen in black, gold-inlaid full armour, with red at the edges of the main pieces. His face painted in grey and pink hues, he stands, baton in his right hand, against the red velvet curtain and the red-velvet-draped stand where his helmet rests. The brushwork is smooth throughout the whole composition, and the highlights, whether on the subject's face, the armour, or the drapes, bring about a soft sheen. The design of the armour, the folds of the drapes reaching the floor, the sitter's formal and yet animated pose, and the interplay between his idle left hand and his sword hilt, both dynamically shaped, imbue the composition with a brisk rhythm which binds together the figure of Philip IV and his royal attributes. The contrast between these two portraits, both now at the Metropolitan Museum of Art, is the more revealing as it underlines the mastery of Maino, then a painter of renown, and the distinct originality of young Velázquez.

Different in both pose and treatment from Velázquez's *Philip IV* is his companion portrait of the *Count of Olivares* (plate 44). The sitter's corpulent figure, also clad in black, is made rather ponderous by the vivid display of the red cross of Calatrava, the heavy gold chain, drawn firmly across the chest — instead of falling in the light curve of the King's — and the other symbols of his high offices, the key of the Lord of the Bedchamber and the spurs of the Master of the Royal Horse, dangling from his belt. His forceful gesture emphasizes the mundane nature of his power, as his left hand rests on the sword hilt under the weight of the cloak draped on the shoulder, and the right one upon the table top, the finger curving over the edge, the two weighted with shadows. A strong light falls across his face accenting, as do the varying

[1] The latest catalogue of Spanish paintings at the Metropolitan Museum of Art, published in 1940, does not include Maino's portrait of *Philip IV in parade armour* which came in 1944 to the museum, where it bears a label attributing it to a 'follower of Velázquez'. This fine likeness of Philip IV was openly imitated in a rather mediocre portrait which shows the King, accompanied by a dwarf, standing on a platform, behind which one can partly see a page holding a horse, and, beyond, a landscape view (Madrid, Palacio de Viana). See José López-Rey, 'Maino y Velázquez: Dos retratos de Felipe IV en el Metropolitan Museum of Art de Nueva York', *Colóquio*, Lisbon, October 1963, pp. 15–19; 'A portrait of Philip IV by Juan Bautista Maino', *The Art Bulletin*, New York, December 1963, pp. 361–3, and 'Sobre la atribución de un retrato de Felipe IV a Gaspar de Crayer', *Archivo Español de Arte*, Madrid, April–September 1966, pp. 195–6.

textures of pigment also, the wrinkles and other peculiarities of appearance, and leaving the left side in shadow.[1]

The indicated differences between these two companion portraits are so obvious that they have led some scholars to cast doubts on the authenticity of one or the other, or even of both pictures. Such doubts arise from the idle assumption that Velázquez's sense of composition and handling of pigment was unvaried within any one given time, and that such dissimilarities in execution as are noticeable between any two paintings bearing his name are evidence either that they were painted at different periods, or that at least one of them is not by his hand. Assumptions of this kind, often made in relation to great masters, overlook the complexity of a creative artist's work and lead to conclusions which are not more convincing for the simplicity of argument to which they lend themselves. In the case of Velázquez, available data make such simplifications untenable.

As we know, dissimilarities in pictorial handling appear quite early in Velázquez's art, and are apparent not only in companion pieces, such as *The Immaculate Conception* and *St. John writing the Apocalypse*, but also within one single picture, as in *The adoration of the Magi* (plates 27, 28 and colour plate II). Rather than being disconcerting, such dissimilarities reveal the freedom and consistency of Velázquez's work. He made use of dissimilarities in the treatment of light and shade, or in the quality of the brushwork, for various expressive purposes, often to emphasize the artistic reality of the images that he put on canvas. He consistently used them to express the polarity of the human and the divine or the contrast that he saw between the King as the embodiment of a divine right and the King's minister as the personification of wordly power.

The young master achieved another resounding success at the Court with an equestrian portrait of Philip IV, painted entirely from life, which he completed in 1625. It won praise from courtiers and poets and aroused envy among the painters, as Pacheco, who was then in Madrid, recorded. The King rewarded Velázquez with three hundred ducats plus a life annuity in the same amount, and allowed the portrait to be displayed at the favourite spot of the Madrilenian cognoscenti and wags, a public walk across the convent of San Felipe.

That equestrian portrait is now lost. However, there is at the Prado Museum a bust portrait of *Philip IV in armour* painted by Velázquez, probably also about 1625, though he later re-painted it. A radiograph reveals that, as originally executed, this portrait still represented the King with a round chin and a short neck (plate 46).

Some years later, most likely between 1626 and 1628, Velázquez repainted the full-length portrait of the King which he had executed in August 1623 and which, as radiographs have

[1] There is at the Hispanic Society of America, New York City, another full-length portrait of Olivares, which I, like all other Velázquez scholars, beginning with Beruete, have catalogued as by the Master. The cleaning that it underwent in 1958 has left it in a 'poor state of preservation', as I have pointed out elsewhere (*Velázquez: A Catalogue Raisonné*, no. 507, and plates 40 and 41, reproducing the picture before and after the mentioned cleaning). It bears an inscription which, as I recorded in my catalogue entry, has been read as *Año 1625* by Miss Elisabeth du Gué Trapier ('Velázquez. New Data on a Group of Portraits', *Notes Hispanic*, New York, The Hispanic Society of America 1944, vol. IV, pp. 36–63). I am now convinced, however, that this inscription is an old inventory number rather than a date.

recently shown, had been somewhat damaged. It was not a restoration, though, that Velázquez undertook. Rather, he repainted the whole composition, substantially altering the royal sitter's pose, introducing changes in his costume, and, more significantly, endowing him with distinctly different features, going even further in that than in the other likenesses of 1623-4 (plates 43 and 45). In the resulting new portrait, there is no floor line and the sense of space is achieved by a subtle interplay of light and shade (plate 48). The King's face and hands are unmarked by shadows or any natural flaw; his chin is somewhat pointed, and his neck quite elongated; the verticality of his figure has been somewhat enhanced by the change in his stance and the omission of the looped gold chain; yet his gesture is as effortless as in the earlier portrait.

As for the bust portrait of *Philip IV in armour*, which had also remained in the royal collection, Velázquez repainted it in much the same spirit and presumably about the same time, making the King's chin pointed and his neck elongated; he also added a red scarf across the King's armour. The brushwork texture of this scarf, made of vivid highlights and a variety of red hues, underscores the rose tones of the sovereign's face and the serene light that bathes it (plate 47).[1]

In the bust portrait of 1623 or 1624, as well as in the full-length of the latter year, Velázquez had still depicted Philip's chin as round and his neck as short (plates 43 and 45). Yet, in those painted after 1624, he made the King's chin look somewhat pointed and his neck long (frontispiece and plates 47, 48, 80, 98, 109, 120 and 151). This appears more obvious if one compares the portrait of 1626-28 with either of the earlier ones, since in the three of them the King wears identical collars and his face is seen from the same point of view (plates 43, 45, and 48).

The use of such pictorial devices to improve the sitter's appearance did not, of course, originate with Velázquez. He used them as another means of achieving his image of the King as a quasi-divine person. Flattery could hardly have been his motive, as he had won his first and astonishing success at the Court precisely with a true-to-life likeness of Philip which was praised to the utmost by the King himself, Olivares and all the courtiers. Moreover, if the portraits of Philip IV executed throughout the years by other painters, even in the workshop of Velázquez, are any indication, the prevailing taste at the Court continued to favour likenesses of the King which were truer to life than those that came from Velázquez's hand — a preference that Philip himself seemingly came to share in his melancholy last years. As it happened, Velázquez always left it for his assistants to meet that taste.

About the same time, 1626-28, Velázquez portrayed the Infante Don Carlos, who was two

[1] Six portraits of Philip IV painted by Velázquez in the 1620's, including two visible only by means of X-rays, have come down to us. Their chronological sequence is as follows:

   (i)   The full-length, hidden under a later portrait, at the Prado Museum. Most probably the one finished on 30 August 1623 (plates 42 and 49).

   (ii)   The bust portrait in black, Meadows Museum, Dallas. Painted after August 1623 and before December 1624 (plate 43).

   (iii)   The full-length at the Metropolitan Museum. Finished by 4 December 1624 (plate 45).

   (iv)   The bust in armour, hidden under a later portrait, at the Prado Museum. Painted about 1625 (plate 46).

   (v)   The full-length, painted over (i), at the Prado Museum. Painted in 1626-28 (plate 48).

   (vi)   The bust, in armour and with a scarf, painted over (iv), at the Prado Museum. Painted in 1626-28 (plate 47).

years younger than his brother, the King (plate 50). The portrait of the Infante, though, is quite different from that of the monarch: the light on his face is intermingled with shadows which make somewhat weightier his character traits, and highlights make vivid the wrinkles and textural qualities of his black costume and gold bandolier, as with a worldly gesture he nonchalantly holds a glove in his right hand and his hat in his left.

As shall be seen, the differences I have been illustrating between Velázquez's depiction of the person of the King and that of other sitters runs through the whole of his art, and only a superficial attitude can ignore them or explain them away as accidental or without significance.

THE NEW AND THE OLD

By his appointment in 1623 as painter to the King with a regular stipend, young Velázquez joined the exclusive company of three painters who were at least double his age and who had achieved recognition in the preceding reign: Bartolomé González, Eugenio Caxés, and Vincencio Carducho.

Carducho and Caxés had been trained in the taste and routine of mannerism, which had ceased to be a creative attitude before they could be fullfledged artists. Like other painters of their background, in Spain and elsewhere in Europe, they groped or forged ahead into the new taste by casting naturalist images, usually as secondary counterthrusts, within the classic framework of their compositions. Bartolomé González (1564–1627) had mainly been engaged in painting portraits of royal persons; though older in years than either Caxés or Carducho, he was more attuned to the times, for he had grown up in the live Titianesque tradition of his master, Juan Pantoja de la Cruz (1553–1608), and had later been attracted to Caravaggism (plate 17).

Velázquez's success at the Court had thus far been based mainly on his mastery as a portrait painter. He had, however, gone on painting *bodegones*, and his 'forceful example' had led other painters to do likewise. Indeed, even old Pacheco, to whom we owe the information, felt compelled to paint a *bodegón* piece when he was in Madrid in 1625.

Early in 1627, Don Juan de Fonseca died, leaving a sizeable number of paintings which Velázquez appraised at the request of the heirs on 28 January. The portrait that Velázquez had painted of his early protector was not among them. Included, though, was *The waterseller*, which Fonseca had acquired from his protegee, perhaps as a gift.

Velázquez appraised *The waterseller* at four hundred *reales*, higher than any other painting in the collection. It was bought by Don Gaspar de Bracamonte, another of the courtiers instrumental in securing Velázquez's early success, for a lesser amount, three hundred and thirty *reales*, which, however, was equalled only by two anonymous portraits, one of the King and the other of the Cardinal Infante Don Fernando, and surpassed by no painting in the sale.[1]

Bodegones and naturalist portraits were looked down on as not quite proper subjects by Vincencio Carducho, who, as a writer on art, hovered inconclusively between the mannerist doctrine, learned in his youth, and the baroque concepts which he seems to have

[1] José López Navío, 'Velázquez tasa los cuadros de su protector D. Juan de Fonseca', *Archivo Español de Arte*, January–March, 1961, pp. 53–84.

acquired from his fashionable literary friends, one of whom was the great Lope de Vega.

It is likely that some of the men of letters whom Carducho frequented contributed ideas for the allegorical engravings which illustrated his *Diálogos de la Pintura*, a book which has the appearance of a collective undertaking, even though the eight *dialogues* are undoubtedly the work of Carducho. One of the main aims of the book is to prove that Painting is a liberal art, and that, consequently, painters ought to be exempted from taxation as had been argued, by El Greco among others, since early in the century. In 1629, Carducho had brought out in book form, under the title *Memorial informatorio por los pintores*, seven briefs written in support of his and other painters' claim by authors of varying literary persuasions. Velázquez was not among the pleaders.

In the *Diálogos*, published in 1634, Carducho reprinted those briefs as an appendix, which also included the decision rendered by the Royal Council of Finance on 11 January 1633, granting the exception requested by Carducho and his fellow petitioners; facing the text of this decision there is an endpiece that exalts the *act* of painting, regarded by some as purely manual and, hence, as a valid objection to the inclusion of Painting among the liberal arts. A poem by one of Carducho's friends is printed at the end of each dialogue, except the first, and there is after every one of them an engraving with an allegory of Painting.[1] Both the poems and the engraved allegories bear on matters which the corresponding *dialogue* also touches upon, sometimes just in passing.

Carducho makes no claim to the design or invention of any of the nine engravings in the book, five of which are signed by Francisco López, a collaborator and former pupil of his, and the others, as well as the title page, by Francisco Fernández. Therefore, it is hard to decide what Carducho's contribution actually was to the ideas, some of them novel, embodied in the engravings. It ought to be said that he, like most mediocre people, was truer to his prejudices than to the ideas that he appropriated from others. For instance, he favoured the state and other types of formal portrait, in which conventional attributes made explicit the preeminence, deeds or achievements of the royal or otherwise illustrious sitter, but he scorned portraits of ordinary people, as well as naturalistic likeness, which, he felt, ran counter to a learned painter's taste.[2]

---

[1] For the inconographic interpretation of these eight allegories, see George Kubler, 'Vicente Carducho's allegories of Painting', *The Art Bulletin*, December 1965, pp. 439–45.

The engraved title page of *Diálogos de la Pintura* bears the date 1633, but the colophon is dated 1634 in all extant copies. In some of these, the appendix, or *Memorial informatorio por los pintores*, is printed in larger type than the *Diálogos*, and the seven briefs that it contains follow six different folio numerations, two of which are truncated at the beginning. As Carducho explains in the *Advertencia*, he made up some copies by binding together the sheets of the *Diálogos* and remainders of the *Memorial* which he had brought out in larger type years earlier. All the copies of this kind which I have seen lack one or more of the nine engravings which illustrate the book, and retain folio 65, which will presently be discussed, as originally printed.

In all the complete copies which I have examined, both the *Diálogos* and the *Memorial* are printed in the smaller type, then called *Atanasia*, and follow the same folio numeration; the sequence of the briefs in the *Memorial* has been entirely rearranged, and it now begins with Lope de Vega's. As for folio 65, the one originally printed has been cut out and replaced by another, where, instead of an encomium of the Escorial, there is a praise of the Buen Retiro Palace, described as an architectural marvel, still in construction, all credit for which ought to go to the Count-Duke of Olivares.

No thorough bibliographic or critical study of Carducho's *Diálogos de la Pintura* has yet been undertaken.

[2] *Diálogos de la Pintura*, fols. 52 recto and verso, and 110 verso-112 recto.

In short, he despised the new naturalism which he blamed on Caravaggio and identified with the taste for *bodegones*, possibly aiming at bringing Velázquez within the compass of his sarcasm.

The *Diálogos de la Pintura* betrays Carducho's realization that his most cherished ideas about art had become past history, even if it was a history to which hardly any one would take exception. To him, Michelangelo remained unsurpassed as a painter, particularly in point of drawing, and Titian, though not as great an artist, still deserved to be called the master of colour (*dueño de los colores*). These views, rather close to Pacheco's, were not likely to meet with sharp disagreement, not even among those who shared El Greco's opinion of Michelangelo qua painter. On the other hand, Carducho's fear that the art of painting might be rapidly declining was obviously not widespread. Indeed, there was a general feeling of gratification at the fact that 'some modern' painters, to use Carducho's own words, 'excelled' in the live depiction of land-scapes, fruits, animals and like subjects which the old masters regarded as of 'little consequence'. Still more, the naturalist portrait that heightened the actual appearance of the sitter without making it conform to an idea of beauty or decorum was acclaimed as a telling expression of the superiority of art over nature.

It is likely that Pacheco discussed such matters with Carducho, his junior by more than ten years, in the 1620's at Madrid. If so, the old man's clearheaded understanding of modernity must have been disconcerting to his middle-aged colleague.

Francisco de Quevedo (1580–1645), one of the most discerning intellectuals of the time, and certainly the most uncompromising, had written, apparently in 1629, a poem in which he praised the 'distant blobs of colour' — *manchas distantes* — with which the 'great Velázquez' vivified the beautiful and gave meaning to the delicate, achieving truth itself rather than mere likeness in his depiction of sentiments. According to Palomino, Velázquez portrayed Quevedo 'with his spectacles on'; the portrait unfortunately has not come down to us.[1]

In the mid-1620's, Velázquez obviously appeared to other painters as the one rival to be defeated at the Court. This animus must have reached a peak in 1627 when, at Philip IV's command, the young master painted, in competition with Caxés, Carducho and Angelo

---

[1] The lines concerning Velázquez occur in one of the two incomplete drafts of the poem *El pincel*, published as independent pieces by Quevedo's nephew, Don Pedro Aldrete Quevedo y Villegas (*Las tres mvsas ultimas castellanas. Segvnda cvmbre del Parnaso español de Don Francisco de Quevedo y Villegas . . .*, Madrid, 1670, pp. 196 and 201). Luis Astrana Marín held that the two versions were written in 1629, and published them in the form of a single poem (*Obras completas de Don Francisco de Quevedo y Villegas, Obras en verso*, Madrid, 1932, pp. 496–9). José Manuel Blecua has published another incomplete version of *El pincel*, which does not include the lines about Velázquez, quoting the date assigned to the poem by Astrana Marín, and borrowing, as the latter did, some lines from another of the known versions for the sake of completeness (*Francisco de Quevedo, Obras completas. I. Poesía original*, Barcelona, 1963, pp. CXX–CXXI and 249–53). The matter deserves further study from both a literary and a biographical point of view. It should be noted that the one draft in which the lines on Velázquez occur contains also a praise of Pacheco's drawings for the *Libro de retratos*. One of the drawings for this work, begun in 1599, or earlier, and left unfinished by Pacheco, represents Quevedo with his spectacles on, a wreath of laurel on his head, and the red cross of Santiago on both his doublet and his cloak. If this portrait was drawn from life, which there is no compelling reason to believe it was, Pacheco must have executed it no later than 1625–6, when he was in Madrid for the last time. In those years, in 1625 to be precise, Pacheco signed the portrait of *An unknown knight of Santiago*, whom he also represented wearing

Nardi, 'a large canvas with the portrait of Philip III and the unexpected expulsion of the Moriscos' decreed by him.

Angelo Nardi (1584 — mid-1660's) was born in Florence, but spent seven formative years in Venice, from 1600 till 1607, when he went to Madrid, where he established his workshop and became one more unsalaried 'painter to the King'.[1] He was the sort of uncreative fellow who, being as receptive to his elders' ideas as to those of the younger generation, is regarded as a promising man by nearly everyone while yet his work steadily blurs out of interest. The compositions which he had executed in Madrid up to the mid-1620's show his dependence on Titian's and other Venetian masters' works.

Philip IV appointed Juan Bautista Maino and the Roman architect Giovanni Battista Crescenzi as a two-man jury; both found Velázquez's picture superior to the others; the King agreed with their verdict and as a reward he appointed Velázquez Usher of the Chamber. It was the same position that six years earlier, shortly before Velázquez's first stay in Madrid, Philip IV had awarded to Rodrigo de Villandrando, distinguishing him above all the other Court painters. For Velázquez, it was the first in a long series of royal distinctions that he was to receive throughout his life. Philip was six years younger than Velázquez. In that year of 1627, both were in their twenties.

On 7 March 1627 Velázquez was sworn in; his new office, regarded by Pacheco as a great honour, entailed the use of a rent-free apartment and the services of a physician and of a chemist. It was, moreover, in the wake of that success that the Master was able to reach a settlement with the treasury of the royal household which had been remiss in making the payments due to him. As it was finally worked out, in documents dated 18 and 27 September 1628 and 8 February 1629, he was to receive a daily allowance of twelve *reales* in return for foregoing his claims and as payment for the 'original portraits' which the King might command him to paint.[2]

---

spectacles (Lawrence Art Museum, Williamstown, Mass.). It may be that Velázquez originated the portrait of Quevedo with the glasses on — which would explain why Palomino called attention to this detail — if he actually portrayed him. The Master could have painted the portrait referred to by Palomino in 1622, when he was first in Madrid, or between 1623 and 1629, when he left for Italy, or perhaps between his return in 1631 and 1639, when Quevedo was imprisoned by order of the King far from Madrid, to which he never returned.

As I have stated elsewhere, contrary to the opinion held by most scholars, it is not certain that any of the extant oil portraits of Quevedo wearing spectacles was executed after the one that, according to Palomino, Velázquez painted (*Velázquez: A Catalogue Raisonné of his Oeuvre*, nos. 530–4).

[1] The available data on Nardi have been summarized by A. E. Pérez Sánchez, *Borgianni, Cavarozzi y Nardi en España*, Madrid, 1964, pp. 25–30.

[2] The cited documents state that the twelve-*reales* daily allowance is equal to that of the King's barbers. As Cruzada wrote, only by taking this fact out of its historical context could one read in it any disparagement of either Velázquez or the painter's profession (*Anales de la vida y de las obras de Diego de Silva Velázquez*, Madrid, 1885, p. 45). A like instance concerning an Italian artist is that of Andrea Sacchi, who from 1637 to 1640 'was placed in Cardinal Antonio Barberini's household among three slaves, a gardener, a dwarf and an old nurse' (Francis Haskell, *Patrons and Painters*, London, 1963, p. 7). Like all others, administrative documents ought to be read within the context of usage. For instance, in 1950, both charwomen and university professors in the United States of America were granted Social Security benefits at the same time and by the same law. Surely it would be a distortion of fact to see in it a disparagement of either group.

III. Velázquez, detail from Two young men at table (plate 33).
London, Wellington Museum

Nor was that all. According to Pacheco, Philip IV, who had several times promised to grant Velázquez's wish to visit Italy, was impelled by the painter's success in the 1627 competition to make good his promise. Velázquez, however, did not set out for Italy till July 1629, perhaps because he wanted first to have spelt out his settlement with the treasury, which took close to two years, perhaps too because he did not wish to miss the impending visit of the famous Peter Paul Rubens to the Spanish Court.

Before the end of 1627 Velázquez clashed again with Carducho and Caxés. This time the issue was the position of salaried titular painter to the King left vacant by the death of Bartolomé González. There were twelve applicants for the position, and Velázquez, Carducho and Caxés had to determine which of them had the necessary qualifications and recommend them in order of their merit. Van der Hamen, a friend of Carducho, was among the eight applicants unanimously excluded perhaps because, in spite of his efforts at figure-composition, he was primarily considered a still-life painter and, as such, not fully qualified for the position.

Though Velázquez, Caxés and Carducho placed Antonio de Lanchares first, the wording of Caxés and Carducho's joint recommendation suggests that they rather favoured Félix Castelo, a former pupil of Carducho, whom they placed second, listing Nardi as their third choice and Pedro Núñez del Valle, then held to be a painter of promise, as the fourth. Velázquez wrote somewhat acidly that he had no knowledge of Castelo's competence, while he knew about Nardi's, whom he therefore listed as his second choice, giving the third place to Castelo, and the fourth to Núñez del Valle.

Lanchares was undoubtedly a better painter than either Nardi or Castelo. Actually, however, none of the three was worthy of an affirmative choice, and Philip IV, whose sense of values was high when it came to art, decided not to fill the position for reasons of economy. There the matter rested till Lanchares's death in 1630. Less than a year later, early in 1631, Philip IV appointed Velázquez's friend, Nardi, even if somewhat parsimoniously, to the vacant position which he still coveted. As for Carducho and Caxés, they kept losing ground with the King; even though Caxés petitioned time and again for an appointment as Usher of the Chamber, pointing out that Philip IV had so honoured both Villandrando and Velázquez, his wish remained unfulfilled.[1]

RUBENS AT THE COURT

Rubens arrived at Madrid in August 1628. Even though he made this second trip to Spain in the political service of his sovereign, Philip IV, it was his personality as a painter which was to the fore at the Court. He brought with him eight of his own paintings for the King who had them hung in the 'new chamber' over the entrance hall of the Royal Palace among other outstanding pictures — one of which was Titian's allegory of Philip II after the victory of Lepanto (Prado Museum, no. 431). Then, since the political matters relative to the contemplated peace between the Catholic Spanish King and the Protestant monarch of England, who as Prince of

---

[1] Caxés's petition was supported time and again by the *Bureo*, the royal office in charge of such matters, but the King never granted it (see Caxés's personal file at the Archive of the Madrid Royal Palace).

Wales had been in Madrid a few years earlier, did not take much of his time, he gave himself to his art. He had been given a studio at the Royal Palace, where Philip IV often visited him, and it is safe to assume that Velázquez would not have missed the opportunity of seeing the famous master at work. Among the many paintings that Rubens executed either for the King or for private individuals, there were a considerable number of copies after Titian and quite a few portraits. Velázquez, with his admiration for Titian and his own mastery of portrait painting, must have been particularly interested in those facets of Rubens's art. This interest may even have been increased by the fact that Rubens painted no fewer than five portraits of Philip IV, as well as several of the Queen and other members of the Royal family.

In spite of the promise, if it was a promise, made by Olivares to Velázquez that he would be the only painter to portray Philip IV, the young master could not be jealous of the great Rubens. On the contrary, after his daily contacts with his hollow colleagues at the Court he must have found refreshing the challenge of the older master's works, success, and words.

We know from Pacheco,[1] who doubtless had it from his son-in-law himself, that during the nine months that Rubens stayed in Madrid he had little intercourse with other artists, except Velázquez, with whom he had corresponded before, possibly in 1626 when the Fleming was instrumental in Paul Pontius's commission to engrave an allegorical portrait of Olivares after a likeness of the head by Velázquez. It was the young Court painter who accompanied Rubens to the Escorial — the visit to which had been paramount in Velázquez's mind when he left his native Seville for the first time. Pacheco also tells that the great Flemish master spoke favourably of his younger colleague's works.

In closing his encomium of Rubens, Pacheco praises 'the greatness, beauty and richness of his intellect', which shines in his paintings as the mainstay of his success with Kings and Princes, though, Pacheco explains, it is only the painter's own hand which truly helps him and which earns all the honours that he receives. These words probably reflect, or are a commentary on Velázquez's feelings about a painter's creative and social success that he saw embodied in Rubens and about which he is likely to have written to his father-in-law. Be this as it may, the paragraph with which Pacheco closed his eulogy of Rubens is particularly significant as it immediately precedes his enthusiastic narrative of Velázquez's life.

Of the portraits of Philip IV painted by Rubens at Madrid, Pacheco singles out for praise one showing the sovereign on horseback 'with other figures, very striking'. It depicted the twenty-two-year-old monarch on a chestnut horse, holding the baton in his hand; in the upper part, Faith was seen offering a wreath of laurel to him and holding a cross on a globe supported by two angels, while Divine Justice was hurling a thunderbolt at her enemies; on the ground an Indian, representing Philip IV's kingdoms in the New World, carried the royal helmet.

This allegorical portrait was greatly admired at the Court then and in later years. As for Velázquez, he went on representing the person of Philip IV as the quintessence of kingly power, dispensing with what was doubtless to him the redundancy of allegory — and in doing so he won acclaim too.

Velázquez's admiration for Rubens's creative power and resplendent success had a short-

[1] *Arte de la Pintura*, vol. I, pp. 152–55.

lived impact on his work, noticeable in *Bacchus* and *Democritus*, both painted in 1628–9 (plates 57 and 55). It is, nevertheless, likely that, as he came to realize the unfettered aim of Rubens's copies after Titian, his own response to the Venetian master's handling of pigment, light and space grew warmer and freer, as can be surmised from the pictorial handling of the wraps about Bacchus's loin. It was probably also then that Velázquez put on canvas the *Head of a stag*, apparently a fragment of a larger painting. By masterful use of rough impasto he achieved a sweeping contour line that makes the animal's head stand out as a dynamic shape against a grey blue sky (plate 83).[1]

BURLESQUE OF THE FALSE GODS

On 22 July 1629 Philip ordered that Velázquez — he had just formally granted him leave to go to Italy — be paid one hundred ducats for 'a picture of Bacchus that he has done on my service' (plate 57). Obviously the painting had been delivered by the artist after 9 February of that year when he agreed to the financial settlement covering all the works he had painted for the King up to that date. It is likely, however, that he had started work on so large a composition much earlier, probably some time in 1628.

Since about 1828 the prevailing view has been that this work, known as 'the painting of Bacchus' in Velázquez's day, depicts an actual event which calls for a title such as 'The Drinkers' or the like. That of *The triumph of Bacchus in burlesque*, recorded by Palomino in 1724, reflected a real understanding of the painting and was certainly more apt. In more recent times the discussion of the picture has been rather unrewarding probably on account of the idle

[1] López-Rey, *Velázquez: A Catalogue Raisonné*, no. 150. The painting is heavily varnished; its size is: h. 0·66 m; w. 0·52 m. It is known that Velázquez painted a *Head of a stag* between 1626 and 1636; it was last recorded as rescued from the fire that gutted the Madrid Royal Palace in 1734; its size then was about 1·11 m. in height and 1·25 m. in width (measurements inadvertently reversed in my catalogue, where I listed it under no. 149 as 'lost, unless it is to be identified with no. 150'). Perhaps, though not surely, it is the painting of the same subject listed, with no painter's name, as measuring about 1·25 m. square among the canvases rescued from the 1734 fire which in 1747 were 'rolled-up' in storage.

In 1966, a painting, *Trophies of the chase*, representing an owl with widespread wings and the heads of a stag, a boar, a bear, a wolf and a fox, was found in the royal palace at Riofrío, near Segovia; it measures 1·22 m. in height and 1·465 m. in width, including three strips added at the top and on both sides. The inference has been drawn that the major part (1·07 m.× 1·25 m.) is that of Velázquez's *Head of a stag* rescued from the 1734 fire (Diego Angulo Iñiguez, 'La cuerna de venado, cuadro de Velázquez', *Reales Sitios*, vol. 4, 1967, no. 12, pp. 13–25). I examined the painting in June 1967, and concluded that the owl had been added after the stag's antlers were painted. However, I could not see any telling qualitative difference in the execution of the various animal heads, a failure which may, of course, have been due to extensive repainting. The stag's head is awkward in execution; the antlers are studiedly highlighted at every turn and point, and they are further overemphasized by the shadows that they cast on the background. The whole work recalls *Weapons on a board*, a painting inscribed *Dⁿ Diego Velázquez Fe:*, though it certainly is not by his hand (Prado, on show in 1960 under no painter's name; not included in the 1963 Museum's catalogue; no. 173 of my *Velázquez* catalogue).

Trophies of the chase was described as including an eagle rather than an owl and attributed to Velázquez in 1845, before Isabel II of Spain bought it, together with other lesser paintings, from the Marquis of Salamanca for the unpretentious palace of Riofrío, where it was inventoried in 1883, under no. 563, as by an 'anonymous' painter; its size was then recorded as: h. 1·35 m.; w. 1·64 m.

points on which it has centred. The point has, for instance, been made that, though the composition with its nine life-size figures is an open-air scene, it was painted in the artist's studio rather than on the slopes of the Guadarrama Mountains, at some distance from Madrid. The question has also been raised whether it represents a Flemish fête, which Rubens would have described to Velázquez, or some popular scene that he happened upon. Moreover, the variety in the handling of various figures has been taken as evidence that Velázquez did each one separately, the corollary being that he failed to bring about a sense of impressionist unity — a kind of unity which, I may interpolate, was alien to Velázquez's art, much as the Impressionist painters were to admire him. The suggestion has also been made that such differences in handling argue in favour of the assumption that Velázquez partly repainted the composition after his return from Italy in 1631.

Before proceeding further it must be said that the picture was damaged in the fire that gutted the Royal Palace in 1734; as a result, the composition darkened considerably and unevenly; the canvas was, moreover, cut down on the sides. The vine-crowned man sitting in the foreground to the left has been blurred into a brown shape that hardly fulfils its intended repoussoir function; it fails to add to the dynamic intercrossing of diagonals, now mainly supported by the man being crowned and the nude youth holding a glass. This intercrossing of diagonals underscores the heads of Bacchus and of the hatted drinker as two off-centre focal points; it also builds a unifying rhythm which runs from the roomy area where the god officiates, across the huddle of tosspots, up to the standing beggar — identified as such by his open palm — at the back of the group.

As the reveller clad in a yellow jacket and dark breeches kneels in a communion-like pose by a brown earthen jug and a greenish glass, his face sinks away in shadows under the vine wreath which Bacchus is crowning him with. Blotches of shadow make more clodlike both the flabby god and his soft-muscled nude attendant. Similar shadows and rather rougher impasto emphasize the grimacing features of the four carousers bunched together on the other side, in contrast to the face of the standing beggar which Velázquez has just shadowed forth. The composition is made the more dynamic by the lusty counterpoise of the vine-crowned Bacchus to the toper in the shapeless hat, and by the white bowl of red wine, which by its vivid textures and reflections marks another centre, and an intense one, in the *bodegón*-like composition.

The picture is, of course, a baroque, double-edged parody of the false world of the fable and of sinful human ways, and the laugh is made heartier, healthier, and pregnant, as the clowning tosspots vie in their bearing with the loutish nudes of Bacchus and its attendant; the underlying religious sentiment is keyed to the figure of the beggar who, lightly sketched, looms in the background over the drunkards who ignore him.

The virtue of Charity, then readily identified with alms-giving, almost invariably led the Catholic mind to the contemplation of the Cross where Jesus shed His blood for the redemption of Mankind. In Velázquez's burlesque of Bacchus and his soulless fellows, the beggar is made to underplay his part in a pithy baroque manner, while the false god emphasizes his, as does his counterfigure, the drunkard, who holds up a bowl, his dull senses still responsive to the wine's pungency, his mind obviously blank to its symbolic Eucharistic meaning.

There is no need to suppose that Velázquez made sketchier or less distinct the figure of the beggar — or any other — after he returned from Italy. For about 1629, when he was paid for this painting, the famous Francisco de Quevedo wrote the poem in which he praised him for his '*manchas distantes*', that is, distant blobs of colour.

Quevedo may have seen this painting of *Bacchus* before writing his poem; he may also have seen *The Supper at Emmaus* (plate 52) which Velázquez probably painted about the same time. In this work, which represents the moment when Christ breaks the bread and His divine nature is revealed to His astonished companions, the artist once more rendered the difference between the divine and the human. Luminous tints and smooth brushwork model the figure of Jesus, whose humanity, which connotes His humility, is expressed by weightless shadows on the faint rose tones of His face; a rosy glare that lits up His pink tunic sets Him apart as an unearthly presence from the reality of His gesturing companions, whose coppery-brown flesh tones harmonize with the yellows, dusky browns, and darkish blue of their surroundings and heavily-textured costumes. The natural characteristics of age and expression are depicted on the disciples' faces, modelled by energetic strokes and shadows though without the heavy impasto which weighs down the visages of the topers — one of whom, incidentally, resembles the disciple in the background (plates 52 and 57).

Christ after the flagellation contemplated by the Christian Soul appears to have been painted by Velázquez also before leaving for Italy, probably some time between 1626 and 1628. The torso of Jesus, with His arms stretched toward the column, and that of *Bacchus*, with his hands extended to the kneeling reveller, are rather alike in execution and shape; both, markedly curved at the back, are modelled by a similar interplay of light and shade (plates 51 and 57). However, contrary to Bacchus, Christ looks monumental in relation to the other figures in the composition, the Christian Soul and the guardian angel. Velázquez has achieved a subtle depiction of the humanity of Christ as the measure of both His humility and the immensity of His sacrifice.[1] The readiness with which the Redeemer submits to torture and humiliation is not lessened either by the rope which ties His hands together or by the blood, a vivid red, which drops from His body and limbs to the ground. The harmonious rhythm that pervades Jesus's serene face, shackled arms and sprawling legs has as a foil the nervous modelling of the plaintive Christian Soul.

THE PAINTER'S ITALIAN JOURNEY

In August 1629 Velázquez left for Italy preceded by letters of recommendation to the Spanish ambassadors in the states he was to visit.[2] The King had three hundred ducats advanced

[1] When the painting, at the London National Gallery, was cleaned and somewhat restored in 1963, the halo round the head of Christ became slightly bluer and a trifle emphatic. A study for the figure of the guardian angel, in charcoal on yellowish paper, was destroyed by the fire that gutted the Instituto Jovellanos, at Gijón, during the Spanish Civil War, in 1936 (see López-Rey, *Velázquez: A Catalogue Raisonné*, no. 631, plate 61).

[2] According to Pacheco, Velázquez sailed from Barcelona on the day of St. Lawrence, that is, on 10 August. Data concerning Velázquez's first journey to Italy other than that provided by Pacheco or collected in *Varia velazqueña*

to him on account for paintings not yet completed, and ordered that he should continue to receive all his emoluments for the duration of his absence, the length of which was not even indicated. The Count-Duke of Olivares secured a royal order by which Don Juan de Velilla, Secretary of State, requested the ambassadors from the Italian states in Madrid to provide Velázquez with passports and letters of recommendation. The request was complied with, not without some apprehension that the true aim of the painter's visit to Italy might be espionage. The suspicion probably arose from the knowledge that Velázquez's position at the Court was, in point of fact, far superior to what his office of Usher of the Chamber would suggest; the young painter was not only a favourite of the King, who often watched him painting, but of the King's chief minister as well; he was, moreover, sailing with the famous General Spínola, who had been appointed governor of the State of Milan and was to take command of the Spanish armies in Italy. If the petty ambassadors suspected, as they might have been expected to do, that politics rather than art was the true aim of Velázquez's trip to their lands, they were at least aware that it was as a portrait-painter that he was well known, and so they wrote in their cautious dispatches.

Landing at Genoa on 19 September, Velázquez proceeded a few days later to Milan, probably still in the company of Spínola; he then set out for Venice, presumably making a halt at Verona, to whose *Capitano*, or politico-military chief, he had a letter of introduction.

In Venice he stayed at the home of the Spanish ambassador, Don Cristobal de Benavente y Benavides. Since there was unrest in the city, where, moreover, Spaniards were then most unpopular, the ambassador ordered that some of his men should accompany his guest whenever he left the house to see the city. 'Leaving that unquietness', as Pacheco put it, Velázquez started with his servant on his way to Rome. The first stop was Ferrara, where he spent two days, and was extended many courtesies by the papal legate, Cardinal Giulio Sachetti, who had been nuncio in Spain. The Cardinal insisted that Velázquez should stay at the palace and have his meals with him, which the painter courteously declined on the excuse that he did not keep regular meal hours. Sachetti then assigned one of the Spanish gentlemen on his service to look after Velázquez, and to show him the things of major interest in the city.

The last evening of his stay Velázquez went to take leave of his host, who kept him for more than three hours, talking about various matters, and ordered the gentleman who had been attending Velázquez to accompany him the following day 'to a place called Cento' sixteen miles away. Velázquez's visit to Cento lasted only a little while; though he was 'very well entertained', he dismissed his guide, and decided to proceed immediately to Rome, through Bologna, where, however, he did not stop, not even to present the letters he had for the Archbishop, Cardinal Ludovico Ludovisi, and for the papal legate, Cardinal Bernardino Spada, though he understood that they were in the city.

It might be that, as some scholars have suggested, Velázquez visited Guercino at Cento:[1]

can be found in Palomino, *El Museo pictórico*, pp. 900-3; Antonio Rodríguez Villa, *Ambrosio Spínola, primer Marqués de los Balbases*, Madrid, 1904, pp. 547-8, and Johannes A. F. Orbaan, 'Notes on art in Italy', *Apollo*, July 1927, pp. 28-9.

[1] This suggestion has been turned into an apparent statement of fact by Denis Mahon (*Studies in Seicento Art and Theory*, London, 1947, p. 69, n. 111), and repeated as such by other writers.

it is, indeed, conceivable that Cardinal Giulio Sachetti, a patron of Guercino, would have induced, or prevailed upon, Velázquez to go to Cento for that purpose. If so, some significance ought to be attached to the fact that Pacheco, who undoubtedly follows Velázquez's own account of the journey, does not refer to Guercino either in this passage or anywhere else in his *Arte de la Pintura*. Guercino was then carrying on 'an extremely successful mail-order business in large altar-pieces', as has been aptly said.[1] The thought occurs that Velázquez, whose aims and achievements as a painter, to say nothing of his vital purpose, differed essentially from Guercino's, might have found that the latter overbuilt his compositions and that his brush-stroke was jejune. This might have had some bearing on his decision not to visit Cardinals Spada and Ludovisi, since the latter, like Sachetti, was an admirer of Guercino.

It is most likely that he stopped at Florence as he had intended to do when he secured letters of introduction from Averardo Medici, Florentine ambassador in Madrid, a protocol-minded individual whose main concern, according to a dispatch that he wrote on 22 September 1629, was that Velázquez, the 'favourite painter' of both Philip IV and Olivares, should not be treated with either too much or too little courtesy. It is probably to this stay in Florence that Don Gaspar de Fuensalida referred in 1658.[2]

In Rome, where he was to stay for about a year, Cardinal Barberini, the Pontiff's nephew ordered that he be lodged in the Vatican Palace; he was given the keys to several rooms, the main one of which was decorated in fresco by Federico Zuccaro. Finding that lodging too lonely and out-of-the-way he left it, first assuring himself, however, that the Vatican guards would let him in without difficulty whenever he wished to return to draw after Michelangelo's *Last Judgment* or Raphael's works. And he spent a good many days so occupied.

Pacheco's statement that his son-in-law left his lodging at the Vatican Palace because it was out-of-the-way and he did not wish to be so lonely, reveals that Velázquez enjoyed city life and intercourse with other people. It is well documented that throughout his life he won the friend-ship of a good many men who, by reason of background, profession and social station, must have been rather discriminating in their choice of friends.

Much as he cared for city life, however, he feared the heat of the Roman summer. Hence late in April 1630, he set eyes on the Villa de' Medici, thinking that it would be a convenient place to spend the summer, for it had a high and breezy location and a good many antique statues, from which he could study, adorned its walls, halls and gardens. The Spanish ambassador, the Count of Monterrey — Olivares's brother-in-law — took care of the matter, and within a few days, on 4 May, the reply came that a room had been made available for Velázquez at the villa. For more than two months he stayed there, most likely glad of the opportunity to study antique sculpture, which he had learned to admire in his Sevillian days, by copying from the fine pieces he had at hand, among them reliefs from the Ara Pacis, and the Niobe and Niobide now at the Uffizi. Unfortunately all these drawings are lost, as are most of the many that Velázquez made throughout his life.

It was an illness, a tertian fever, that forced the painter to move down into the city, near the

---

[1] Ellis Waterhouse, *Italian Baroque Painting*, London, 1962, p. 115.
[2] In his testimony concerning Velázquez's qualifications for admission in the Order of Santiago.

residence of the Count of Monterrey, who did him many kindnesses, providing him with the services of his own physician, as well as with medicines, and sending him sweets and specially cooked meals; the Count, moreover, frequently sent someone from his own household to call on the sick painter.

From Pacheco's narrative, it appears that, while at Rome, Velázquez made 'studies' for the most part, one of them being 'a famous self-portrait'. It is also known that the Countess of Monterrey, on the advice of her brother, the Count-Duke of Olivares, had her portrait painted by Velázquez. Neither of these portraits has been convincingly identified among the Master's extant works.

On his way back to Spain he made a halt at Naples where his older fellow-countryman, José de Ribera (1591–1652), was the outstanding painter. The sister of the Spanish monarch, the Infanta María, had stopped at the vice-regal court in April, and stayed there till 18 December, when she resumed her journey to Hungary where she was to marry the King, Ferdinand III. Velázquez made a portrait of her to be taken back to Philip IV (plate 67).

The painter must have left Naples around the same time as the Infanta, about 18 December, for he was in Madrid in January 1631. The Count-Duke of Olivares received him cordially. He ordered him to go at once to kiss the hand of His Majesty and thank him, for Philip had not let himself be portrayed by another painter during Velázquez's absence and had waited for him to paint the first portrait of Prince Baltasar Carlos, born shortly after the painter's departure for Italy.

TITIAN'S GREATNESS AND VELÁZQUEZ'S FREEDOM

Of the works painted by Velázquez in Italy, Pacheco mentions only 'a famous self-portrait', now lost, and the 'fine portrait' of the Infanta María (plate 67). Palomino, writing early in the eighteenth century, adds that the Master painted at Rome in 1630 both *The forge of Vulcan* and *Joseph's bloody coat* (plates 59 and 58). Palomino states further that Velázquez, in the days that he spent in Venice, made many drawings, especially from Tintoretto's large *Crucifixion*, at the Scuola di San Rocco, and that he painted a copy of another work by the same master, 'where Christ is depicted giving the communion to His disciples', possibly the one at the Scuola di San Rocco, too.

Velázquez had most likely been acquainted with Tintoretto's *Crucifixion* since his apprentice days, for Pacheco owned what he described as part of a preliminary cartoon for it, and was familiar with the whole composition from an engraving, probably the one made by Agostino Carracci in 1589. Pacheco admired the dexterity and daring of Tintoretto, whom, however, as he made clear, he could not recommend as an example to follow.

A painting of *The last supper* listed as by Velázquez in the inventory of the Madrid Royal Palace drawn up in 1666 by Mazo, the Master's son-in-law, may have been the copy after Tintoretto's painting which, according to Palomino, Velázquez presented to Philip IV, and which has not come down to us.

From what Pacheco reported, obviously on the basis of Velázquez's own account, and from what Palomino added, seemingly borrowing data collected in the 1650's by Alfaro, one of the Master's pupils, Velázquez spent a good deal of his time in Italy drawing or painting after old masters' works, particularly Tintoretto's, Raphael's and Michelangelo's, as well as trying his hand at 'studies' in oils. Pacheco mentioned only the subject of one of these studies, that 'famous self-portrait', painted 'in the manner of the great Titian', which, as he put it, he kept for the admiration of true connoisseurs and to the honour of art.

As Pacheco came to see it — most likely through Velázquez's eyes — Titian's greatness lay in his masterly use of sketchy strokes to achieve relief and depth by dint of light and shade. Velázquez used sketchy strokes in *The forge of Vulcan* and in *Joseph's bloody coat*, and more markedly in the two small studies of *Villa Medici*, probably painted during his summer stay there (plates 64 and 65). In execution there is a similarity between these studies, which are fluidly painted with impasto used for luminous accents of form, and the landscapes in the two large compositions, particularly the one in *The forge of Vulcan*.

In both *The forge of Vulcan* and *Joseph's bloody coat*, there is a live contrast between well-drawn figures and those shaped as blobs. Such contrast exists also in *Bacchus*, painted earlier in Madrid (plate 57). There are, however, outstanding differences between the works executed by Velázquez before his Italian journey and those which he painted in Rome. In these, indeed, the space is deeper and the colouring richer in hues and glow. Another difference brings tantalizingly to mind Velázquez's lost studies after Raphael, whom he later came to dislike: the proportion of the human figure in both *Joseph's bloody coat* and *The forge of Vulcan* is more slender than in either *Bacchus* or *Christ after the flagellation*, painted by Velázquez before he left Madrid (plates 58, 59, 57, and 51). This is also the case with *Christ on the Cross*, datable to 1631 or 1632, shortly after the Master's return from Italy (plate 53).[1]

It would be idle to try to retrace Velázquez's thoughts as his mind's eye ran through Raphael's and Michelangelo's works and seized upon Titian's brushstroke. Since his apprentice days he had been approaching the confrontation which took place in the Vatican when he started drawing from Michelangelo's and Raphael's frescoes. Pacheco, true to his convinctions, must have advised his young apprentice to take the path of Michelangelo, Raphael and their followers as the way to master drawing and to achieving smoothness, beauty, profundity, and power of expression. He must also have warned him against the sort of sketchy and indistinct painting which, as he wrote, imitates neither the manner of the ancients nor the truth of nature.

It was in Madrid that the young master learned to admire Titian's and other Venetian masters' works. This admiration was necessarily heightened as he saw the enthusiasm and freedom with which Rubens made copies after Titian's works at the Spanish Court, and later by the copies after Tintoretto that he himself made at Venice. In Rome, he finally faced the achievements of Raphael and Michelangelo, whose greatness had been impressed on him, and came to grips with them. It is a thousand pities that the drawings he then made are lost, for they might have revealed to us the interplay of his understanding of those great masters and his own creative disposition.

[1] This painting, now at the Prado, is considerably darkened; it was already so in 1826 when it was for sale at Paris (see López-Rey, *Velázquez: A Catalogue Raisonné*, no. 14).

Another grievous loss is that of the self-portrait painted by Velázquez at Rome in 1630 'in the manner of the great Titian'. It must have been significantly different in execution from the 'fine portrait' of the *Infanta María*, which he painted later the same year (plate 67).

Scholars of various persuasions have commented that the modelling of the *Infanta María*'s well-drawn face is somewhat dry, though her blond hair is fluidly painted,[1] a contrast of the kind which can also be found in the larger and more elaborate compositions of 1630, *The forge of Vulcan* and *Joseph's bloody coat*, neither of which could, of course, be described as painted in the manner of Titian, in spite of the sketchy passages common to both. Pacheco was a discerning connoisseur; hence his characterisation of Velázquez's self-portrait as a Titianesque masterpiece confirms that the quality of Velázquez's brushwork was not invariably uniform at any one period, not even at any one year, of his creative life.

Either while in Italy or soon after his return to Spain, Velázquez must have written to Pacheco of his enthusiasm for Titian, whom he very likely regarded as the stem of creative freedom. As some of Velázquez's works painted in the early and mid-1630's reveal, it was after his return to Madrid that his kinship with Titian became more noticeable. It was, however, as his paintings also reveal, a vital kinship that precluded imitation; that, in fact, quickened the sense of individual creation.

THE RETURN TO THE COURT: WORK, CHORES AND REWARDS

Soon after his return to Madrid, Velázquez began to work on the portrait of *Prince Baltasar Carlos*, which the King had been waiting for him to paint and that he finished in March 1631 (plate 68). This portrait of the Prince was followed by the full-length of *Philip IV* in brown and silver, executed that same year or the following, when Velázquez also repainted entirely a portrait of *Queen Isabel* which he had painted before leaving for Italy, modifying the costume and the hairdo in accordance with the new fashion of the day, probably in order to pair it with the new portrait of the King (plate 69 and frontispiece).

Portraits of the sovereigns and other royal persons, in great demand among people of various social stations, were sold at painters' and dealers' shops, as well as on the streets and in other public places. Most of them were, of course, perfunctory works, copies of copies, so many steps removed from the original that they neither bore a resemblance to the sitter nor showed any sense of royal decorum. One of Velázquez's occasional chores as a Court painter was to determine whether they were offensive on either point.

In October, 1633, Velázquez and his colleague, Carducho, had to view over eighty such portraits confiscated from various painters, whose names are recorded, though with no lasting claim to attention. They let twelve of the portraits pass, and recommended that the others be returned to their painters, instructing them to erase and paint anew the heads of the sitters in every one, as well as the rest of the figure in a few. A portrait of Philip IV was singled out as particularly offensive because it represented the King wearing green breeches and hose.

[1] Beruete, *Velázquez*, 1906, p. 38; Moreno Villa, *Velázquez*, 1920, p. 33, and Gerstenberg, *Velazquez*, 1957, p. 68.

Don Jerónimo de Villanueva, protonotary of the Kingdom of Aragon, stated in 1634 that Velázquez had received several payments, totalling one thousand ducats, for the following eighteen pictures acquired for Philip IV: 'Cambiaso's *Susannah*, an original by Bassano, Titian's *Danae*, the picture of *Joseph*, the picture of *Vulcan*, five flower pieces, four small landscapes, two *bodegones*, a portrait of *Our Lord, the Prince*, and another of *Our Mistress, the Queen*'.

The listings 'the picture of *Joseph*' and 'the picture of *Vulcan*' sound as if they referred to well-known, readily identifiable works. As is generally held, they can only be *Joseph's bloody coat* and *The forge of Vulcan*, which, according to Palomino, Velázquez painted in Rome.

As for the portraits of the Prince, that is, Baltasar Carlos, and the Queen, they probably were replicas or workshop copies after Velázquez's originals. Indeed, according to the terms of the royal order of 9 February 1629, meant for the benefit of the painter, he was to receive no payment in addition to his regular emoluments for the 'original portraits' which the King might command him to paint. It is improbable that the Protonotary of Aragon would have bought original portraits of the Queen and the Prince for the King, together with sixteen sundry pictures, just to get round a royal order which, needless to say, was not too binding on the monarch.

The pictures had been evaluated by Francisco de Rioja — whom we know as a friend of both Pacheco and Velázquez. Cruzada held that one thousand ducats for a group of paintings, which included a 'masterpiece by Titian' was a rather paltry sum. Yet, if we read carefully, it is notable that the one painting mentioned as 'original' is Bassano's and it would appear that the references to the Cambiaso and the Titian are to copies.

As Cruzada himself pointed out, Velázquez was often paid under one hundred ducats, in addition to his regular emoluments, for pictures executed for the King. Consequently, one thousand ducats for the lot, though not a generous price, would not be an unusual one if one realizes: first, that, apart from two, or perhaps four, paintings by Velázquez, the lot included only one original work, by one of the Bassani, which was probably not regarded as exceptional, since its title or subject is not mentioned; secondly, that, as we shall presently see, it is unlikely that any of the other pictures was by any well-known master; and finally, that at least half of them — five flower-pieces and four small landscapes — would at the time have commanded low prices on account of their subject or size.

The possibility cannot be excluded that Velázquez himself made the copies of Cambiaso's and Titian's works, perhaps while in Italy. One of Titian's *Danae*, now in the Naples Museum, was then in the Collection Farnese in Rome, and another had been in the Spanish royal collection since the 1550's (Prado Museum).[1] Yet, as neither of the copies is extant, and the pertaining document is unclear, speculation on this point would be idle.

As for the five flower-pieces, it is safe to assume that Velázquez had purchased, rather than painted, them for the King. Pacheco, writing at that time, regarded flower-pieces as a trifling subject, and cited only Van der Hamen as a painter who had succeeded in painting them with vigour and art. Had Velázquez painted flower-pieces, it is unlikely that Pacheco would not have mentioned it.

The four small landscapes and the two *bodegones* might have been Velázquez's works as far as

[1] Pedro Beroqui, *Ticiano en el Museo del Prado*, 2nd ed., Madrid, 1946, p. 139.

subject matter is concerned, though of course they might as well have been by some other painter. It is in any case worth underlining that in the 1630's *bodegones*, whose validity as an art form Velázquez had so powerfully asserted, were in favour at the Spanish Court.

On 21 August 1633, Velázquez's fourteen-year-old daughter, Francisca, married Juan Bautista Martínez del Mazo, a painter about whom nothing is known before that date. The wedding was at the church of Santiago in Madrid. As his daughter's dowry, Velázquez passed on to his son-in-law the position of Usher of the Chamber, which he had held for several years. The King's permission to do so had been preceded by granting to Velázquez the privilege of designating, for a financial consideration, an individual to be appointed constable of justice. At the time, there was an interdiction against this old lucrative privilege, but, after some legal quibbling, the interdiction was waived in favour of Velázquez with the stipulation that it would, however, remain in force for others.

A few years later, on 28 July 1636, an astute observer of life at the Court, commenting on the King's recent appointment of Velázquez as 'Gentleman of the Wardrobe, without duties', remarked that the painter's ambition went higher; that he, indeed, aimed at becoming 'Gentleman of the Bedchamber', as he, in fact, did nine years later, and at wearing the robe of a military order like Titian, which he achieved late in life. As Ortega y Gasset noted, these predictions reveal not only the sagacity of he who made them, but also that neither did Velázquez pursue his ambitions for advancement at the Court, nor did the King grant them, in a haphazard manner, since, to both, royal preferment did mark a *cursus honorum*.[1]

JESUS AND THE GODS

Five paintings datable at the time of Velázquez's 1629–31 Italian journey have come down to us: two large compositions, each including six figures, a colour sketch for one of these, and two small landscapes of *Villa Medici*. The large compositions, *Joseph's bloody coat* and *The forge of Vulcan*, have at least one of the models in common (plates 58 and 59). Though they were originally identical in size, there is no reason to conclude that they were intended as companion pieces; nor is there any indication that they ever hung in the same room.

In *Joseph's coat*, the painter made use of a plain perspective device to set the figures in space — a device that he used in just one other painting, the portrait of the jester *Don Juan de Austria*, painted soon after his return to Madrid (plate 105). It has been plausibly suggested that this perspective rendition closely conforms to the manner discussed and illustrated in Daniello Barbari's *Pratica della Prospetiva* of 1568, a copy of which was in Velázquez's library at the time of his death.[2] It would seem, indeed, that the possibility of clearing the space around the human figure by means of geometric or architectural schemes exercised Velázquez's imagination while he was in Italy and even for a while after his return to Spain. Yet, it is significant that, if he painted *Joseph's coat* at Rome in 1630, he also painted then *The forge of Vulcan*, in which he did not underline the geometric design of the interior and did achieve spatial airiness.

[1] José Ortega y Gasset, *Papeles sobre Velázquez y Goya*, Madrid, 1950, p. 262.
[2] Gerstenberg, *Diego Velázquez*, pp. 217–19.

Velázquez, well read as he was in architecture — if the books he kept till his death are any indication[1] — persevered in what from early in his career as a painter appears as his aim: mortising, as it were, the depiction of the human figure or group with that of spatial depth, as he did in *The fable of Arachne* in the late 1640's (plates 127-9).

It is worth pointing out here that an art treatise can throw about as much light on a painter's paintings as a book of rhetoric can on a poet's poems; either may express what earlier creative men were understood to have achieved, or what the painter or poet was admonished to do on the authority of past achievement or current speculation. In short, books of rhetoric or art treatises can provide us with a clue to the views that a creative artist may have learned by rote in his youth, grown up with, or come to know in later years. On the other hand, whatever the time and circumstances of a creative artist's acquaintance with a book of rhetoric or art treatise may have been, the meaning of his work is not to be found therein.

As in the case of *Bacchus* (plate 57), it has become customary to assume that *The forge of Vulcan* and, to a lesser degree, *Joseph's coat*, were repainted by Velázquez after 1630, the reason given being that in each composition there is at least one figure which is more 'impressionistic' than the others.

It is a fact, conclusively proved by X-rays and at times made all too plain by overzealous cleanings, that Velázquez substantially repainted no small number of his works after the pigment he had originally laid on the canvas had dried and hardened; to determine the length of the intervening time, which may have been a matter of months, or years, is however, not always possible. Even when radical changes rather than just *pentimenti* are evident, one should not jump to the conclusion, lacking other evidence, that Velázquez made them after having regarded the picture as finished. We know that Velázquez often worked at a leisurely pace; it is, moreover, documented that there were times when he was working at more than one picture — and it would be in the nature of his baroque imagination to find in the unfinished canvas, where the paint had already dried, an invation to change.

Beruete is mainly responsible for the view that the differences in the handling and texture of pigment noticeable within a number of individual works by Velázquez are to be explained as the result of later repaints by the Master himself. In the case of *The forge of Vulcan*, he was convinced that Velázquez had repainted it 'towards the end of his life' since 'there are in the head, and also in the body' of Vulcan 'a boldness, a freshness of touch, and a happiness of execution at which the Master only arrived in his latest works'.[2] A good many of the pictures which Beruete included among Velázquez's latest works are now known to have been painted one or two decades earlier; some, indeed, not later than the mid-1630's, which cuts the ground from under his argument.

In *The forge of Vulcan* and in *Joseph's bloody coat* the build of most of the figures is strongly accented by a light which comes from high up outside the composition, and in both a sense of airy depth is achieved by the fluid landscapes in the distance and by the blobs into which the background figures are shaped: the shadowy figures of the two youths standing beside Jacob against a light wall in the Biblical scene, or the lit-up half-length nude seen

---

[1] See n. 3, p. 20 above.   [2] Aureliano de Beruete, *Velázquez*, London, n.d. (1906), p. 35.

against the shadow at the chimney corner in the mythological painting (plates 58 and 59).

Velázquez, who made many studies at Rome, must have made at least a few for these large paintings. Unfortunately, only one, a colour sketch for the head of Apollo, has come down to us (plate 60): painted in full light, it shows the god's youthful countenance contoured by a filmy shadow which, in the final composition, overspreads the whole face. This sketch corresponds more closely to the outline of Apollo's face and neck as first painted by Velázquez in *The forge of Vulcan*, before he somewhat modified the contour of the god's face, a change which is clearly visible in a radiograph (plates 61, 62).

Apollo's figure, clad in an earth-yellow mantle, is as fleshy and dappled with shadows as that of Bacchus in the earlier and considerably less airy composition; his shadowed face stands against a thick-textured yellow light as he discloses Venus' and Mars' infidelity to Vulcan, who is as thick-hided a blacksmith as his assistant Cyclopes. The cuckolded Vulcan stops in his work, the surprise on his face made the more bumpkinlike by his bushy moustache and by his fast grip on the hammer. The comedy is maintained by the gestures of the three Cyclopes in full view and by the intent stare of the one in the background, whose figure keys the diagonals which fan the composition open.

For a cogent pictorial contrast one could compare the light-soaked figure of Apollo — the sensorial brilliancy of whose flesh, mantle, laurel-crown and aureole is still one with the brilliantly depicted coarseness of his companions and surroundings — with the figure of Jesus at Emmaus, translucent in the midst of His earthly surroundings and gesticulating companions.

THE PRINCE AND THE DWARF

In March 1631 Velázquez finished the portrait of *Prince Baltasar Carlos with a dwarf* (plate 68). The blond, sixteen-month-old prince, wearing a gold-embroidered dark-green costume, stands majestically on a dais, his right hand on a baton and his left one on the sword hilt. In the foreground, to the left, there is a chestnut-haired dwarfish girl in a dark-green dress lined in red and a white apron; holding a silver rattle in one hand and an apple in the other, she turns her head as she looks intently across the composition.[1] The smooth modelling of the Prince's luminous face and the uneven handling of the shadowed visage of the dwarf contrast, as much as do their bearing and pose; as the dwarf's glance and gesture ties her to her surroundings, the Prince towers over everything around him; the varying hues of purplish red which dominate in the composition become particularly luminous on the sash across his formal costume.

Painters in Spain and elsewhere had for a long time included dwarfs in some of their royal portraits, even when there was only one royal sitter. As we know, in 1619 or soon after, Villandrando had represented Philip IV, then a Prince, resting his right hand on the head of *Soplillo*, his favourite dwarf (plate 38).

In Villandrando's portrait, there is no contrast, except for the stature, between the figure of Philip and that of *Soplillo*, not even in their stance or gesture, much less in the brushwork

[1] José Camón Aznar has been the first to point out that the dwarf's costume, which includes a necklace, is that of a girl (*Velázquez*, Madrid, 1964, I, p. 437).

used to depict them; indeed, the dwarf quietly merges, as one more attribute, into the Prince's regalia. As for Velázquez's portrait, where the Prince and the dwarf are about the same height, there are contrasts in their stance and gesture, and, more significantly, in the handling of pigment. It is mainly this contrast that makes the child-dwarf appear as a foil to the majesty embodied in the figure of the child-Prince.

Before leaving for Italy, Velázquez had portrayed a dwarfish Court fool, *Calabazas* (plate 104), and throughout the succeeding years he made at least seven more individual portraits of such jesters, though only once — in the so-called *Meninas* — did he again represent one in the entourage of a royal person. As we shall see, any of those portraits of dwarfs or jesters, if compared with those of either the Prince or the King painted at the same or nearly the same time, reveal the sort of difference in the brushwork treatment which distinguishes the person of Baltasar Carlos from that of his dwarf in the portrait of 1631.

Equally meaningful is the contrast offered by two works executed by Velázquez at roughly the same time: a likeness of *Baltasar Carlos*, painted in 1632, in which the Prince's face is as luminous as in the portrait of 1631, and the portrait of *Doña Antonia de Ipeñarrieta and her son*, of about 1631–2, in which the child's face, like his mother's, is finely modelled in light and shade (plates 70 and 71).

PORTRAITS OF THE KING

Beruete suggested that it 'is probable that on his arrival in Madrid, Velázquez hastened to paint the new portrait of the King, perhaps the one now in the National Gallery', at London.[1] It is, indeed, reasonable to assume that Velázquez, on learning that, during his absence, the sovereign had allowed no other painter to portray him, should have been eager to paint a new likeness of Philip. There is moreover no reason, stylistic or otherwise, to suppose that the portrait of the King in brown and silver at the London National Gallery (frontispiece) was executed significantly later than the one of the Prince with his dwarf.

Substantial *pentimenti*, now quite noticeable, indicate that Velázquez was not quickly satisfied with his work. That he regarded it as of particular importance is attested by the fact that this is one of the two portraits of the King that he is known to have signed with his title, 'painter to Your Majesty', appended to his name — the other being the lost equestrian portrait of 1625.[2]

In this portrait, as in earlier ones, the likeness of Philip, though keen and quick, does not depend on the depiction of the accidental. The same is the case with later portraits of the

---

[1] Beruete, *Velázquez*, p. 39.

[2] Velázquez is only known to have signed three other paintings, in addition to the two mentioned portraits of Philip IV, after his appointment as Court painter; all three are also portraits, and two of them were of momentous importance to him: the lost *Philip III and the expulsion of the 'Moriscos'*, painted in the crucial competition of 1627, he signed in Latin, and the portrait of *Innocent X*, painted in 1650, carries a dedication in Italian, signed by the artist as painter to His Catholic Majesty. The other signature has come down to us in a fragment of a picture: the hand of an ecclesiastic holding a paper with the inscription: *Illmo Señor — Diego Velázquez* (plate 122).

In 1936, the portrait of Philip IV, in brown and silver, underwent a cleaning which removed some distortions of the original composition, probably due to the dark varnish which covered the surface, and with them any doubt whether the painting was not entirely by the Master's hand; it also rendered a little too obvious Velázquez's *pentimenti*.

sovereign, such as those in hunting costume (plate 98) or on horseback (plate 75), of the mid-1630's, the one in field uniform painted in 1644 (plate 109), or the bust dating from the early 1650's, when, though Philip was rather infirm, Velázquez still represented him as unblemished by age or any other temporal accident (plate 151). This depiction of the august character of the person of the King was not grasped by Velázquez's assistants, followers and imitators; they, in fact, more often than not, emphasized the flaws of age and appearance in their copies or derivative portraits of Philip IV. It may even be that some thought that by doing so they were improving upon Velázquez's naturalism. There seems always to have been only a small number of those capable of fully apprehending the true import of contemporary creations, even when they advocate them. Followers, whose minds are generally more sweeping than sharp, are almost invariably to be counted among the point-missers — which, in a small way, is gratifying to the art-historian as it makes it somewhat easier to tell their works from those of the Master whom they followed.

Among Velázquez's pupils, assistants and followers, there were obviously some who assimilated one or more aspects of his art; yet it would seem that they did not quite grasp the polarity of his naturalism which imbues the depiction of the human figure with Catholic meaning; at least, they did not fully realize that the differences in his pictorial handling of figures were means necessary for the Master's manifold portrayal of human nature or temporality, to his depiction of man as stirred by appetite, or even as a simulacrum of lust whether of the flesh or of knowledge; or to achieve an image within the reach of the human mind of the spotless nature of the humanity of Jesus or of His Mother; or, again, to give shape to the quasi-divine character of the person of the King, without symbols or allegories.

We have already compared in this light the portraits of Philip IV (plate 48) and his brother, the Infante Don Carlos (plate 50) both painted in 1626–28. Equally meaningful for the 1630's is a comparison of the portrait of the King in brown and silver (frontispiece) with either that of Don Diego del Corral y Arellano (plate 63) whose face is made unquiet by broad strokes and vivid lights and shadows, or the one of the husky royal master of the hunt, Juan Mateos (plate 73) whose character traits are accented by a nervous modelling in shadow — which the hands, sketched in with rough impasto, make the more emphatic. Likewise, if we look at the portraits *Philip IV* (plate 98), *Infante Don Fernando* (plate 96), *Prince Baltasar Carlos* (plate 97), painted between 1632 and 1636 for the royal lodge called Torre de la Parada, all clad in hunting dress, it becomes obvious that the King's face, as well as that of the heir to the throne, is more luminous and freer from shadows than that of the Infante. A consideration of Velázquez's three outstanding equestrian portraits will presently give further support to this view.

THE GREAT HALL OF THE BUEN RETIRO

In 1630 the ground was broken for a new Royal Palace, the Buen Retiro, at Madrid. Hastily, and it would seem poorly, built, it was partially in use two years later, but it was not till April 1635 that all the rooms were completed, including the ceremonial *salón*, or Great Hall, which late in the century became known as *Salón de Reinos*.

The idea of building a new palace on the outskirts of Madrid where Philip and his Court could repair to an architectural setting brighter than the one provided by the old Alcázar had originated with Olivares.[1] It was then said, and has often been repeated since, that his purpose was to keep the King amused and forgetful of the affairs of State which the Count-Duke was handling with more confidence than success. Such design has never been unusual at the seat of power. Nor is there anything uncommon in the fact that the new palace was intended to convey the greatness of the established political régime — the absolute monarchy in this case.

This move of the Count-Duke in his gamble for more power, as well as the interests and sentiments on which he played — whether those of the weak-willed King, of eager entre-preneurs, or of thoughtful as well as frivolous courtiers — and the praise and taunting that the whole affair attracted, would be just one more historical anecdote of the kind were it not for the fact that both Philip and Olivares valued Velázquez, who by then called himself 'painter to His Majesty and to the Count-Duke', as the artist that he was.[2]

The decoration of the new palace was a vast artistic project in which Velázquez, high in office and highly regarded at the Court, probably had an active part. A good many works were brought from other royal palaces in Spain, as well as from Portugal and Flanders, and they were still coming as late as 1639 when both the King and his painter were already busy with another project, the Torre de la Parada.[3]

The Great Hall is about all that remains of the Palace of the Buen Retiro, except for the so-called *Casón*, a building which has undergone too many changes, some recently. No longer a part of a vast architectural complex, and divested of the ceremonial function for which it was intended, it hardly suggests the idea of grandeur that it originally conveyed. Yet in 1635 when it was first on display, with its paintings and decoration, the *Salón*, as it was immediately called for short, was seen as the embodiment of majestic grandeur.

Nearly all the paintings that then decorated the hall have found a permanent place at the Prado Museum. Unfortunately there is extant no graphic record of what must have been a magnificent decorative ensemble. However, the order in which the paintings were most likely arranged has at least been worked out by Tormo as convincingly as the references to them in a poem published in 1637 allow.[4]

This poem, Manuel Gallegos's *Silva topográfica*, mentions as *in situ* every one of the paintings known to have been painted for the *Salón*, with just one exception, *The surrender of Breda* (plate 87). This is, however, one of the pictures listed as in the *Salón* by Don Francesco de'

---

[1] On the Buen Retiro Palace, see: Elías Tormo, 'Velázquez, el Salón de los Reinos del Buen Retiro y el poeta del palacio y del pintor', *Pintura, escultura y arquitectura en España, Estudios dispersos,* Madrid, 1949, pp. 127–246; María Luisa Caturla, *Pinturas, frondas y fuentes del Buen Retiro,* Madrid, 1947; *Un pintor gallego en la Corte de Felipe IV: Antonio Puga,* Santiago de Compostela, 1952, pp. 10–13, and 'Cartas de pago de los doce cuadros de batallas para el Salón de Reinos del Buen Retiro', *Archivo Español de Arte,* vol. 33, 1960, pp. 333–55; and Yves Bottineau, 'Felipe V y el Buen Retiro', *Archivo Español de Arte,* vol. 31, 1958, pp. 117–23.

[2] In the minutes of a meeting of the *Cortes del Reino* held in Madrid on 9 September 1633, it is stated that Velázquez, appearing as a petitioner, is '*pintor de Cámara de Su Magestad y del el Señor Conde Duque*'.

[3] Pedro Beroqui, *El Museo del Prado,* Madrid, n.d. (1933), vol. I, pp. 27–9.

[4] See n. 1 above.

Medici, Commendatore de Sorano, the Tuscan Ambassador, in his report on the completion of the Buen Retiro Palace dated 28 April 1635.[1]

Early in August 1634, Velázquez was at work on paintings for the *Salón*, some of which he had not yet finished on 28 March of the following year, just one month before Sorano reported on the completion of the Palace. On 14 June 1635, he acknowledged payment for a total of 2,500 ducats for an unspecified number of paintings, including several from his hand, which had been executed for the Hall. Entirely by him are the equestrian portraits of Philip IV and of Prince Baltasar Carlos (plates 75 and 76); his hand is also recognizable in the equestrian portrait of Queen Isabel, and, to a lesser degree, in those of the King's parents, which were, however, mainly executed by other painters (plate 74).

The surrender of Breda was one of twelve lengthwise, life-size battle scenes intended to perpetuate victories won by Philip IV's armies since the beginning of his reign in 1621, some as recently as 1633. Over these battle-scenes of recent times ran like a frieze ten paintings of the labours of Hercules.

[1] Sorano listed twelve subjects, with no indication of the painters who had painted them. However, according to documents published by M. L. Caturla ('Cartas'), the number of battle-pieces executed for the Great Hall was thirteen. Only eleven of them have come down to us; their measurements vary within the following limits: height, from 2·9 m. to 3·09 m.; width, from 3·11 m. to 3·81 m. All are now at the Prado Museum; their painters, subjects, and inventory numbers are as follows: Velázquez, *The surrender of Breda* (no. 1172); Maino, *The recapture of Bahía* (no. 885); Zürbarán, *The relief of Cadiz* (no. 656); Pereda, *The relief of Genoa* (no. 1317a); Jusepe Leonardo, *The surrender of Julich* and *The taking of Brisach* (nos. 858 and 859); Caxés (with help of Antonio Puga), *The recapture of San Juan de Puerto Rico* and *The recapture of the Island of Saint Christopher*, one of them actually finished by Luis Fernández (nos. 653 and 654); Vincencio Carducho, *The victory of Fleurs, The relief of Constanza*, and *The storming of Rheinfelden* (nos. 635, 636 and 637).

It is documented that Zurbarán received payment for the extant picture of *The relief of Cadiz* and for another of the same subject executed by him at the same time and for the same destination, which has not come down to us. It is also documented that Félix Castelo completed a picture of an unspecified subject for the *Salón* before 23 April 1635, when he received the final payment for it; the total fee, 350 ducats, indicates that it was a large composition, and it is reasonable to assume that it was a battle-piece.

Caturla holds that Zurbarán's lost *The relief of Cadiz* was mistitled by Sorano, who thought that it represented *The dislodging of the Dutch from the Island of Saint Martin by the Marquess of Cardereyta* — an error that would have arisen from the fact that Cardereyta had also played an important role in the naval action fought off Cadiz in 1625. As for Castelo's work, Caturla has suggested that it should be identified with *The recapture of the Island of Saint Christopher*, one of the two pictures which had been commissioned to Caxés (*Archivo Español de Arte*, vol. 33, 1960, p. 340). Yet, the available evidence contradicts this suggestion. Indeed, Castelo received a first payment for his painting for the *Salón* on 1 August 1634, about three weeks before Caxés received his first payment for the works commissioned to him for the same destination. Moreover, Puga, in his testament of 1 March 1635, claimed that he had worked on Caxés's painting for the Buen Retiro at the latter's home, and Caxés's widow received a final payment for both pictures, even though one was completed by Luis Fernández. It appears consequently more likely that Castelo's painting was *The dislodging of the Dutch from the Island of Saint Martin by the Marquis of Cardereyta*, listed by Sorano and now lost. A painting of 'the Marquis of Cardereyta with the Spanish armada', corresponding in size to those in this series, was inventoried, without artist's name, at the Buen Retiro Palace in 1701. As for the two pictures of *The relief of Cadiz*, it is probable that only one was hung in the *Salón*, where Sorano recorded it as one of the twelve battle scenes.

Another Spanish military victory, *The rescue of Valenza del Pó in 1635* was painted by Juan de la Corte for another chamber in the Buen Retiro Palace some time later. According to the royal inventory of 1701, the head of the victorious general, Don Carlos Coloma, was by Velázquez. The picture disappeared from the Madrid Palace at the time of Napoleon's invasion of Spain (1808–14); its present whereabouts is unknown.

The Hercules paintings, as well as two battle scenes — one of them now lost — were by Zurbarán, who was paid for all of them on 13 November 1634. Vincencio Carducho painted three battle pieces all bearing the date 1634. Eugenio Caxés, who had been commissioned to paint two of the military subjects, secured before his death (on 15 December 1634) the help of Antonio Puga to complete them; Puga, though, fell seriously ill, and another painter, Luis Fernández, was commissioned to finish one of the pictures, for which he was paid on 14 April 1635.

Late in March 1635, Maino was still at work on the painting that he contributed, *The recapture of Bahía by Don Fadrique de Toledo*, a victory won by the Spaniards over the Dutch on 1 May 1625. Pereda and Jusepe Leonardo seem also to have delivered their works shortly before the opening of the Great Hall for, like Maino and Velázquez, they were not paid in full till mid-June.

There is no documentary evidence that any of the paintings which formed part of the decoration of the Great Hall was not *in situ* by the end of April 1635, when the Ambassador from Florence wrote his report. A collection of poems on the Buen Retiro Palace was published in 1635, at the time of the inauguration of the *Salón*; its references to paintings have till now been overlooked or dismissed as inconsequential, perhaps because, unlike Gallegos's, they are not of an enumerative or descriptive nature. Nearly all these poems were written by courtiers, and express views and sentiments which obviously were then readily acceptable. Two sonnets, one on the portrait of Philip IV and the other on that of Baltasar Carlos, could only refer to the paintings in which Velázquez represented the King and the Prince on horseback, for no other independent portrait of either hung in the *Salón*.

It would indeed have been unthinkable to open the ceremonial hall without the portraits of the King and the Prince *in situ*. For that hall was conceived as a display — or *amphiteatro* to use the word then appropriate — of the Spanish monarchy with the reigning sovereign and the heir to the throne at its most luminous centres. Such is the idea that runs throughout the mentioned collection of poems published for the occasion — considerably more than half of which, including the opening one, have the *Salón* for their specific subject.

The name of Velázquez is mentioned in none of the poems. The sonnet on the portrait of Baltasar Carlos designates its painter as a 'heroic man' whose style is 'never rude' — a play on words which enhances the true grandeur of his art. As for the sonnet on the portrait of Philip, the strand of imagery which runs through it makes us see the painter displaying his own majesty in the presence of that of the King.[1]

[1] Diego de Covarruvias i Leyva, *Elogios al Palacio Real de Buen Retiro escritos por algunos ingenios de España. Recogidos por . . . ,* Madrid, 1635, fol. D2. The sonnet about the portrait of Baltasar Carlos is by Don José Pellicer de Tovar, and the one on the portrait of Philip IV by Dr. Felipe Godínez; they read as follows:

Esse Mayor que todo el edificio	*Felipe, El que con tantas atenciones*
Magnifico Salon, Theatro grave	*Tu nombre copia, o su grandeza imita,*
A donde aun el silencio apenas cave	*No se si te dá gloria, o te la quita,*
Por ser siempre menor que su artificio	*Tu mismo a ti parece que to opones.*

(Continued on page 68.)

Actually there were two likenesses of Philip IV in the Hall: one was the equestrian portrait by Velázquez; the other, included in Maino's *The recapture of Bahía*, was a replica of the portrait of the King as a young man painted by the same master in 1623 or 1624, one or two years before Philip's soldiers recaptured the Brazilian palace. If the book of poems I have referred to is any indication, Maino's painting was praised above all others in the *Salón*.

In a manner not uncommon at the time, Maino intertwined the narrative of the event with allegorical images, thus enhancing the prodigious nature of the military victory. Set off against the rest of the composition by rocks, there is a large scene of a wounded man being tenderly cared for; the young matron sitting on the foreground, three children grouped with her, appears as a live embodiment of the virtue of Charity — her intent pose enhanced by her elongated statuesque neck (plate 90).

Though prominently set, this is just an episode in Maino's narrative and, in point of composition, rather a foil to the scene which fills the space at the right from the bottom up to the top. There Don Fadrique de Toledo, the victorious commander, displays a tapestry with the image of the King to the assembly of soldiers and civilians who pay their homage. The King, looking the youth he was when that military success was achieved, is not seen alone. Victory, helped by Olivares, is crowning him with a laurel wreath, and while the goddess offers the sovereign a palm, the chief minister holds in his left hand his own sword, crushing underfoot, as does the King, the bodies of Heresy, Envy and War.

Maino's composition must certainly have satisfied Olivares's need for self-assertion as it unmistakably depicted him as the maker of the King's military victories. That the point was not missed is attested by the book of poems on the Buen Retiro Palace referred to above. Maino, indeed, is the only artist mentioned by name in it, and his painting the only one whose subject is identified, and repeatedly so.[1]

In the equestrian portrait of Philip painted for the *Salón* Velázquez achieved, as will presently be discussed, a telling image of the absolute monarch without relying on either allegorical figures or incidental narrative. Hence, whether it was by design or vital accident, there were in the ceremonial hall of the Buen Retiro two focal likenesses of Philip IV: in Velázquez's, the King's quasi-divine person appeared alone, dominating the expanse of the

---

Esse que dà esculpido tanto indicio
De quanto España de su Reynos sabe,
Y sin que el ocio su materia acabe
Lisonja Real embuelta en beneficio

Esse exemplo eloquente, estudio mudo
Purpureo Baltasar, que os ha labrado
Varon Heroyco en nunca estilo rudo

Esse pues, consultad, que alli enseñado
En vivas lenguas de vno y otro Escudo
Quedareis a mas glorias empeñado.

A sido equivocar admiraciones
Que la pintura a la verdad compita,
La fè que erije templos, solicita
Cultos a la Deidad, no emulaciones.

Mas si inspirando tu, que se construya
A tu nombre esta fabrica; en presencia
De tanta Magestad luzio la suya.

Esse es tambien obsequio de la sciencia
Pues osò competir, porque era suya
La gloria de su misma competencia.

A new limited edition of this collection of poems was issued in Valencia in 1949.

[1] The titles of four of the poems mention both Maino's name and the subject of his painting.

earth; in Maino's he was seen as the source of political and military power in the turmoil of a narrative and allegoric world in which his right-hand servant took the semblance of a demigod. Any interpretation of that lost baroque ensemble ought to take into account so live and telling a polarity.

Likewise, in discussing the paintings of the labours of Hercules, which ran like a frieze above the depiction of the victories won by Philip IV's armies, one should bear in mind that one emblematic significance of Hercules current at the time was that of the antiquity of the Spanish monarchy, and that Olivares was then regarded as the Hercules of Philip IV — himself seen as the Atlas of Castile.[1]

The word play, where one word or image is used as a prismatic whole from which bursts a plurality of significances, was a common and often effective device of the baroque writer. Painters, too, were intent on expressing at one time more than one meaning — which those truly creative did, not by just playing on the various emblematic significances of a given figure, but rather by fashioning on the canvas strands of imagery of their own. Other artists of the period appear to have done likewise, and it would seem that spectators and readers had their ears, eyes, and minds open to it.

This digression may be useful for an understanding of the overall decoration of the ceremonial hall, obviously planned to express a plurality of meanings with the antiquity, the present power and the bright hopes of the Spanish monarchy as live centres. There is no evidence that Velázquez was entrusted with the planning of that pictorial ensemble. But probably his advice was sought at one point or another during the planning and execution of the project. As for the paintings which he painted for it, they stand unmistakably apart from those by other painters, showing that Velázquez gave new substance and shape to the world in which he, as well as his less creative contemporaries, had his roots.

THE EQUESTRIAN ROYAL PORTRAITS

The equestrian portraits of Philip IV, his Queen, his parents — Philip III and Queen Margarita — and Prince Baltasar Carlos hung in the ceremonial hall of the Buen Retiro. Those of Philip IV and the Prince are entirely by Velázquez. As we know from the book of poems of 1635, the reigning sovereign and the heir to the throne appeared as focal points in the display of the Spanish monarchy that the *Salón* was meant to be.

It is generally held that Velázquez began the other three portraits before his journey to Italy, leaving them to be completed during his absence by another painter, and that it was only years later, under the pressure resulting from the hurry with which everything pertaining to the Buen Retiro Palace had to be done, that the Master decided to freshen them up. Quite naturally it was the portrait of Isabel de Bourbon, the reigning Queen, that he himself reworked extensively, painting anew her head and bust after the likeness he had painted of her in 1631–2; he also painted afresh the white horse and made important changes in the landscape. In fact, a recent and successful cleaning has revealed that, as it turned out, this portrait was almost

---

[1] See, for instance, *Elogios al Palacio del Bven Retiro*, fols. A2, C2, E (poems by Luis Vélez de Guevara, 'Arminda', and Juan de Paredes).

entirely repainted by Velázquez (plates 69 and 74). As for those of Queen Margarita, expertly cleaned in 1968, and of Philip III, most of the repainting was done by assistants, though some passages suggest that Velázquez touched up both portraits, particularly that of the Queen.

The portraits of Philip IV and the Prince were most likely finished in 1634, or just before April 1635, when they were in the *Salón*. We know from Pacheco that Velázquez was given to making studies and doubtless he made some in connection with these two portraits, though no extant picture has convincingly been identified as such. The inventory drawn up at the time of his death shows, however, that he had in his apartments a *Prince Baltasar Carlos on horseback* sketched, in colour, most probably by his hand;[1] it is also likely that the *Philip IV on a chestnut horse* listed in the same inventory was by him.

Horses were a familiar sight in the seventeenth-century life when nearly everybody, including Velázquez, was used to riding on horseback, a fact of which some critics and historians brought up in horseless cities appear to be not quite aware. Though Pacheco noted in some detail the proportions of the horse, he commented that it was so common an animal that it could almost always be imitated from nature.[2]

No doubt on undertaking those equestrian portraits, or, for that matter, any of his major works, Velázquez must have thought of such similar compositions by other masters as were alive in his mind. He was by then acquainted, or even familiar, with other artists' equestrian compositions, some of them outstanding. True, there is no indication that he had been in Padua, where he would have seen Donatello's *Gattamelata*. There is, however, reason to believe that, on his way from Venice to Rome, in 1629, he stopped at Florence, where he could hardly have missed seeing the pedestalled *condottieri* in Uccello's and Castagno's paintings at the Cathedral. Undoubtedly, as he walked about the streets of Venice, protected by the Spanish ambassador's men, he paused, forgetting for a while the unrest of the city, to look up at Verrochio's *Colleoni*; and doubtless later on, while at Rome, he did not ignore the famous *cavallo* of Marcus Aurelius.

Long before, even since his appointment to the Court, Velázquez had had at hand at the Royal Palace several equestrian compositions, including the one of *Charles V at the battle of Mühlberg* (Prado, no. 410 — plate 78), in which Titian achieved a masterful likeness of the Caesar as warrior, with no depiction of battle or troops, or any allegorical figures. Four paintings of horses, probably unfinished works by Ribera and others, were also at the Palace. Velázquez himself, as early as 1625, had won acclaim with a portrait of Philip IV on horseback, now lost.

[1] The entry in the inventory reads: '*El Principe Nro. Sr. a cauallo, en bosquejo*'. Pacheco makes it clear that *bosquejo*, or *metido de colores*, is always in paint; though he is aware that some painters use only black and white, or reddish and white pigments, his advice is to employ a full range of colours, especially for the heads and flesh of human figures sketched from life (*Arte de la Pintura*, vol. II, pp. 78, 127–8).

There were also in Velázquez's studio three unfinished large canvases, representing respectively a white, a chestnut, and a grey horse, without any human figure; it is likely that they were by the artist himself, though the possibility cannot be excluded that some of them were among the four canvases of similar subject and size inventoried at the Royal Palace as early as 1600.

[2] Pacheco, *Arte de la Pintura*, vol. I, p. 419; vol. II, p. 133.

Three years later before leaving for Italy, he had seen Rubens, the old and famous master, painting the equestrian portraits of the reigning Philip IV and of the long-dead Philip II (Prado, no. 1686 — plate 79), both of which were allegorical compositions. It was probably at that time that he began the equestrian portraits of Philip III and the two Queens which, as it turned out, he later repainted for the Great Hall of the Buen Retiro. The one of *Philip III*, little more than sketched by him, shows a certain link with Rubens's manner, particularly in the posture and modelling of the horse; yet, like the others, it shows that Velázquez, contrary to Rubens, had no penchant for allegories.

THE KING AND THE PRINCE, EQUESTRIAN

As Velázquez was setting up the canvases for the equestrian portraits of Philip and Baltasar Carlos, he may well have turned over in his mind memories of like compositions by other artists or by himself, more intent — one would assume — on excelling than on imitating them. However, he did not depend on any other work for the composition of either of these portraits.

The one of the Prince was to hang high, above a door, in the Hall of the Buen Retiro (plate 76). As it has been pointed out, this explains the exaggerated curve of the pony's barrel. It should be added that Velázquez made use of that circumscribing condition for his own expressive ends, and thus achieved a monumental perspective setting for the equestrian figure of the young Prince — which one misses at the height at which the picture now hangs in the Prado Museum.

All writers on the subject have remarked on the delicacy with which the painter brushed in the likeness of the fair-haired, blue-eyed Prince, with no emphatic modelling of his features which appear the more airy as highlights accent the fluidity of the head's contour. It is, indeed, one of Velázquez's luminous 'distant blobs'. The sitter's rose-and-ivory-hued face — where even the shadow cast by the brown hat is diaphanous — is fully illuminated, as are his green and gold dress, his pink flying scarf and his brown pony. Also thinly painted and brilliant, gossamer-like, is the sloping landscape; its green and blue hues deepen the space round and below the figure of the Prince, as his mount, in an arrested posture, paws the air above the brownish foreground thus heightening the monumentality of the composition.

As for the portrait of the King (plate 75), Beruete perceptively noted that its execution is 'even freer' than that of the Prince, and that Philip IV is 'here represented in the fullness of absolute power and grandeur, in the brilliancy of such triumph as the most fortunate heroes of ancient or modern times have seldom known'. Since Beruete was censorious of Philip IV, he concluded that 'Velázquez in this picture, more than in any other, seems to have wished to redeem by idealization of the outward form the unworthiness and moral ruin of his model'.[1] The critic was certainly right in his views about Philip who, penitently, considered himself weak-willed and a sinner, hopelessly incapable of making himself worthy of his royal task.

There seems to have been a friendly closeness between Philip and Velázquez from early in their association. Pacheco tells us that the King kept a key to Velázquez's studio — which

[1] *Velázquez*, pp. 79–81.

was at the Palace — and had a chair there where he sat almost daily watching the painter at work. It is permissible to assume that Velázquez would not have gone on painting un-interruptedly during the King's visit, and that conversation took place between the two men. It is even likely that Philip, who was given to speaking or writing about his weaknesses to those he trusted, had a confidant in his painter. Whatever their relations may have been, Velázquez, like any other observing person close to Philip, must have realized the shortcomings that led the King throughout his life to put up an ineffectual fight, made all the more agonizing by the sincerity of his religious sentiments, against both his sensuous proclivities and the enemies, heretics most of them, of his kingdoms. Yet, in his portraits of the sovereign, beginning with the bust-length of 1623 or 1624 (plate 43), Velázquez never aimed at a characterization of Philip's natural bents. Nor did he ever represent the King, allegorically or otherwise, as a warrior in either action or victory.

In 1628 when, at the peak of his success, Rubens was in Madrid, he made several portraits of Philip IV.[1] One of them, now lost, was a religious allegorical composition, representing the King on horseback as victorious over his enemies. In those which are extant, the Flemish master gave his royal sitter an animated though stately appearance, with vivacities of light and shade modelling the lively face; it has been quite rightly said that Rubens 'painted the King as an elegant nobleman'.[2]

Velázquez, whose prestige was then rising at the Court, had to reckon with those portraits; he probably watched the famous master painting them, and certainly witnessed their success. Yet he never imparted any sensuous liveliness, Rubenslike or otherwise, to his portraits of the King. Neither did he ever emphasize the luxury of the King's costume or adornments, not even when he portrayed him in magnificent attire, as he did in 1631-2 and in 1644 (frontis-piece and plate 109). In this respect, a comparison of two portraits of Philip in black dress, one painted by Rubens in 1628-9 and the other by Velázquez in 1626-8, is enlightening, for it shows that, contrary to Rubens, Velázquez did not see the King as just one more nobleman (plates 36 and 48). Indeed, however close to, or familiar with, the spectacle of Philip's melan-choly or sensuous moods and frustrating ways Velázquez may have been, it was rather the quasi-divine nature of the monarch that he put on canvas, leaving for others to record what was accidental in Philip's appearance, as well as the external attributes of his royal power.

Some time before 1638 Pacheco wrote — he must have had it from his son-in-law himself — that when, after his return from Italy, Velázquez made the equestrian portrait of Philip IV, obviously the one we are now discussing, he had the monarch 'seated for three hours at a time, all that élan and grandeur suspended'. The Spanish expression, 'suspendido tanto brio y tanta grandeza', has a lilt which is somewhat startling in Pacheco's text and may well reflect Veláz-quez's own words.

It is plain that Velázquez did not depend for the composition of this portrait on any of the works familiar to him. Unlike Rubens he made no use of allegories; nor did he represent the King, as the Flemish master had done with Philip II, on a scale made colossal by the low

[1] Pacheco, *Arte de la Pintura*, vol. I, p. 153.
[2] F. Saxl, 'Velázquez and Philip IV', *Lectures*, vol. I, London, 1957, p. 314.

horizon line and the diminutive figures that fill a battle-field in the middle distance (plate 79). Monumental though it is, there is nothing colossal about Velázquez's composition, which in just this regard bears comparison with Titian's *Charles V at the battle of Mühlberg* (plate 78).

Titian represented Charles V at Mühlberg as a warrior in full armour, setting out from the lee of a tree's shadow into the open; the forward motion is made vivid as the Emperor grasps the lance and the curvetting horse lowers its head and raises its forefeet off the ground. The live diagonal of the lance enhances this sense of motion and, at the same time, it sets off the erect trunk of the Emperor who, his character traits accented, masters with his bearing and mien the action into which he stirs his mount. So unerring a live personification of the idea of the Caesar is what makes this one of the greatest portraits of all time; in its own day it led Pietro Aretino to fancy that, rather than by Titian, it had been painted 'by the hand of that idea that Nature imitates in live and spiritual design' — a cogent expression of what the vying of art and nature was understood to mean in those years of the Renaissance.[1]

In Velázquez's *Philip IV* there is no accent on human character, action or time; the surface texture, fluidly brushed in, is luminous at every point — the King's half-armour and the pink and gold of his costume, the white and chestnut hues of the horse, and the greys, greens, and blues which extend to the background in the landscape. This portrait must have appealed to those who held that the King's duty, unlike a captain's, was not to fight but to rule, as Gracián put it in 1640.[2]

The equestrian group is in full profile but for Philip IV's head, which is slightly turned to the right, thus adding to the effortless pose with which he holds the baton in one hand and the bridle in the other, while the spirited horse rears back in mid-gallop, arresting his own movement and that of the King's scarf, into a monumental pose. Lit up from an invisible centre in front of him, the halcyon figure of Philip outshines the radiant expanse which spreads around and below into the horizon — a limpid image of the quasi-divine nature of the absolute monarch.

More often that not, Western painters have achieved verisimilitude in their portraits. Yet a portrait's truth to the sitter's physique — seldom verifiable for long, or by many — has rarely been of lasting consequence. What has always mattered, at the time the portrait was painted and ever after, is the sentience of the image into which the painter has fashioned his sitter. The painting, indeed, is the thing, even when minute likeness has been the painter's aim and achievement.

In *Philip IV, equestrian*, Velázquez achieved a painting of monumentality unadorned by either allegorical array or architectural pomp; in it, the person of the King is at one and the same time vividly seen on the earth and yet not of it. We know from seventeenth-century sources, other painters' portraits of Philip IV, including copies of this one, and even from the first likeness of him which Velázquez put on canvas in 1623 and painted out soon after (plates 48–49), how divergent from all others, how compelling and inimitable was the image of the King achieved by the Master in the ten portraits which have come down to us (frontis-

---

[1] *Lettere*, Paris, 1609, vol. V, fol. 53v., and José López-Rey, 'Idea de la imitación barroca', *Hispanic Review*, vol. XI, July 1943, pp. 253–7.

[2] Baltasar Gracián, *El político* (Madrid, 1961, pp. 39 and 55).

piece, and plates 45, 47, 48, 75, 98, 109, 120, and 151). Compelling, unique and vital that image remains, to the point, indeed, that what may have been closer likenesses of Philip appear today as of little more than anecdotal significance.

OLIVARES, EQUESTRIAN

Most writers on Velázquez have observed that his portrait of Olivares on horseback (plate 77) is as fluidly painted as those of Philip IV and Prince Baltasar Carlos, though it is less luminous than either of the others. The chief minister, wearing black half-armour inlaid with gold, gold-braided dark trunks, a purplish scarf and a grey hat with mauve plumes, is on a chestnut horse at the edge of a cliff against a cloudy sky made sombre by the blue-grey smoke which rises high from a burning town in the background. Both his commanding gesture — with the baton raised in his right hand — and his high-spirited mount are directed to the battle raging below in the middle distance; yet he faces towards the spectator.

Cruzada, and others after him, suggested that the battle depicted is the one fought in the autumn of 1638 at Fuenterrabía, where the French were defeated by the Spaniards.[1] Even though Olivares, never really an army man, had not moved from Madrid, the victory was credited to his strategy and leadership. As the King rewarded him with a great many honours, the Count-Duke seized the occasion to recover his prestige, which had been on the wane for some time. It would have been at that triumphal time, late in 1638 or shortly thereafter — it is suggested — that Velázquez painted his equestrian portrait.

Yet, as shown before, the role of Olivares as the maker of the monarchy's military victories was current at the Court by 1635, when it found pictorial expression in Maino's painting for the Buen Retiro Palace. Since, in point of execution, the equestrian portrait of Olivares admittedly resembles those of the King and the Prince painted about that time, there is no reason to suggest that it was painted significantly later. As for the military action depicted, no specific one was probably intended; indeed, the battle scene would have been the more expressive of Olivares's power and success for not referring to a particular event.

The dynamic, bold rhythm of the composition is carried by live diagonals — the horse, the sword, the baton, the smoke, the cliff — which, as it happens, are keyed to Olivares's bearing. Slashing lights enliven the modelling of the horse, and the textures of the rider's costume and of the mount's trappings look rich and weighty as they sparkle with vivacities of touch. As in the equestrian portraits of Philip and his son, Olivares's head is painted vividly; it is, indeed, as Beruete noted, the highest light in the picture; yet the shadows on it are narrowed rather than thinned and the character traits are incisively rendered. It is in this cogent pictorial whole that the Count-Duke embodies in his gesture of command and of self-assertion both the turmoil of the bloody battle depicted below and the bustle and glow of victory — a lusty image of worldly success plainly different from Velázquez's portrayal of the King's absolute power and grandeur.

Any portrait, even if a masterpiece, lends itself to anecdotal interpretations and seems to ask

[1] Cf. Cruzada, *Anales*, p. 118; Enrique Lafuente Ferrari, *Velázquez*, London, 1943, p. 22; G. Marañón, *El Conde-Duque de Olivares*, Madrid, 1952, pp. 66-7; and Trapier, *Velázquez*, p. 236.

for the iteration of commonplaces. Hence it is not surprising that flattery has been found more than once to be the key to the understanding of Velázquez's three equestrian portraits: flattery of the charming little heir to the throne, of the inept and profligate monarch, and of the ambitious chief minister. Very likely Velázquez's equestrian portraits, as well as others, gave rise in his day to some caustic remarks about the sitters not quite looking their parts. Yet it is unlikely that the portraits were held to be faulty on this score or suspected of flattery. That a majestic quality was observed in Velázquez's works is obvious in Gallegos's poem on the Buen Retiro Palace; as indicated before, this poem refers to or describes and praises a great many paintings, but the emphasis is on those by Velázquez, each one of which is given prominence at one time or another. Without entering into a full discussion of Gallegos's views, I may point out that time and again he bestows on Velázquez's art the attributes of the monarchy; thus, his brush is 'sovereign', or 'a sceptre' which attains a 'miraculous monarchy', a deathless world in which the artist depicts in a 'sovereign manner' all the affections of the soul, and even what is invisible; and this art-created world chooses Philip IV as monarch, thus offering him a 'more lasting empire'.

It might again be argued that Gallegos was just currying favour with both the King and his painter. Yet even those minded to regard Gallegos's poem as a piece of double-barrelled courting, must realize that some of Velázquez's contemporaries saw the world which he created and the one in which he lived as heightening one another and having the person of the King as their common centre — which the Master's portraits reveal by themselves.

VELÁZQUEZ'S PORTRAYAL OF MILITARY VICTORY

The surrender of Breda (plate 87) represents Ambrosio Spínola, one of the ablest generals in the service of the Spanish monarchy in the course of the Thirty Years' War, receiving from Justinus of Nassau the keys of the conquered city.[1] Since his youth Spínola, a Genoese descended from an old and wealthy family of merchants, had served in the armies of the Spanish King. He made a military reputation for himself in Flanders where, in 1604, he conquered Ostend, for which he was rewarded with the Golden Fleece. Later, in 1621, as he was besieging Jülich, Philip IV, who had just come to the throne, made him Marquis of los Balbases. It was in 1624 that he was ordered to take Breda, the key fortress of Antwerp, which was defended by Justinus of Nassau.

The siege of Breda was a momentous test of power between the Netherlands and Spain, eagerly watched by the rest of Europe; it was also a decisive contest between two famous generals, both well versed in the arts of fortification, who had their renown at stake. A good

---

[1] For accounts of the surrender of Breda published before Velázquez painted this subject, see Saxl, 'Velázquez and Philip IV', *Lectures*, vol. I, pp. 315–18, and Marqués de Lozoya, *La Rendición de Breda*, Barcelona, 1953, pp. 8, 14–19. Saxl stated that he had 'not read in any account that Justinus delivered up the keys' (op. cit., p. 317). Nor have I, not even in the passage, cited by Lozoya, in which Gonzalo de Céspedes y Meneses, after describing the surrender, mentions that Don Fernando de Guzmán was sent with the news to Madrid (*Historia de Don Felipe IIII, Rey de las Españas*, Barcelona, 1634, p. 226).

many observers from various lands were attracted to the spot where Spínola, reputed to be the first engineer of his time, matched wits with Nassau, quickly counteracting time and again his ingenious schemes for breaking the siege. Finally, as the beleaguered city was entirely cut off from the outside, hunger forced Justinus to seek an honourable capitulation. Spínola, though the victory was already his, granted unusually generous terms.

The formal surrender took place on 5 June 1625. The citizens who so wished were allowed to leave the city with their possessions and the defeated army were granted the privilege of marching out carrying their arms and colours. Spínola sat on horseback outside the city attended by some of the noblemen in his army. He had forbidden his troops to jeer at, or otherwise abuse, the vanquished Dutch, and, according to a contemporary report, he himself saluted Justinus, who came forth first, followed by his wife riding in a carriage, and the leaders of his defeated army, and they returned his salute with 'composed countenances and voices, and with a modest enclining of the banners'.[1] Another account relates that the victorious general spoke words of encouragement and cheer to Justinus and his wife, and ordered some of his Spanish and Flemish officers to escort them.

Spínola's benignity caught the imagination of the Spaniards, and even though some held that he had been overgenerous in granting the capitulation, its terms were ratified. Magnificence and magnanimity were then not only cognate words but kindred sentiments as well, and the Christian belief in the fleeting nature of human splendour and glory made them more so, even in the course of bitter religious wars.

None of the accounts of the surrender published within a few years of the event mentions that Justinus delivered the keys of the city to Spínola. It was, however, in that episode, real or inferred, that some Spaniards saw the transcendent significance of Spínola's success and clemency. Indeed, the capitulation took place on 5 June 1625, and before that year ran its course, Calderón de la Barca wrote a play, *The Siege of Breda*, to celebrate the victory. The play closes with the delivery of the keys by Justinus, who in so doing sees Fortune turning even the most powerful monarchies into dust, while Spínola tries to raise him from the gloom of defeat with time-honoured words: 'the valour of the conquered makes the conqueror famous'. With these words, in which there is self-regard though not self-complacency, the conqueror's stature is enhanced by that of the conquered, while the banners of Spain are raised on the fortress and there is victorious music and shouting.[2]

The surrender of Breda differs essentially from the other extant pictures of military victories which hang at the Buen Retiro. Nearly all of them — the exception being Maino's *The recapture of Bahia* — resemble one another in their compositional pattern; whether their subject is a battle or an act of surrender, the victorious Spanish general is at one side on a rise above the

---

[1] G. Barry, *The Siege of Breda*, Louvain, 1627, p. 145. Cf. Herman Hugo, *The Siege of Breda* (translated from the Latin), [Brussels?], 1627, pp. 140–2.

[2] Calderón's play *El sitio de Bredá* — with which Saxl obviously was unacquainted — was first performed in 1625, shortly after Spínola's victory, won in June of that year. See Emilio Cotarelo y Mori, *Ensayo sobre la vida y obras de D. Pedro Calderón de la Barca*, Madrid, 1924, p. 123; Harry Warren Hilborn, *A Chronology of the Plays of D. Pedro Calderón de la Barca*, Toronto, 1938, pp. 9, 12.

area where a land or a sea battle is depicted on a markedly lesser scale, as if on a back drop.

Velázquez must have made several drawings as studies for *The surrender of Breda*, though only two are extant (plates 89 and 91). The overall composition appears to have been 'drawn in paint' on the canvas, to use an expression applied at the time of Velázquez's death to a painting left unfinished by him. As he then went on with his work, his mind's eye would time and again be challenged into further creation by the very shapes which he had brushed on the canvas and which he painted off, often with light strokes that, as it happens, keep them as live evidence of the act of creation (plates 86–7). The same process is noticeable in earlier and later Velázquez works, such as *Bacchus* and *The Royal Family*, to mention only two.

It has always been visible to the naked eye that Velázquez first brushed in the figure of Spínola as embracing Nassau with both his arms, and that he later changed the position of the Spaniard's left arm. Radiographs have shown the overlapping of many other changes hidden to the naked eye. For instance, the Master altered more than once the view of the horse on the foreground. More significant is the disclosure that the lances, which were to become a cardinal compositional element, were not initially part of the composition.[1]

Radiographs of this and other Velázquez paintings, as well as the *pentimenti* plainly visible in many of them, help us to understand the thrusts and counter-thrusts with which he shaped his works, responding to pictorial challenges of his own. Our major interest focuses, of course, on Velázquez's works as completed by his hand, which endowed them with an effortless appearance.

In *The surrender of Breda*, an aerial perspective articulates the whole composition in depth and breadth, bringing together the essentials of the narrative: the trenches, waterworks and block-houses in the background; the light-hued, pink, yellow or blue army dresses of the defeated men who march past with their arms and colours in the middle-distance; the scattering of

---

[1] Two of the outstanding elements in the composition of *The surrender of Breda*, the lances and the group of Spínola and Nassau, have lured some writers into a search for works by other artists which might have influenced Velázquez's. José Ortega y Gasset crisply commented on the *naïveté* of a method which results in regarding any picture executed before April 1635 whose composition includes soldiers holding their lances up — or for that matter, a group of two men embracing or bending to each other — as a source for *The surrender of Breda* (*Papeles sobre Velázquez y Goya*, Madrid, 1950, pp. 74–5). However, the number of works supposed to have influenced the composition of this masterpiece keeps growing at random and *ad nauseam*; those most frequently or most recently suggested are the following: Bernard Solomon's smallish wood-cut representing *Melchizedek presenting Abraham with bread and wine*, which illustrates Claude Perrin's *Quadrines historiques de la Bible*, Lyon, 1553; an illustration to *Concordia* found in some editions of Alciati's *Emblemata* brought out by Christian Wechsel between 1534 and 1545; a drawing dated 1565 by Jan van der Straet (Stradanus) which is an allegory of Philip II's role as mediator of the treaty of Cateau-Cambrésis (Ashmolean Museum); Martin de Vos's illustration of *Melchizedek presenting Abraham with bread and wine* in Gerard de Jode's *Thesaurus sacrarum historiarum*, Antwerp, 1579; Antonio Tempesta's frontispiece for Otho Vaenius's *Batavarum cum Romanis bellum*, 1612; three paintings by Rubens, *Melchizedek presenting Abraham with bread and wine*, *Reconciliation between Henry III and Henry of Navarre*, and *The Cardinal Don Fernando and the King of Hungary after the battle of Nördlingen*; El Greco's *Despoiling of Jesus* and *Martyrdom of St. Maurice*; Veronese's *Susanna and the Elders* and *Jesus and the centurion*; Dürer's *Large horse*, and Christopher Jobst's tapestry cartoon of 1615, *The Surrender of Hersfeldt* (Kassel, Archiv). It is rather unlikely that Velázquez was acquainted with some of the works supposed to have influenced his composition of *The surrender of Breda*. For instance, both Rubens's *The Cardinal Infante Don Fernando and the King of Hungary after the battle of Nördlingen* and Velázquez's *The surrender of Breda* were shown publicly for the first time in April 1635, one in Antwerp and the other in Madrid.

Dutch soldiers who wearily cluster together, to the foreground, as a distant column of smoke rises higher than their pennons; and the unwearied Spanish officers who, bareheaded for the solemn occasion, are massed around their flag, behind their leader, while their troops, whose lances bar the space above, look on from under their slouched hats.

In either cluster the gesture and bearing of the soldiers are keenly expressive of a variety of emotions, moods, or dispositions, which makes them truly human groups. There are faces which are sharply illuminated and modelled in the round; the features of others are distinctly shaped by graduated shadows; some, whether lit or shadowed are what Quevedo called distant blobs. This imaginative handling of light and pigment endows both human groups, and for that matter the whole composition, with a sense of depth and airiness.

It is a full-toned picture, with a richness of yellow, ochre, blue, green, rose, and purple hues, fluidly brushed in. It portrays both the misery and the splendour of the scene of surrender as its brilliant tints sweep into a luminous whole the dust-hued colours sparingly used in the depiction of the field and the defeated.

The group of Dutch soldiers comes to the fore, where a few stand on a mound, fatigue showing in their faces and in the manner in which they hold their pennons; others are comely figures, like the blobs, one in shadow, the other in light, of the two young men seen in profile — who recall Apollo in *The forge of Vulcan* (plate 62) — or the light-splashed youth, clad in white and blue, who quiets with a gesture of his right hand the fellow officer whispering at his ear.

The victorious and the defeated generals meet in a sort of clearing bounded by two slight elevations in the foreground, on one of which Spínola's horse stands restlessly while Dutch soldiers wearily group themselves on the other. Spínola stands on a patch of green circled by the barren ground which Nassau steps across. Live diagonals maintain whole and dynamic the overall composition, intercrossing, running parallel, or meeting in the far-off distance. The most obvious are the one marked by the Dutch soldier standing, back to the spectator, in the foreground and the Spaniard with the musket on his shoulder seen across him, which is intersepted by that established by the two horses; or the parallel ones underscored by the weapons on the shoulder of the Spanish and the Dutch musketeers; or those which, running along the front row of their group, funnel through into distance.

As Justinus of Nassau, with a slow and heavy tread, steps out from his soldiers to surrender the key of the city, Spínola's arm — its broad, liquid contour a transparent tissue over the bright hues of the defeated troops marching past — bridges the distance between the two, a courtly smile on his pale, intelligent face directed at the mortified hurt on Nassau's weather-beaten visage, where the eyes are heavy with fatigue. The figure of the conquered certainly is not just a foil to that of the victor in this composition where Velázquez has swept even dusty hues into luminosity. Rather, as Spínola puts his arm on Justinus's shoulder, the bearing of the one enhances his human likeness to the other, and the victor's gesture mortises in one image the Christian sentiment of charity, and hence of humility, and the heroic sense of mercy, and hence of greatness — 'noblesse' might have been the word for it (plate 88).

It is possible that, as has been suggested, Velázquez painted from life some of the officers who were at hand at the Court nine or ten years after the surrender of Breda, though none of them has been convincingly identified. Spínola died in 1630 and consequently could not have sat for the painting. Yet Velázquez had journeyed with him to Italy in 1629 — from Madrid to Genoa, if Pacheco's report is accurate — and this has led to the surmise that the painter may have sketched the likeness of the great general at that time. There is, however, no documentary reference to Velázquez's having painted then, or at any other time, a portrait of Spínola from life, and it would have been unlike Pacheco, who made a point of recording his son-in-law's early successes, not to mention that so famous a man had sat to Velázquez. In any case it is reasonable to assume that Spínola's traits, shape, and mien were alive in Velázquez's mind at the time when *The surrender of Breda* was painted. As for Justinus of Nassau, Velázquez never saw him. Consequently the painter must have made use of other artists' works for at least this one of the two main figures in the composition, perhaps even for both. And yet the two appear equally vivid in gesture and expression, as vivid, indeed, as any portrait that Velázquez ever painted from life. This fact should be taken into account by those who are minded to decide on the basis of the life-like quality of a portrait whether or not Velázquez painted it from life.

Nor was Velázquez ever in Breda; available to him, however, were maps, descriptions and engravings of the city, the battle-field and the surrender.[1] The background view of the painting reveals familiarity with, and freedom from, the details they provide (plate 93). Vitally, the truth of *The surrender of Breda* is not truth to the physique of the various participants in the action, or to the location, circumstances or fripperies of the happening, but rather to the play of sentiments that the painter discerned in the event.

Velázquez painted in a live, naturalist manner what he had seen, or learned, or envisioned, whether a sitter or a popular, historical, mythological, or religious story; yet he painted it as it had worked itself through his mind. He was, indeed, creative. Certainly, he was steeped in a live pictorial tradition rooted in Spain and more deeply in Italy, and in a Catholic sense of life which was then particularly keen and forceful in Spain. Needless to say, such circumstances would not necessarily have turned him into the artist that he was. Still, his works bring them to mind. Nor should we assume that this is so because he worked to a fixed programme — which no true artist ever does. Yet the consistency of his *oeuvre* vitally reveals a polarity of the religious and the worldly which is of his day, that is, baroque, and creative and hence his own; and it is so that his work stands as unique in the continuum of historical time.

OTHER PAINTERS' PORTRAYAL OF MILITARY VICTORY

The sentiments that Velázquez embodied in *The surrender of Breda* are unlike those which other painters of his, or, for that matter, earlier times depicted in works of similar subjects. A

[1] As Saxl suggested ('Velázquez and Philip IV', *Lectures*, vol. I, p. 316), it is very likely that Velázquez knew the extraordinarily large engraving (more than three feet high) depicting the siege and surrender of Breda which Jacques Callot made in 1628 by commission of the Infanta Isabel Clara Eugenia, Governor of the Netherlands. He doubtless had also seen the engravings, some with details of the siege, which illustrate Herman Hugo's *The Siege of Breda*, which had been available in Latin, Spanish, and other languages since the late 1620's.

case in point is *The surrender of Seville*, signed in 1634 by Francisco de Zurbarán, who most probably painted it for the Shod Mercederian Convent in Seville (plate 94).[1] It shows Ferdinand III, the Saint, King of Castille and Leon, receiving the key to Seville from the Moors, against whom a decisive victory was won in 1248. This event remained charged with feeling throughout most of Philip IV's reign. As we know, a closely related event, the expulsion of the Moriscos, decreed by Philip III in 1609, was chosen as the subject for the competition in which Velázquez, Caxés, Carducho and Nardi took part in 1627 by royal command.

In Zurbarán's *The surrender of Seville*, the gesticulating and gaudily garbed Moors contrast in both colour and expression with the sedate figures of Ferdinand III and his religious and military cortege. The defeated Moors are, indeed, made to look laughable by the over-done expression of obeisance which pervades their faces and gestures — all of which is in keeping with the climate of sentiment which prevailed at the time and which pervaded some of Lope de Vega's plays, quite popular then.

For another contrast, we may look at Jusepe Leonardo's *The Surrender of Jülich*, the city during the siege of which Spínola received the title of Marqués de los Balbases and which he succeeded in conquering on 3 February 1622. Jusepe Leonardo was approximately of the same age as Velázquez, having been born at Calatayud, Aragon, about 1600 or soon after. As his friend Jusepe Martínez wrote, and as compositional elements in his works tend to confirm, Leonardo was a pupil of Eugenio Caxés.[2] Yet, like other painters active in the Madrid of the 1630's, he tried without success to approximate Velázquez's manner and at least once lifted a figure from one of his works,[3] though he actually never cared for the famous Master's sense of composition or came close to his way of fashioning a form and its ambient air. He became insane in 1648 and died at Saragossa eight years later.

Like *The surrender of Breda*, *The surrender of Julich* was painted for the Buen Retiro and it too represents Spínola receiving the keys of a city from a vanquished Dutch general, while the defeated troops march past with their arms and colours in the distance (plate 95). The surrender takes place on a rise above a view of the battle-field, and the city is depicted on a much smaller scale as if on a drop curtain, with no aerial blending of the two spaces. That was Leonardo's, and others', manner of emphasizing the main episode and detailing at the same time other incidents of the narrative. In the foreground scene, the Dutch general, fear showing on his face, kneels as a Spanish officer directs him to surrender the keys to Spínola who, sitting on a restless horse, bends slightly to receive them. The victorious general is the apex of a pyramid which has for sides the diagonal which leads to the kneeling Dutch general and the one leading to the Spanish officer firmly planted on the left. The contrast between the victors and the

---

[1] See José López-Rey, 'An unpublished Zurbarán: The surrender of Seville', *Apollo*, London, July 1965, pp. 23–5.

[2] *Discursos practicables*, p. 115. In the light of Jusepe Leonardo's documented paintings, including *The taking of Breisach* mentioned in n. 2 below, it is groundless to regard him as a 'disciple' of Velázquez, as has been done (Martin S. Soria, 'José Leonardo, Velázquez's best disciple', *The Art Quarterly*, vol. 13, 1950, pp. 267–80).

[3] In *The taking of Breisach* (Prado, no. 859), also painted for the Great Hall of the Buen Retiro, he imitated somewhat awkwardly the horse in Velázquez's equestrian portrait of Olivares at the Prado Museum, and in *The surrender of Jülich* (Prado, no. 858), he plainly imitated one of the horses in Rubens's *Riding school*, of 1608, now at the Berlin Museum (Olle Cederlof, 'Kallorna till "Las Lanzas"', *Konsthistorisk tidskrift*, vol. 26, 1957, pp. 43–62).

conquered is heightened as the two Dutch soldiers by their general's horse recoil at the hurt and shame of the surrender. It is a narrative of victory, with emphasis on incidental fripperies, dramatized for the victor's sake; its composition, rather commonplace in the 1630's, conveys a crudity of feeling not unlike that which pervades many a still or motion picture which has recorded similar twentieth-century events.

THE ROYAL HUNTING LODGE

Hardly had the Buen Retiro Palace been completed when Philip IV started another project which kept Velázquez busy for several years. In January 1636 the King decided to make fully habitable his hunting lodge at El Pardo, near Madrid, known as the Torre de la Parada.[1] As part of the refurbishing programme, he ordered a large number of paintings from Rubens and Velázquez. By the autumn, the two painters were busy with their commissions. Rubens — who was nearing the end of his life — made some forty colour sketches over a period of two or three years; their subjects were mainly taken from the *Metamorphosis*. Few of the final works were by his hand, however, as he turned over the execution of most of them to pupils and assistants who, in some cases, were allowed to sign their names.

Velázquez was occupied for even a longer time with the decoration of the Torre de la Parada, presumably not only painting pictures but also selecting and arranging those by other masters. Unfortunately there is no record of when, if ever, the decoration of the hunting lodge was regarded as completed. Nor is there any contemporary description of it. It is said that there are extant, in a private collection, some seventeenth-century pictures of the interior showing its pictorial ensemble but, as far as I know, those pictures have never been exhibited, reproduced, or studied. On 7 April 1701, one hundred and seventy-three paintings were inventoried there. This number might have been either larger or smaller than the original one, since thirty-five years had elapsed since the death of Philip IV, and all the royal residences had undergone a good many changes under the succeeding King, Charles II.

Together with the mythological subjects painted by Rubens or executed from his sketches, there were pictures of animals and hunting scenes by other Flemish masters, such as Paul de Vos and Frans Snyders. Velázquez's works included the portraits of the King, the Prince, and the Cardinal Infante Don Fernando, all three clad for the chase, and of several Court dwarfs; he also painted around 1640 the pictures of *Mars*, *Aesop* and *Menippus* which joined probably then others of classical philosophers painted by Rubens much earlier, about 1603. It would be interesting to learn which paintings were already in the hunting lodge when Philip IV decided to refurbish it, which were discarded, and which added, and, above all, what the resulting ensemble looked like. From what little we know, it would seem that something of the idea of the grotto had been carried into the interior; probably, though, the accent was not on the frolics of man's playful mind but rather on the antics of his coarser nature. Whether by design or

---

[1] For this and most of the following, including all references to the paintings executed by Rubens and his pupils for the Torre de la Parada, see Pedro Beroqui, *El Museo del Prado*, Madrid, 1933, vol. I, pp. 29–30, 34.

accident, it must certainly have offered a significant contrast with the *Salón* of the Buen Retiro at the other side of Madrid.

THE ROYAL HUNTING PORTRAITS

The three hunting portraits painted by Velázquez are life-size; their heights vary from 1·89 to 1·91 m., but their widths differ markedly, the King's being the widest, 1·25 m., and the Prince's the narrowest, 1·03 m. The latter, however, has been cut down on the right by at least ten or fifteen centimetres, and even more if the original composition included three dogs as three extant workshop replicas do. There is no indication that the portrait of Don Fernando was originally wider than its present 1·09 m. The original sizes of the canvases and the changes they have undergone might eventually prove useful for the dating of the paintings as well as for ascertaining the place given to them when they were first hung in the Torre de la Parada.

The portrait of Baltasar Carlos bears the inscription *Anno aetatis suae VI* (plate 97). Since he was born on 17 October 1629, the portrait must have been painted either late in 1635 or in the following year; the latter seems the more likely since it is documented that Velázquez was at work on paintings for the Torre de la Parada in 1636.

The dating of the portraits of Philip and his brother is a somewhat harder problem. The head of the King — who was originally bareheaded — is quite close to that in the portrait that Velázquez painted soon after his return from Italy, that is, in 1631 or 1632 (plate 98 and frontispiece); it looks, indeed, like a replica with no significant variations in point of execution. *Pentimenti* and major corrections are noticeable to the naked eye in the painting. Something of their sequence can be gathered from the early workshop copy in the Castres Museum (plate 99). Velázquez, after sketching the figure on the canvas, altered its stance considerably, as revealed by the substantial *pentimenti* running from the waist to the feet. At that point in the process of composition, the King was represented holding the cap in his left hand, as he appears in the copy in the Museum of Castres. At a later moment Velázquez painted out the cap — whose shape is now seen overlaying the earlier *pentimento* about the waist — and depicted the King wearing it. Laboratory tests might give an indication of the length of the interval between those two major changes. Yet the execution of the painting suggests a date rather close to the London portrait of Philip in brown and silver and that of Baltasar Carlos with a dwarf, and consequently it could not have been painted much later than 1632 or 1633. As for the copy at the Museum of Castres, it must have been executed by an assistant before Velázquez had entirely finished the original, surely before he altered the composition by representing the King with the cap on rather than bareheaded.

The portrait of Don Fernando is executed in very much the same manner as that of his brother except for the pictorial handling of the face which, as is always the case with Velázquez, is smoother in the King's (plate 96). Don Fernando was not quite twenty-three years old when he left Madrid on 12 April 1632 with the King and his other brother, Don Carlos, on a journey to various Spanish cities, including Barcelona, where Philip left him as Governor;

two years later he was sent from there to Flanders, also as Governor; he died in Brussels in 1641 without ever having returned to Madrid.

It is quite likely, though by no means certain, that Velázquez, in his capacity as Usher of the Chamber, accompanied the King on that journey, in the course of which he could have portrayed Don Fernando in Valencia, Barcelona, or any other city where the royal party stopped. That Philip, even before his decision to refurbish the Torre de la Parada, would have liked to have a portrait of his brother Fernando clad for the chase, would seem natural since hunting was the favourite sport of both and they shared many hours indulging in it.

We learn from Pacheco that it was in the entourage of the Cardinal Infante, the then fourteen-year-old Don Fernando, that Fonseca first succeeded in creating an atmosphere favourable to Velázquez at the Court in 1623. Indeed, the young painter's initial success came when he was commanded to paint the portrait of the Cardinal Infante, though, to his greater advantage, it was then thought more advisable that he should first portray the King. It is in consequence likely that Velázquez made a portrait of Don Fernando before the one in hunting costume — which, as the broad brushwork indicates, and the sitter's appearance confirms, must have been painted after the artist's return from Italy in 1631. Yet, as it happens, this is the only likeness of Don Fernando unquestionably by Velázquez which has come down to us.

In this portrait, Don Fernando hardly looks older than his twenty-three years in 1632. Therefore, if the Master painted it later, he must have worked from a sketch made at about that time. As with the portrait of Philip, there is, however, no stylistic reason to suggest a date later than 1632 or 1633. If we compare the landscape in either picture with that in the portrait of Baltasar Carlos as a hunter, painted late in 1635 or in 1636 (plate 97), we realize that the depth of the latter sets it apart from the others, and links it rather with those in the equestrian portraits painted by Velázquez for the Buen Retiro no later than 1635 (plates 74–76). The conclusion suggests itself that the hunting portraits of Philip and his brother were executed about 1632 or shortly after, perhaps for the Torre de la Parada where the two brothers had spent a good many days together, and that some four years later, when Philip thought of refurbishing the hunting lodge, he decided to add the portrait of his son who had by then reached the age of six. It may have been at that time that Velázquez modified the portrait in which he had represented the King holding the cap in his hand.

In the portrait of Don Fernando, the prevailing tints are grey and ochre, which contrast with some light-green strokes and with the vivid, almost saturated, blue of the mountain in the background. In that of Philip, ochres, used in a wide range of hues, dominate over the greys and greens, filling the whole composition with an amber warmth which enhances the luminous face of the King. The portrait of Baltasar Carlos, now extensively restored, is lighter in hue and evenly luminous, the greys and greens of the landscape being keyed to the blues of the sky.

As in other sets of royal portraits, Velázquez has rendered in a different pictorial manner the face of the King. Only the subtlest of shadings have been used in the modelling of Philip's face, which is lit up by a light coming from a source other than the one which falls on the dog by his side and finer than that on the landscape. Shadows, however, are used to accent the features of

Don Fernando in much the same manner as in the portrait of the Infante Don Carlos painted by Velázquez much earlier, about 1626 or 1627 (plate 50); moreover, the lights on his face have the same source as those which fall on the dog beside him, and show the same vivacity of touch as those which light up the landscape.

THE PORTRAYAL OF ANTIQUITY

A large number of life-size mythological paintings were executed by Rubens and his assistants for the Torre de la Parada; to these were added two, or perhaps three, pictures of ancient philosophers executed more than thirty years earlier by the Flemish master. Velázquez, too, seems to have painted several similar subjects for the same place.

The life-size pictures of *Mars, Aesop* and *Menippus* are generally, though not unanimously, held to have been painted for the Torre de la Parada where they were recorded in 1701 (102, 101 and 100). This is, of course, too late a date to be regarded as evidence of the paintings' original destination. There is, on the other hand, no indication that they had been elsewhere earlier.

The three paintings are tall and narrow. *Mars* is 1·82 m. in height and 0·97 m. in width. As for *Aesop* and *Menippus*, both are a bit smaller: 1·79 × 0·94 m.; their height, though not their width, coincides, either exactly or within one or two centimetres, with seven paintings of subjects from antiquity by Rubens and his pupils known to have been executed for the hunting lodge in the late 1630's, or to have been transferred there from other royal residences. These seven Rubens compositions differ among themselves markedly as to width, lending themselves to a grouping in pairs which, alas, is not very conclusive.

The fact that these two paintings by Velázquez are of the same height and, in one case at least, of the same width, as several Rubens compositions known to have been executed for, or brought to, the Torre de la Parada — where all the said works were in 1701 — makes it reasonable to infer, though not to conclude, that the three works by Velázquez were executed for the hunting lodge.

Aesop and *Menippus* have been variously dated from 1628, that is, before the Master's first Italian journey, to 1660, the year he died. The range of disagreement is narrower for *Mars*, for which the earliest date suggested is 1640–42, and the latest 1653–58. Needless to say, Beruete placed the three works in the painter's last years. The current catalogue of the Prado Museum suggests 1639–40 for *Menippus* and *Aesop*, and some time between 1640 and 1642 for *Mars* — which is plausible, though it would be more accurate, if less specific, to suggest that the three were painted roughly about the same years, with 1640 as the pivotal date.

In pictorial treatment, and inherent meaning, *Aesop, Menippus* and *Mars* show an analogy with the second portrait of the jester *Calabazas*, which there is no reason to suppose was painted after 1639 when he died, and with that of the dwarf *Francisco Lezcano*, of the early 1640's, both of which seem to have been at the Torre de la Parada (plates 106 and 110).

It has been repeatedly suggested that *Mars* shows a resemblance to an antique statue in Villa Ludovisi, Rome, as well as to Michelangelo's *Lorenzo de' Medici* in San Lorenzo, Florence, which Velázquez may have seen in 1629. It is, indeed, conceivable that ideas of one or the other sculpture, or both of them, came to his mind when he was at work on the painting. Be this as it may, Velázquez's composition, in which an unheroic god of war sits on a couch propping himself with his staff, is essentially different from either sculpture (plate 102).

Velázquez's *Mars* is a huge gawky figure, whose flabby torso, framed by broad shoulders and brawny arms and legs, sinks in a shade as his uncouth, dull and quite human features, touched up by light on the chin and nosetip, shadow forth under a glittering helmet. The god's slack pose is emphasized by the luminous rim of the tilted steel-blue helmet and the diagonal of the glistening Moorish shield which tops a heap of pieces of armour in the foreground.

The glittering armour and the rich textures of the blue loin-cloth and red mantle which falls in folds to the floor underscore the weariness of the figure. The highest light in the composition is the god's left hand, somewhat languidly supporting his head, while the other, hidden under the mantle, props his shape against the staff. It is a masterful scaling down of a god to a human shape — and a worthless one at that — achieved by a pictorial play on his very attributes, without detracting from the plastic integrity of the nude.[1] Indeed, Mars is made into a zany of mythological belief by just the touches of light which, hitting on his hand, chin and tip of the nose, underline his bushy moustache and stolid features.

Scholars and other writers on the subject have seldom failed to emphasize the rascally traits of *Mars* and the beggarly appearance of *Aesop* and *Menippus*, the underlying idea, or even conclusion, being that Velázquez's zest for realism carried him away from his subject to be true to the knave or the wretch posing for it. More recently, however, it has been convincingly shown that Aesop's lacklustre eyes, flattened nose, broad mouth, and thin underlip correspond rather closely with an engraving illustrating Giovanni Battista Porta's physiognomical comparison of man's traits with the ox's, and that the objects depicted by Velázquez at the feet of the Greek fabler — a two-handled bucket with a piece of leather across its edge, to his right, and a hide set up to dry on the other side — are implements and materials of the tanner; they refer to Aesop's fable in which the rich neighbour begins by finding the stink coming from the tannery unbearable till he finally becomes inured to it — the moral being the need to reach equanimity by mastering discomfort (plate 101). Likewise, the books and scroll lying on the ground at Menippus' feet in the companion picture point to his contempt for conventional knowledge and vested interests, and the water jug on a piece of board supported by two stones stands for his cynical philosophy of freedom from human wants (plate 100).[2]

Consequently there can be no doubt that Velázquez kept to his intended subject in each picture. But, of course, the subject of a painting is not the same as its significance, which is embodied in the shapes brushed by the painter on the canvas.

In the late 1620's, Velázquez had painted a picture of the laughing *Democritus* (plate 55), a subject which, together with the weeping Heraclitus, had found room in Giovanni Battista

[1] An interesting contrast is afforded by *Vulcan forging rays for Jupiter*, executed after a Rubens sketch by one of his assistants for the Torre de la Parada (Prado, no. 1676). In this picture, almost identical in size with Velázquez's *Mars*, a shield and pieces of armour are also placed at the feet of the god, but their function is to scale his figure up to heroic proportions.

[2] Gerstenberg, *Diego Velázquez*, pp. 221–4.

Marino's *Galeria*.[1] Rubens had painted both subjects in 1603 in Spain (Prado nos. 1680 and 1682), and the two pictures were among those taken to Torre de la Parada where they probably joined Velázquez's *Aesop* and *Menippus*, which are of the same height. Other painters had earlier represented men of antiquity as guiding thinkers of genius. Ribera was doing so about the time that Velázquez was in Naples in 1630. Rembrandt — to cite the one seventeenth-century painter equal to Velázquez in the effortless use of pigment for sheer expressiveness — was still to paint some such pictures, including the one in which he fashioned the classical bust of Homer into a three-quarter-length likeness of the blind poet, whose monumental and richly-hued human shape is pervaded by the rhythm that he is seen beating out with his hands (Mauritshuis, no. 584).[2]

Velázquez's *Aesop* wears unconcernedly a tattered brown robe, while *Menippus*, his legs also in brown rags, is snugly wrapped in a cloak, grey and tattered like his hat. Each of them stands against a neutral background, shadows narrowing the space marked by the floor-line. Everything is subdued and fluidly painted but the wasted faces and gnarled hands, which are accented beyond the descriptive by vivid textures of rough impasto. Each is centred in the midst of the unemphatic symbols of his way of thought, intently looking outside, his bovine or sharp eyes and his ruminating or knowing expression stressing the carnality of his features and, with it, the purely human nature of his knowledge.

Seen within the Master's *oeuvre*, his pictures of *Mars, Aesop* and *Menippus* rank with his portraits of Court fools and jesters, in all of which the sitter's coarse carnality is vividly accented. Within a broader context, that of Velázquez's Spain, *Aesop* and *Menippus* appear as pictorial counterfigures to the *pícaro*, the literary type who lives by his wits and sinks beyond salvation in his purely human, and as such forever faultfinding, knowledge, as age and accidents misshape him into a wretch. As for *Mars*, it has been pointed out more than once that it was not unusual in Velázquez's day to regard mythology as a merry farce, and that Quevedo laughed at the pagan gods and saw in Mars a sort of celestial Don Quixote.[3] Nor was this derisive attitude peculiar to Spain. Catholic writers in other countries, such as Marino, freely indulged in it on occasion.[4]

Hence Velázquez's depiction of mythological or classical subjects — well based as it was on humanistic knowledge — corresponded to a climate of sentiment which in his day led to seeing the world of antiquity as one of purely human nature and thought. Yet, there is no caricatural distortion in his pictures of subjects from antiquity, which are, on the contrary, endowed with the pulse of life. For instance, the caricatural traits, sharply defined in the engraving illustrating Porta's comparison of man's traits with the ox's, are composed into a live human presence in Velázquez's painting of *Aesop*.

Certainly Velázquez's humanistic knowledge is woven into his compositions, but it ought not to be identified as their theme. What he appears always to be intent on is the life he is in —

---

[1] *La Galeria del Cavalier Marino distinta in pitture & sculture*, Venice, 1620, pp. 173–5.
[2] See F. Saxl, 'Rembrandt and Classical Antiquity', *Lectures*, vol. I, pp. 298–310.
[3] Cf. J. O. Picón, *Vida y obras de Don Diego Velázquez*, p. 54; Trapier, *Velázquez*, pp. 262–3.
[4] *La Galeria, passim.*

whose splendour, drollery, coarseness, delicacy, misery, truth and deceit are heightened, but not distorted, by his mind, at ease within the range, embracing both the divine and the human, of his religious belief. Hence his vivid portrayal of the ephemeral human shape and mien — which explains the lasting appeal of his naturalism.

CLOWNING OF THE SENSES

The available documentary evidence shows that, contrary to views held by earlier scholars and occasionally favoured by recent ones, seven of the eight extant portraits of Court fools, dwarfs and other jesters by Velázquez were painted before his second journey to Italy.[1] The sitters for five of them had died before his departure from Madrid in November 1648 or passed away within the next eleven months, long before his return; the latest reference to the jester whose portrait Velázquez left unfinished is also of 1649, and there is no stylistic reason for concluding that any of these six portraits was executed after the sitter's death. The seventh, *Don Diego de Acedo*, is well documented as having been executed in June 1644. As for the remaining one, *Don Juan de Austria*, there is documentary indication, supported by stylistic considerations, that it was painted in 1632 or soon afterwards.

The earliest of these portraits is one of the buffoon *Calabazas* holding in one hand a small bust portrait of a woman, and in the other a pinwheel. This children's toy, known in Spanish by a large variety of names, such as *rehilandera, rehilete, reguilete* or *molinillo de papel*, had long been regarded as an attribute of Folly. As has been pointed out, a woodcut illustration to *Pazzia* in Cesare Ripa's *Iconologia*, published at Padua in 1630, represents a man riding a cane with a children's pinwheel in his hand.[2] For a broader understanding of the subject, I should add that Mateo Alemán in his picaresque novel, *Guzmán de Alfarache*, a seventeenth-century best-seller, first published at Madrid in 1599 and soon translated into every major European language, had personified idle dreaming in the figure of a boy riding a cane and carrying a pinwheel in his hand.[3]

The nervous, somewhat tight modelling of *Calabazas's* face, highlighted on the nose and mouth, particularly at the corners of the lips, recalls the figure of Bacchus in the large composition of 1628–29 (plates 57 and 104), which leads to the belief that this portrait must also have been painted before Velázquez set out on his Italian journey in 1629.[4]

[1] José Moreno Villa found most of the documents bearing on this matter in the archive of the Madrid Royal Palace (*Locos, enanos, negros y niños palaciegos*, Mexico, 1939). For a general discussion of the representation of such court retainers in art, see E. Tietze-Conrat, *Dwarfs and Jesters in Art*, New York, 1957.

[2] Henry S. Francis, 'Velázquez: Portrait of the jester Calabazas', *The Bulletin of the Cleveland Museum of Art*, November, 1965, pp. 117–23.

[3] Samuel Gil y Gaya's edition, Madrid, 1965, II, p. 14. On the words *rehilandera, rehilete*, etc., see J. Corominas, *Diccionario crítico y etimológico de la lengua castellana*, Madrid, 1954, III, under *rehilar*.

[4] Beruete thought that Velázquez had painted it in 1631 (*Velázquez*, Berlin, 1909, pp. 64 and 91); Allende Salazar dated it about 1626–27 (*Velázquez*, vol. VI of *Klassiker der Kunst*, 1925, p. 30), and Mayer also dated it about 1626 (*Velázquez, A Catalogue Raisonné of the Pictures and Drawings*, no. 445). All other qualified Velázquez scholars familiar with the actual portrait have regarded it as an authentic work by Velázquez.

There has been uncertainty as to whether this is the painting described in the first inventory of the Buen Retiro

Palace, compiled in 1701, as Velázquez's portrait of 'Calabacillas with a portrait in one hand and a letter in the other' ('*Calabacillas con un Retrato en la mano y un villete en la otra*'). Most connoisseurs of Velázquez have tended to dismiss the disparity between the letter mentioned in the inventory and the pinwheel seen in the painting, occasionally with the suggestion that *villete* was a careless description of the paper windmill. They were encouraged to do so by a description of the painting published in 1784 by Antonio Ponz, who neither was nor claimed to be a connoisseur (*Viaje de España*, ed. C. M. del Rivero, 1947, p. 552). Ponz, referring to a group of portraits in one of the rooms of the Buen Retiro, wrote that 'that of a buffoon amusing himself with a pinwheel, and some others are in the taste of Velázquez'. In Ponz's days, the paintings at the Buen Retiro were not permanently located there; many had been taken and others were now and then being taken, to and from the Palacio Real at the other end of Madrid (*op. cit.*, p. 551).

In view of the doubtful value of the data then available on the matter, I did not mention the Buen Retiro among the former locations of *Calabazas with a portrait and a pinwheel* in my catalogue of Velázquez's oeuvre, published in 1963. Nor did I find it necessary to mention Miss Trapier's conclusion, shared by other literal-minded students of Velázquez, that the disparity between the 1701 inventory entry and the portrait of *Calabazas* holding a pinwheel instead of a letter led to the conviction that this painting, which she gave no indication of having seen, could not be by Velázquez (*Velázquez*, New York, 1947, p. 115).

I have recently come across several unpublished documents which, together with others which have often been cited, make it possible for me to clarify what appears to have been a long-drawn out comedy of errors revolving around Velázquez's *Calabazas with a portrait and a pinwheel*. All these documents are preserved in the archive of the Madrid Royal Palace.

As one who had unqualifiedly concluded that *Calabazas with a portrait and a pinwheel* was by Velázquez on the stylistic evidence provided by the portrait itself, I have, of course, been pleased to discover documentary evidence that corroborates my conclusion and confirms my conviction that in matters of attribution the painting, or whatever the work of art in question may be, is the thing. Before summarizing my findings, I should like to remind the reader that errors occur and accumulate even today in inventories, those of a royal collection as well as of a shoe factory, compiled by computer as well as by hand.

The Palace of the Buen Retiro was begun in 1630 and finished in the spring of 1635. Paintings from the Palacio Real, at the other end of Madrid, were then taken there. The *Calabazas with a portrait and a pinwheel* must have been among them, for it was not included in the inventory of the Palacio Real drawn up in 1636, after the decoration of the Buen Retiro was completed, nor in that of 1686. In fact, like the portraits of the jesters *Don Juan de Austria* and *Pablo de Valladolid*, now at the Prado (plate 105 and colour plate IV), painted by Velázquez in the early or mid-1630's, it was inventoried for the first time in 1701, when all three were in the same room of the Buen Retiro. There is no earlier documentary reference to any of the three.

The unnumbered entry of the 1701 inventory describing Velázques's likeness of *Calabazas* as representing the sitter with a portrait in one hand and a letter in the other, was repeated almost identically under no. 614 in 1716, when Don Manuel Marentes became the new keeper of the Buen Retiro and a numbered inventory of its contents was compiled (*Calabacillas con Retrato en la mano y un Billete en la otra*).

On 19 July 1789, Mariano Salvador Maella (1739–1819), assisted by two of his fellow Court painters, began a new inventory of the paintings at the Buen Retiro. He adopted a new numeration which ended with no. 572, having abandoned his task when less than half of the paintings had been inventoried. No portrait of *Calabazas* was listed. However, Maella included, under no. 178, a painting which had never before been recorded in the royal collections or anywhere else: a portrait of *Velazquillo, the buffoon*, with no painter's name ('*Retrato de Velazquillo el Bufon*).

Shortly after Maella interrupted his task, the keeper of the Buen Retiro, now Don Pedro Gil de Bernabé, took it upon himself to draw up a thorough inventory, which he completed on 7 September 1789. The numeration adopted by Maella seven weeks earlier was retained, but obviously the entries were checked not only against Maella's incomplete inventory but also against that of either 1701 or 1716, or both. Still more important, the entries, 1387 in total, were checked against the paintings themselves. As a result, the entry 178 which in Maella's inventory read 'Portrait of Velazquillo, the buffoon' with no painter's name, was changed to 'Another [painting] by Velázquez: Portrait of Velazquillo, the buffoon, which the old inventory says is of Calabacillas, holding a portrait and a pinwheel in his hands' ('*178. Otra de Velázquez, Retrato de Velasquillo el Bufon, y el Ynventario antiguo dice ser de Calavacillas con un Retrato en la mano y un reguilete*').

Apparently, an auditory error on the part of the amanuensis to whom the 1701 inventory was dictated resulted in his substituting *villete* for its like-sounding *reguilete*, that is, letter for pinwheel. It is also apparent that, in July 1789, a confusion concerning the names of the portrait's painter and sitter led to using the diminutive name Velasquillo for the latter, and to the omission of Velázquez's name. Some weeks later, the diligent Don Pedro Gil de Bernabé corrected the inaccurate 1701 description of the portrait on the evidence provided by the painting itself, spelled out anew its artist's name, and called attention to the confusion which had arisen concerning the name of the sitter.

In 1794, Maella and the two fellow painters who had assisted him five years earlier undertook the compilation of another inventory of the paintings at the Buen Retiro, which they finished on 25 February of that year. They consistently followed the numeration, and often the phrasing, of the inventory drawn up by Don Pedro Gil de Bernabé. Unfortunately, though, they shortened several entries, including no. 178, which was made to read: 'Another [painting] by Velázquez: Portrait of Velasquillo, the buffoon' ('*178. Otra de Velázquez: Retrato de Velasquillo el bufon*').

There can be no question that the portrait of *Velasquillo, the buffoon*, which I, like all other Velázquez scholars, had listed among the Master's lost works, is no other than *Calabazas with a portrait and a pinwheel*.

Included in Maella's 1794 inventory of the Buen Retiro were paintings which were no longer there. This was a consequence of the situation to which Ponz had referred ten years earlier. Such a state of affairs was obviously a matter of concern for Don Pedro Gil de Bernabé, who on 5 May 1794 recorded by number all the paintings actually at the Palace in a list that was duly certified. He, moreover, made marginal notations in his inventory of 7 September 1789, indicating the paintings which had since been removed from the Buen Retiro, their new destination and the date of their removal. Thus, we know that Velázquez's *Calabazas with a portrait and a pinwheel* was still at the Buen Retiro on 5 May 1794.

According to a certified document, drawn up on 24 May 1803, when Don Pedro Gil de Bernabé was still the keeper of the Buen Retiro Palace, Maella had been entrusted at an unspecified date with the restoration of eighteen paintings from the palace, including no. 178, that is, Velázquez's *Calabazas with a portrait and a pinwheel*. It may have been then that the background and the sitter's right hand were restored, and that his right eye was repainted, perhaps to lessen his strabism, likely to offend Maella's flabby taste. This repaint was removed in 1965, when the painting was cleaned and some minor damages were restored.

In 1808, when Napoleon's troops occupied Madrid, their headquarters were established at the Buen Retiro Palace. General Billiard, the French military governor of the city, sent to the keeper of the palace an order, issued on 4 July 1808 by the Spanish first minister of State, regarding the works of art. In compliance with this order, Don Pedro Gil de Bernabé, accompanied by a French colonel and a Spanish civil servant, verified one by one the paintings housed at the Buen Retiro, using Don Pedro's annotated inventory of 7 September 1789 as a master list. Eight paintings were found to be missing, and duly recorded as such. Further, lists of the inventory numbers of the paintings in each room were drawn up and signed by the French officer occupying it, or by his representative. From one of these lists, we learn that as of 5 July 1808 Velázquez's *Calabazas with a portrait and a pinwheel* was in the former chamber of the King which had been allocated to the chief inspector general of the French armies in Spain. This is the latest known document attesting to the presence of the painting in Madrid. For the inventory of the Buen Retiro compiled on 11 February 1814, after the French armies had been expelled from Spain and the palace had in fact ceased to be a royal residence, listed the paintings that 'existed' there in 1808 with no indication of those which had disappeared in the course of the war. The entry corresponding to the painting we are concerned with repeats in a shorter form that of 7 September 1789: '178. Another [painting] by Velázquez. Portrait of Velasquillo, the buffoon, which the old inventory says is of Calabacillas' ('*178. Otra de Velázquez. Retrato de Velasquillo el Bufon, y el imbentario antiguo dice ser de Calabacillas*').

The painting appeared next in Paris, where it was shown as the property of the Duke of Persigny at the 'Exposition Retrospective' in 1860. Persigny's father, Antoine-Henri-Marie Fialin, had renounced his aristocratic claims and joined the French army as a *sous-officer* early in 1808; he was assigned to one of the units sent to Spain, where he died four years later at the battle of Salamanca. Fialin is only briefly mentioned in the biography of his son written by Honoré Farat (*Persigny: Un ministre de Napoléon III, 1808–1872*, Paris, 1957, p. 7).

The looting of Spanish art collections, royal, ecclesiastic or private by high ranking and petty officers, as well as by ordinary soldiers, of the French army was widespread during the years 1808–14, when Madrid was twice occupied by the French and twice liberated from them. It is reasonable to surmise that Velázquez's *Calabazas with a portrait and a pinwheel* was then taken, or sent, to France by one of the looters. (See José Lopez-Rey, 'Velázquez's *Calabazas with a portrait and a pinwheel*', *Gazette des Beaux-Arts*, October, 1967, pp. 219–26).

As in the face of Bacchus, the smallness of Calabazas's eyes, vacuously looking somewhere outside the composition, is underscored by the light that broadens the sockets; the squint is accented by a highlight, pictorially balanced by another on the teeth. The distortion of the jester's features is also rendered by the shadows that harden the left side of the face and by the lights that dislocate, as it were, the mouth to the same side. His empty smile quickens our eye to the contrast between his smallish head and torso and his gangling limbs completed with big hands and feet. As he stands, his figure is made unquiet not so much by his gesture as by the interplaying diagonals of the toy pinwheel, the folding stool, and the shadows on the floor. There are, however, no caricatural traits. Indeed, the likeness of the misshapen buffoon has the fullness of an individual presence.

Next in point of time are the portraits of the buffoons *Don Juan de Austria* and *Pablo de Valladolid*, both of about the same size, larger than the earlier *Calabazas*. The dating of *Don Juan de Austria* in 1632 or soon afterwards is suggested by a clothier's bill submitted to the King's accounting office that year; it lists several pieces of different fabrics to be made into a costume complete with cape and cap for this jester, whose services at the Court from 1624 till 1654 were only occasional. The materials listed coincide, almost to the last detail, as to stuff, colour and quantity, with the velvet and silk attire, in black and rose which he wears in Velázquez's portrait (plate 105). Court jesters used to mime famous personages, and sometimes they had costumes especially made for such impersonations.

The name Don Juan de Austria, probably given to this jester by Philip III or some other royal person, was that of the hero of the naval battle of Lepanto (1571), Charles V's son, memories of whom were very much alive at the time of Philip IV, when the buffoon may have been encouraged or commanded to impersonate his illustrious namesake. Velázquez has represented him in a martial pose, one hand on the sword and the other on a baton. The Master was doubtless aware that there was then at the Royal Palace a life-size portrait of Philip III by Pedro Antonio Vidal in which the late monarch was represented holding the baton in his right hand and resting the left on the sword, while he stood between a terrestial globe and his helmet and gauntlets neatly arranged on a black pillow on the floor (plate 39).[1] The comparison invited by Velázquez's *Don Juan de Austria* made plainer and more laughable the ridiculous appearance of the dressed-up jester. Though, as we have just seen, Velázquez's portrait illustrates a practice and a sentiment of the time, its full significance lies well beyond that.

The composition recalls the two large pictures painted by the Master at Rome in 1630. As in *Joseph's bloody coat* (plate 58), the lines of the tiled floor emphasize the perspective that leads towards an open wall in the background — a device found only in these two paintings in the whole of Velázquez's *oeuvre*. In point of modelling, on the other hand, the face of Don Juan de Austria recalls that of Vulcan in the six-figure composition painted by Velázquez in 1630, too (plate 59); another analogy between this mythological picture and the portrait of the jester is the markedly diagonal arrangement of the objects on the floor intended to further the sense of spatial depth in each work.

[1] Of Pedro Antonio Vidal, we only know that he was active in 1617, and that this portrait of Philip III, now at the Prado Museum, was ascribed to him in the 1636 inventory of the Madrid Royal Palace.

IV. Velázquez, Pablo de Valladolid. Mid 1630's. *Prado*

Velázquez turned *Don Juan de Austria*, as he would later do with *Mars* (plate 102), into a military simpleton, whose spiritless mien is emphasized by the contrasting splendour of his attire and the mock naval battle seen in the background, just as the shape of his weary figure is stirred by the interplay of the diagonals indicated by the baton in his hand and the armour and weapons at his feet.

No such distinct interplay of diagonals occurs in the portrait of *Pablo de Valladolid*, of the mid-1630's (colour plate IV). In this work, the jester's declamatory gesture and stance enliven the empty space, as his well-rounded figure merges into ambient air, and his countenance is made both piteous and comical, and as such quite human, by vivacities of touch which highlight the tip of the nose, the slack mouth and the eyes, smallish and quiet in their large sockets. Velázquez has brushed in a full and yet substanceless shape of a man, standing in a space void of everything else, depicted just by dint of hue and shade, without even a floorline.

These three portraits of buffoons offer, as a group, a view of the consistency and flow of Velázquez's art with his first Italian journey as a turning point. The nervous, somewhat tight brushwork of *Calabazas* gives way to the rather sketchy strokes of *Don Juan de Austria*. In these two works, however, there is an architectural depiction of space, more fluidly achieved in *Don Juan de Austria*, which is totally expunged in *Pablo de Valladolid*, a seemingly effortless masterpiece which was to remain unequalled even within the Master's *oeuvre* — a painting, incidentally, that in later centuries won him such creative students as Goya and Manet.

It was probably in a like vein that Velázquez conceived the portrait of *Don Cristobal de Castañeda y Pernia* (plate 103). This jester is known to have been at the Court from 1633 till 1649; his claims to military ability had earned him the nickname of 'Barbarroja', made famous in the preceding century by an Algerian pirate; he was also much celebrated for his clownish performances as a bull-fighter, and seems to have been regarded as first among the King's jesters.

The portrait, most likely begun in the late 1630's was left unfinished by Velázquez and has remained so, though another painter worked on it, mainly on the grey mantle draped on the sitter's shoulder. The Master's brushwork is unmistakable in the painting of the head and hands, as well as in the live outline of the whole figure. Barbarroja is clad in a red Turkish costume of sorts, which includes a head-piece not unlike a fool's cap. His energetic gesture is one with his fiery expression, the latter being stressed by a bristling moustache that, like those of *Vulcan* (plate 59), *Mars* (plate 102), and *Don Juan de Austria* (plate 105), gives a farcical touch to his countenance without distorting it into a caricature. The jester's pose of defiance is pictorially accented in a spirit akin to that of comedy by his hold on the empty sheath, even stronger than the one he has on the bare sword. Unfinished as the portrait is, it reveals Velázquez's mastery in quickening a sitter's likeness into a human shape of passions or appetites, made the more piquant by a trace of chaff.

A like work is the portrait of the dwarf *Sebastián de Morra*, which could not have been painted before 1643 when the sitter arrived at Madrid from Flanders to enter the service of Prince Baltasar Carlos; he died in October 1649, when Velázquez was in Italy. The bearded dwarf, in a green dress and gold-braided red overgarment, is sitting on the floor. The depiction of empty space is much the same as in the just discussed unfinished portrait. The dwarf's petulant temper is rendered by the play of thick light upon shadow, which adds to the distortion and carnality of his features, and by his droll pose; his fore-shortened legs, with the upturned soles of the shoes on his little feet, and the low floorline make his torso look large, and the quite symmetric pull of his shortish, forceful arms give to his chest the appearance of a monumental bust, which conflicts with the diminutive and richly braided overgarment which hangs from his shoulders hardly touching the floor where he sits (plate 107).

Not long before Calabazas's death, which occurred in October 1639, Velázquez portrayed him again (plates 104, 106). This time the buffoon was represented sitting on a low bench, flanked by two gourds, each of a different variety, a visual pun upon his name and mindlessness since *calabazas* is Spanish for both simpleton and gourds. The sketchy delineation of space is very similar to that in the portraits of *Barbarroja* and *Morra* (plates 103 and 107); the high floor-line underscores the dwarfish torso of the jester, whose gangling limbs and flowing green robes are piled in a heap that comes to the foreground; his head is a shadowy blob roughened out by thick lights and circled around by the striking brilliancy of a white lacy collar; the smallish eyes are sunk in the sockets, made broad by dense shadows and deep by a thick light which extends from across the nose to the cheekbones skirting the lower side.

Velázquez could not have portrayed *Francisco Lezcano* from life later than 1645, for the sitter, also known as the *Boy of Vallecas*, was absent from the Court from then till 1648, and died the following year while the Master was still in Italy. Nor is there any stylistic reason to suppose that this portrait is markedly earlier or later than the one of *Don Diego de Acedo*, painted by the Master in June 1644. The moronic dwarf, clad in green (plate 110), is picking at the edges of the playing cards that he idly holds in his hands. He sits clumsily against an overhanging cliff which lets in a mountainous view; this setting lends a sort of monumentality to his oafish figure, while his relatively enormous hat which fills most of the foreground cuts him down to his dwarfish size — the conflicting appearances coalescing in an image of human shapelessness and spiritlessness heightened beyond the merely descriptive.

As in his pictures of pagan gods or men of antiquity, Velázquez has used foreshortening, highlights, and impasto to stress the carnality of features and earthliness of bearing of dwarfs and jesters, as well as their comical or stupid traits and gestures, and the disfigurement, and accompanying individualization, brought about by passions, appetites, idiocy, and age, singly or together.

Velázquez's portraits of dwarfs and jesters, unlike Callot's works of analogous subjects, show no elaboration of caricatural traits or pervasive rhythm of farce. His mind's eye was not focused on the mode of life and feeling that made those court retainers fashionable. There is, in fact neither laughter nor melancholy in his likenesses of the men whose role it was to act out their feelings and proclivities, even their infirmities, for the King's pleasure. Velázquez's approach to the clowning of dwarfs and jesters was, indeed, stoic; the pictorial stresses which he masterfully used in portraying them emphasize the sitters' human nature, cloddish, enduring, individual.

THE ARTIST AT WORK

In 1635 Pietro Tacca was commissioned to make a monumental equestrian portrait of Philip IV. Since he was to execute it in Florence, he needed a likeness of the King to work from. The sculptor Juan Martínez Montañés, then sixty-seven years old, was called from Seville to Madrid to make a model of the head of Philip; he sculptured it from life in clay some time between June 1635 and January 1636, which was the length of his stay at the Court. His work was found sufficiently impressive for one of the leading Court poets, Don Gabriel de Bocángel, to write a sonnet on it, which was included in a book of poems published in 1637. In the baroque manner current then, the sonnet played upon the human, that is perishable, connotation of clay to exalt the lasting life and shape achieved by the sculptor in the portrait of the King.[1]

Velázquez portrayed Martínez Montañés at work on that very portrait (colour plate V). The sculptor, clad in black, is gazing into the distance, obviously at his royal sitter, holding the modelling tool pointed at the likeness roughed in clay that he supports from the back. The sculptor's head and hands are interrelated in a rhythm of readiness. Montañés's luminous head is modelled with a rich impasto which yet is brushed to a soft tissue in the cheeks and sockets, from whose fluid shadows the eyes, thinly painted, gaze out. This artistic ambivalence mortises in one shape the lusty head and the serene countenance of the sculptor at work. Likewise Montañés's right hand, posed over the clay, is fully modelled, the sensitiveness of the fingers being heightened by the vivacities of a pigment subtly worked from a rich impasto to just a film. As for the likeness of Philip, his main traits are sketched in directly on the grey priming of the canvas, and the sculptor's hand which props the shape of clay is just roughened out with a few strokes of heavy impasto.

These facts have led to suggestions that the picture is unfinished or that Velázquez completed it many years after Montañés's stay at Madrid, which, it is argued, would explain why he did not paint in more detail the sculptured head of the King, since, with the passing of the years, he would not have remembered it.[2] Like surmises have been made about other works, particularly portraits, by Velázquez; with a few exceptions, they have been based on assumptions as to how Velázquez might, or ought to, have painted rather than on a realization of how he did paint.

Velázquez portrayed Martínez Montañés at work in an arrested and intent attitude, similar to the one in which he would portray himself at the easel some twenty years later in the so-called *Las Meninas* (plate 152). The painter's self-portrait in the latter work has been interpreted as an embodiment of the mannerists' views on the imitation of nature by art, in the light of the

---

[1] *La Lira de les Musas*, Madrid, n.d. [1637], preliminary leaf [10].
[2] Cf. Beruete, *Velázquez*, pp. 73–4; Lafuente, *Velázquez*, London, 1943, p. 26, n. 87, and *Velázquez*, Barcelona, 1944, p. 120; Trapier, *Velázquez*, pp. 224–7.

distinction between *disegno interno* and *disegno esterno* formulated in *Cinquecento* treatises.[1] Yet, art-treatises, as I have indicated above, can throw as much, but no more, light on a painter's work as a book of rhetoric can on a literary creation — that is, rather little. They can, of course, inform us of the critical views, practical rules, or artistic aims current at the time, in narrow or wide circles to which the artist in question may have been exposed; and it may be of interest to ascertain just how far the artist conformed, or departed from, such views, rules and aims. Learning, whether theoretical or practical, plays a role, which is perhaps impossible to isolate, in the complex of an artist's creation. But it would, indeed, be a substanceless or misunderstood work whose full significance would just fit a point made in an art-treatise.

There is a meaningful analogy between Velázquez's early *St. John writing the Apocalypse* and the *Martínez Montañés at work* of his mature years: each is represented at a moment of inner concentration on what he is shaping, whether in words or clay, his toiling hand in readiness for the sentient stroke. There is a difference too: the evangelist looks past the depiction of the vision that he is intent on describing towards an indeterminable point outside the picture, while the sculptor looks out of the picture to a determinable though invisible point, his royal sitter. The ineffable nature of the evangelist's experience is rendered by the mumbling of his lips and the far-off look in his eyes (plate 28). The piercing look in the sculptor's eyes, however, makes the presence of the invisible sitter real within the compass of the composition.

Montañés' left hand is sketchy, though in a different manner from the head of clay that it cushions; roughened out with heavy impasto, also used for the wrist cuff, it contrasts with the filmy lights and broad strokes which sketch the likeness of the King. Thus an ambivalent, but by no means confused, image is created as the shape roughened out by the sculptor is made into a painter's sketch; the monumental head of the King, moreover, blends with the background, letting the three-quarter figure of the sculptor dominate the composition — which might not have been the case if Philip's features had been rendered in a more elaborate manner on so large a scale.

Had Velázquez left this work unfinished, it would be necessary to conclude that he chose to do so at a point when he had strikingly expressed on the canvas the act of artistic creation. It appears, indeed, that Velázquez did not limit himself to superimposing, as it were, his own sketch of the likeness of the King on the representation of the head sculptured by Montañés. Actually he fashioned the portrait of the latter into a vivid image of the artist in the act of creation, in the course of which he bends materials — whether clay or pigments — to his expressive purpose, heightening rather than disguising their earthly textures, thus accenting the superiority of the image achieved over the natural appearance that it portrays.

The needlewoman, datable between the mid-1630's and the early 1640's is a fine example of what a plainly unfinished portrait by Velázquez looks like. The head, well modelled in light and shade, is the only finished part, as was noted at the time of the painter's death, and as any viewer will quickly realize; the arms and hands, sketched in, have their rhythm masterfully indicated, though they fall short of the full modelling of the face, which results in a sort of

[1] Charles de Tolnay, 'Velázquez's "Las Hilanderas" and "Las Meninas"', *Gazette des Beaux-Arts*, vol. 35, January 1949, pp. 21–38.

distortion of space and of the limbs, particularly the left forearm. This painting, in its unfinished state, reveals Velázquez's felicity of apprehension of human gesture and the way he went about building a shape within a broadly brushed contour, plainly noticeable in the left hand and shoulders, blending the figure with its ambient air, as seen in the head, whose contour has been thinned into an airy fluid of light and shade (plate 133).

THE KING AND THE DWARF

In January 1643 Philip IV removed the Count-Duke of Olivares from the office of chief minister and banished him from the Court. It was a decision that the Queen and the camarilla around her had been urging on him for a long time. Philip, in what proved to be one of his passing moods of self-assertion, announced that he would now take the affairs of state in his own hands. Yet, within a few days the new chief minister, Don Luís de Haro, Marquis of Carpio — a nephew and political rival of Olivares — was running the government pretty much in his own way. The Count-Duke, who had at first been allowed to retire to his estate at Loeches, near Madrid, was sent into confinement at Toro, far away from the Court. He died there, a bitter man, two years later.

A couple of weeks before the downfall of Olivares, Velázquez had received the royal appointment of Gentleman of the Bedchamber, without duties but with the corresponding perquisites. Less than five months after the new chief minister came into power, the painter was made Assistant Superintendent of Works, to be in charge of such projects as the King might designate — which meant the refurbishing of the old Alcázar made necessary by the transfer of many of the Court functions to the new Buen Retiro Palace.

Apparently Velázquez never took part in the politics of the Court and always remained close to the King. Given Philip's character, it seems likely that he would have occasionally talked about political events to the man who had been at his side longer than any other. But Velázquez — whose exalted view of the person of the King is unmistakable in his painting — never became embroiled in the strife of the camarillas.

The Marquis of Carpio remained in power till his death, which occurred in 1661, one year later than Velázquez's. During his régime, the painter went on accumulating royal appointments, honours and privileges. The son of the chief minister, the Marquis of Eliche, collected a large number of paintings, including ten which were inventoried at one time or another as by Velázquez, though not all of them were entirely by his hand. Some might have come from Olivares's collection, but others were unquestionably painted after the Count-Duke's banishment.

During the twenty-odd years that Olivares was in power, many noblemen had avoided the Court; after his downfall they came back and grouped themselves round the King, desirous of having his authority reasserted. A military opportunity came their way when Philip decided to join his troops engaged in the rescue of the city of Lérida from the French occupation forces. In the spring of 1644, the King, accompanied by a large retinue which included Velázquez, set out on a slow-moving journey to the distant battlefield. When he joined his troops he was wearing an army dress, as he also was when he formally entered Lérida after the French had been chased from the city. The fact that Philip IV had appeared in military dress before his troops was underscored in contemporary accounts of the campaign for then, as now, it was thought that a monarch could encourage, and even reward, his soldiers just by making an appearance before them. Thanks to the interest that the matter then aroused, we have quite precise descriptions of two of the uniforms worn by the King during that campaign — in one of which Velázquez portrayed him early in June.[1]

It was during a halt at the city of Fraga that Philip decided to have his portrait painted. In the last days of May and the early ones of June, an easel was made for Velázquez, the house where he was staying was repaired, and a new window was opened up so that he could 'work and paint'. At the same time the room, or rather alcove, described as just the 'mantel of a chimney', where the King was to sit for the portrait, was reconditioned: it is not quite clear that the alcove was left without flooring, but it is known that a load of reeds was brought to cover the floor each day — three in all — that Philip sat for the portrait, obviously to keep his feet warm.

The documents referred to reveal a procedure which probably was usual for Velázquez as a portrait painter: to work from the model first, and then to finish the portrait in his workshop without the sitter. At least that was the way he went about in the only other instance for which we have a reliable account — from an eye-witness in this case. Jusepe Martínez, indeed, tells how Velázquez during one of his stays in Saragossa — that is, in 1642, 1644, 1645, or 1646 — made the portrait of a young lady, now lost or unidentified. He painted just the head from life, and then 'in order not to tire' her, he brought the canvas to Martínez's house where he finished the rest of the figure. In this particular instance, the sitter was disappointed, so much indeed that she refused to accept the portrait, mainly on the ground that Velázquez had not depicted the collar of very fine point lace from Flanders that she had worn at the sittings.[2]

As for the portrait for which Philip sat in that shored-up alcove illuminated from three windows, and which Velázquez completed in his makeshift workshop at Fraga, the royal sitter, truly pleased with it, sent it to the Queen at Madrid. Velázquez had represented him wearing the red and silver field dress, rather than the red and gold one which, according to the accounts of the time, he sometimes donned during that campaign.

The portrait shows Philip holding the baton in his right, and a black hat with red feathers in his left hand, his fair-hued face and red and silver costume set off by the surrounding umbery warmth. Gliding touches build the King's features in aerial luminosity, without wrinkles or weighty shadows, and fashion at one time the figure and its ambient air (plate 109). This portrait was greatly admired at the Court. The Catalans requested permission to display it during their celebration of the recapture of Lérida, at the church of Saint Martin, in Madrid, where many people came to see it. Within a few days, copies were being made of it, perhaps including the one now at Dulwich College.

Quite different in pictorial treatment — and significantly so — is the portrait of the dwarf

---

[1] For the documents concerning the portraits of the King and of the dwarf Acedo painted at Fraga, see Aureliano de Beruete, *El Velázquez de Parma*, Madrid, 1911.

[2] Jusepe Martínez, *Discursos practicables del Arte de la Pintura*, p. 132.

Don Diego de Acedo painted by Velázquez at Fraga too in June 1644 (plate 108). An attentive reading of the documents bearing on the matter indicates that the painter worked on both portraits at much the same time, and that their execution probably overlapped. The one of the dwarf, however, was finished within the month of June, as a case was then built to ship it to Madrid, while the one of the King may not have been completed till July, when the necessary case was made to send it to the Queen.

The dwarf Don Diego de Acedo, known at the Court as the 'Cousin', performed some administrative functions, such as courier and assistant in the secretarial office where documents were stamped with the facsimile signature of the King. He often journeyed with the Court; in 1642 while at Daroca, he was wounded in the face by one of the soldiers of the guard who had forgotten to substitute blank bullets for the live ones when firing a salvo in honour of Olivares, with whom the 'Cousin' was riding in a state coach.

The quill and inkwell in the portrait appear to allude to the dwarf's administrative duties and the folio in his hands and those surrounding him are perhaps a reference to his bookish disposition. In composition, these tomes emphasize Acedo's dwarfish shape, which is at the same time given a sort of dubious monumentality as his heavy shoulders and big head, under-lined by the slant of the stiff collar, stand out under the weighty shape of a rakish hat against a mountainous backdrop. Needless to say, there was nothing casual about this composition. Indeed, as radiographs of the painting show, Velázquez had represented Acedo bareheaded and wearing a falling collar before achieving the scaling up and down of the dwarfish figure which makes it into a compelling pictorial reality (plates 108 and 115). This scaling up and down of the figure of the sitter to make his oafish shape the more vivid allies this portrait with that of *Francisco Lezcano*, another dwarf who went with the Court on that journey, in the course of which Velázquez may have painted this portrait of him (plate 110).

Contrary to his technique in the portrait of the King, painted at the same time, Velázquez made use of rich impasto to model Acedo's face, where a thick light flows into the shadows without dissolving them, leaving the eyes sparkless; the dwarf's features appear all the more carnal because of the fluid brushwork used for his black hat and costume.

Neither the portrait of Philip in army dress against an umbery background nor that of his dwarf against a backdrop of mountains recalls in any manner the hastily reconditioned alcove where the King posed or the makeshift studio where Velázquez worked, or, for that matter, any specific circumstances of the sovereign's or the dwarf's sittings. Nor can they be regarded as companion pieces, since they differ substantially as to size and had from the very beginning a different destination — one having been sent to the Queen and the other just to the royal palace. Yet, since both were painted by Velázquez within four or five weeks, and most probably simultaneously, they afford as telling an example as one could find of the expressive manner in which Velázquez brushed pigments on the canvas, to depict the human figure as a cloddish shape or as quasi-divine. Between such polar images — which are as opposite from each other as they are mutually necessary for their reality — the likenesses put on canvas by Velázquez in other portraits find their places.

RUBENS'S AND VELÁZQUEZ'S PORTRAYAL OF PHILIP IV

There is no extant portrait of Philip IV with allegorical figures by Velázquez's hand. Nor is there documentary evidence that he ever painted any such portrait. It is true that when, in 1627, he did a large canvas with the portrait of the previous sovereign, *Philip III and the expulsion of the 'Moriscos' decreed by him*, he represented Spain as a matron in Roman armour carrying in her right hand a shield and arrows, and in her left, some ears of grain. That picture, now lost, was, however, painted in competition with three other court painters at Philip IV's command, and it is more than likely that the allegorical figure of Spain was specifically included in the subject that the four participants in the competition were required to put on canvas.

As for portraits of Philip IV, Velázquez must have been more often than not given a free hand. The portraits which have come down to us show that he consistently made vivid the presence of the quasi-divine person of the King by substituting an effortless gesture of innate power for what evidently was to him the redundancy of allegory. He did so even in the equestrian portrait painted for the Buen Retiro, that *amphiteatro* of the Spanish monarchy, in whose overall decoration, as well as in the painting praised above all others — Maino's — allegory was prominent.

Allegories were, of course, quite in vogue in literature and other arts, and allegorical portraits of Philip IV were still painted in Velázquez's time, even by his assistants, as appears to have been the case with the portrait of the monarch with a lion at his feet (plate 111). The portrait of the King painted at Fraga when he was leading his armies against the French might readily have suggested an allegorical composition to Velázquez if he had been allegory-minded. Yet the idea did not occur to him, though others thought of it.

As is often the case when political realities and sentiment reach an unsurmountable crisis, many of the noblemen who returned to the Court after Olivares had been removed from power were filled with a wishful notion of the need to bring back the glorious days of the past. Some such sentiments must have sparked the wish of one of them — perhaps, the new chief minister, perhaps his son, the Marquis of Eliche — to have a picture which would spell out in an allegorical manner the glory and power of the Spanish monarchy now that Philip had victoriously led his armies against the French. Such a picture was indeed commissioned in the form of a copy after Rubens's allegorical portrait of Philip IV on horseback, painted a score of years earlier and then still at the Royal Palace. The commission apparently went to Velázquez, who let one of his assistants copy Rubens's composition, limiting himself to painting afresh the head of the King which, except that it has the hat on, is quite the same as that in the Fraga portrait (plates 109 and 120).[1]

[1] José López-Rey, 'A Head of Philip IV by Velázquez in a Rubens Allegorical Composition', *Gazette des Beaux-Arts*, vol. 53, January 1959, pp. 35–44. The painting was in the collection of the Marquis of Eliche in 1651.

REALITY OF PAINTING

As indicated before, many of the extant portraits by Velázquez have often been described as unfinished. Underlying such view, and frequently mentioned to support it, are one or more of the following facts: an unevenness of texture resulting from the use of both fluid and rough brushstrokes, as in *A Knight of Santiago*, of the late 1640's (plate 117); the sketchy painting of the sitter's hands found in *A young lady*, datable to about 1632–5, in *Juan Mateos* of about 1632, and in *A young man* of about 1626 (plates 113, 73 and 72); or the seemingly chance strokes left by Velázquez in the background of the portraits as if he had wiped his brush on the canvas — an example of which is the *Bearded man* of the late 1630's, where the flowing contour line adds to the unfinished aspect (plate 112). Such 'chance' strokes, however, are also noticeable in paintings which can hardly be considered unfinished. A case in point is *Lady with a fan* probably painted in 1632–5, though not necessarily at the same time as *A young lady*, notwithstanding the fact that both sitters, who resemble each other as closely as sisters or mother and daughter often do, have a very similar pose (plates 113 and 114).

There are pictures, such as *The needlewoman* (plate 133) and *Don Cristobal de Castañeda* (plate 103), already discussed, on which Velázquez obviously stopped working before achieving his end. There is in these two paintings a lack of the atmospheric unity which makes the figure and its ambient air into a pictorial entity in all the portraits mentioned above and, for that matter, in all of Velázquez's finished works.

Studies are a somewhat different matter since, however sketchy they may be, they are not likely to be impaired by want of further work. There are instances, though, in which it is difficult to decide whether a painting ought to be regarded as unfinished or as just a study. Such is the case with Velázquez's short bust of *A girl* (plate 137). The sitter's head is well modelled in light and shade, while the neckline and sleeves of the grey-green dress are summarily indicated with bold strokes of brown; yet, the light that pervades the figure and permeates the background, painted in a grey-green hue darker than the dress, effects the kind of pictorial whole that studies often are.

Ultimately, the decision as to when a painting, whether sketchily or elaborately painted, is finished lies with the painter himself. Yet, works of art are self-existent, even though they express on canvas their maker's vision, and often only their very cast reveals whether or not they are completed. In any case, if outside terms of reference are to be looked for, they ought to be found within the artist's own *oeuvre*.

Sketchy passages appear often in portraits by Velázquez which seem quite finished otherwise, so often indeed that perhaps one should pause before deciding that the Master did not regard those portraits as completed. Their comparatively large number would be of significance for the understanding of Velázquez's art, even if we were to conclude that he often simply put aside his portraits just as he was about to give them the final touches, leaving for instance, no more than one hand to be finished or a few chance strokes to be painted off. The sketchy passages noticeable in such portraits are, moreover, noticeable also in some of his religious, mythological or historical compositions which have always been regarded as finished since his day. Hence it would seem that he used at times, even often, sketchy passages as one more expressive means.

Velázquez's sketchy passages are not distinctive of any particular period of his art, for he used them now and then throughout most of his life, presumably whenever the reality of the sitter, or whatever subject he was depicting, quickened him to do so; presumably, too, at the urge of the artistic reality that was taking shape on the canvas as his work went on.

Even if we assumed that it was a matter of chance, it would be significant that the portrait of Martínez Montañés at work is the painting which shows the widest range from the 'rough' to the 'finished' within the Master's *oeuvre* (colour plate V). Plainly Velázquez has brought into it the theme, as distinguished from the subject, of the artist's mastery of his medium for his expressive ends. He has not only portrayed Martínez Montañés in the process of shaping the King's likeness out of clay, but he has also achieved a live image of the very act of artistic creation, making vivid both the sculptor's and the painter's mastery of their media.

Baroque artists were intent on accenting the texture of their material — whether pigment, clay, marble or bronze — while making it bend docilely to their expressive ends. This — which is quite evident in Bernini, the sculptor and architect — enhanced the superiority of the work of art over both the stuff it was made of and the natural appearances it might portray; it often resulted in a brilliant display of resourcefulness, sometimes bordering on virtuosity, noticeable in so many works of that time. In a broader sense, such brilliant resourcefulness appears akin to that exhibited by creative writers of the period in their use of neologisms, conceits, puns and other word play, by which they underscored the very structure of words while building unique images with them.

Velázquez's sketchy passages in works which appear finished otherwise — whether a shadowy or light-permeated blob, a roughened-out hand, a flowing contour, an unevenness between liquid paint and heavy impasto, or some strokes which smear the background without any representational function — have in common that they make us aware of both the painter's medium and the way he goes about putting his images on canvas. This is as true in *The surrender of Breda* (plate 87) as in *Philip IV in army dress* (plate 109), or *The Coronation of the Virgin* (plate 124), or *Mars* (plate 102), to add only a few to those mentioned before.

In 1865 Manet wrote from Madrid that Velázquez was *le peintre des peintres*[1] — a view that was shared by nearly all the Impressionists. These painters emphasized, of course, the texture of their pigments, nearly always light-hued, by the simultaneous use of liquid paint and heavy impasto, the counterpoint of the 'finished' and the 'roughened-out' within the same painting, even within the same shape, and not infrequently by leaving areas of the canvas entirely untouched. Their world, in which the mind and the senses sharpened each other, was of course, alien to Velázquez's — firm in the clear-cut polarity of the earthly and the divine. Indeed, quite

---

[1] In a letter to Fantin Latour (see E. Moreau-Nelaton, *Manet raconté par lui meme*, Paris, 1926, vol. I, pp. 71–2). Manet's expression, '*le peintre des peintres*', can be translated as either 'the painter of painters' — meaning the first among them — or the 'painters' painter' — meaning the one to be truly appreciated by painters. Manet may have meant both connotations; yet, if one reads his full sentence in the light of what immediately precedes it, the meaning 'first among painters' seems to be stressed: '*Que je vous regrette ici, et quelle joie ceût été pour vous de voir Vélasquez, qui, a lui tout seul, vaut le voyage. Les peintres de toutes les écoles, qui l'entourent au Musée de Madrid et qui y sont très bien représentés, semblent tous des chiqueurs. C'est le peintre des peintres.*'

V. Velázquez, Martínez Montáñes at work. 1635–6. *Prado*

contrary to that of the Impressionists, Velázquez's world was one in which the mind perceived and depicted the sensorial as dense. Yet the Impressionists could, and did, enjoy and admire Velázquez's art without oversimplifying or otherwise distorting its pictorial integrity.

As often happens with felicitous utterances, Manet's pithy remark soon became a catchword, thus losing its original meaning. Painters and scholars of a naturalistic or positivistic bent adopted it. To them, however, the art of Velázquez showed contradictions; to straighten such contradictions out, they devised a line of progressive development which has ever since been zig-zagging back and forth, often groundlessly and at times even running counter to available evidence, including that provided by the paintings themselves. Curiously, the efforts made to establish a line of progressive development in Velázquez's *oeuvre* has resulted in considering the majority of his paintings as either having been retouched by himself endlessly throughout the years or as never having been finished.

There can be no question that Velázquez, like any other painter, left unfinished a number of works, some of which were so listed in the inventory of his possessions drawn up after his death. It is also known that he had a penchant for retouching his own works, which often show *pentimenti*, but there is no clear indication that such changes were not generally made in what he regarded as the course of execution — which very likely was a long one, given the overlapping of royal commissions for paintings, his other duties at the Court, and what seems to have been his own sense of leisure. It is well documented that he made a good many sketches, nearly all of which are lost. Sketches, of course, are self-existent too, and they do not necessarily depend for understanding on the work to which they ultimately led and whose process of composition they help to grasp. Unlike paintings on which the painter stopped working before fully putting on canvas what he intended to brush in, nothing is missing in a sketch.

The problem now at hand, however, is that of works in which Velázquez mortized sketchy passages in a pictorial whole such as *Martínez Montañés at work* (colour plate V), *A young lady* (plate 113), *A woman as a sibyl* (plate 132), *A Knight of Santiago* (plate 117), or *Juan Mateos* (plate 73), to cite only outstanding portraits of the 1630's and 40's. If we compare any of these portraits with *The needlewoman* (plate 133), or, for that matter, with *Don Cristobal de Castañeda* (plate 103) — we can see the difference between a painting on which the Master stopped working whatever the reason, before achieving a pictorial whole, and those pictorial integers embodying sketchy passages for expressive purposes, be it to accent a trait of the sitter, to reveal the painter's mastery of his medium, or to underscore the superiority of the painted image over the natural appearance that it portrays, or to do all three things at one time.

THE DIAPHANOUS WORLD OF CHRISTIANITY

It was probably in the mid- or late 1630's that Velázquez painted *St. Anthony Abbot and St. Paul the Hermit* for the Hermitage of St. Paul in the grounds of the Buen Retiro, where this and other newly built hermitages, monumental statues, fountains, grottoes, ponds, gardens and groves offered a variety of pleasant views. Very likely some of the landscapes with religious subjects painted by Claude Lorrain for Philip IV in those years, and inventoried at the Buen Retiro Palace in 1701, were also originally intended for the new hermitages.[1]

Velázquez's *St. Anthony Abbot and St. Paul the Hermit* is the only extant large composition with small figures unquestionably by his hand (plate 123). The two saints are dynamically grouped at the centre, in the foreground, against an angular crag surrounded by the diaphanous view of a green valley and distant bluish mountains.

Attempts have been made at tracing this composition to one or various sources: the fresco of the same subject by Pinturicchio and his followers, at the Vatican; or two of Dürer's wood-cuts — one of the same saints and the other of St. Joachim and the angel — for the main scene, and Patinir's *St. Jerome* (Prado, no. 1614) for the landscape. It has also been indicated that the background mountains are not unlike those of the Guadarrama near Madrid.[2]

Doubtless Velázquez knew most, probably even every one, of the works just mentioned; likewise he must have been familiar with the distant shape and hues of the Guadarrama mountains which then, as today, were visible from the Madrid Royal Palace. The Master, consequently, might have had in mind any of those works of art or nature. Yet the only similarities with them shown by his work are those to be expected, and hence of little consequence, because of either the iconography of the subject or the natural forms depicted.

Velázquez included in his composition several episodes of the visit of Abbot Anthony to the first hermit. He did so in an imaginative manner, making the narrative proceed unobtrusively from the background along the live lines of perspective depth which span the landscape. Thus, the various scenes are articulated in a vivid rather than enumerative depiction. In the far distance, Anthony is seen asking the centaur the way to Paul's cave; closer to his destination he meets the horned and goat-footed monster; then the action turns to the right where the holy man knocks at the door of the cave built in the crag; this scene is a sort of backdrop for the main one: the two saints, one making a gesture of prayer and the other one of wonder, are dynamically grouped together as the black raven, a small loaf of bread in its beak, flies down to them. To the left, in a barren area off the foreground, the concluding scene, second in point of scale, takes place: two lions dig the grave for St. Paul as St. Anthony prays over his body.

Everything is thinly painted, with impasto used only for highlights, particularly on the luminous faces and limbs of the saints. A silvery light permeates the whole composition, bringing out the richly hued greens and blues of the landscape. The depiction of the hardships of the Thebaid, called for in the Golden Legend's narrative, is embodied in the rugged crag on top of which rises a palm, the tree on whose fruit St. Paul lived for about twenty years, and in the barren ground where the lions dig the grave for him. Surely the surrounding verdurous landscape is not a departure from the narrative. Rather, it heightens the seclusion of the hermit from the luxuriant expanses of the earth — where temptation lurks; it also provides a vast and

---

[1] These paintings are now at the Prado Museum, most of them in storage. As Marcel Röthlisberger has noted, several points concerning them are in need of further research (*Claude Lorrain*, New Haven, 1961, I, p. 155).

[2] See José Moreno Villa, *Velázquez*, Madrid, 1920, pp. 65–6; Diego Angulo Iñiguez, *Velázquez: Cómo compuso sus principales cuadros*, Madrid, 1947, pp. 63–75; Trapier, *Velázquez*, pp. 241–5.

luminous setting for the miraculous event: the heaven-sent loaf of bread. Both significances are supported and impelled by the diaphanous colouring and the upward rhythm of the composition, stressed by the ivy-covered birch tree which rises from the thicket in the foreground, past the forbidding crag, up to the sky.

The *Coronation of the Virgin*, of about 1644, is a lucid pictorial expression of the immaculate nature of the Mother of Jesus, on which the belief in her coronation was postulated (plates 124 and 135). The Father and the Son, both clad in purple tunics and red mantles, hold a crown of roses and green leaves over the Virgin, whose white kerchief leaves her chestnut hair uncovered, and whose blue mantle contrasts with her red gown. It is a masterful opposition of luminous reds and blues, made the brighter by the juxtaposition of purple — in the tunics of the Father and the Son.

The Virgin lightly holds a hand to her chaste breast bathed in light, like her head. A highlight across her luminous face and along her hairline enhances the unblemished symmetry of her features and blends with the most brilliant ray in the rayed-glory of the Holy Ghost above. Her lids lowered, she looks down with an expression of modesty which, compositionally, accents the sense of distance from the earth as angels lift her to the Heavens.

The face of the Son is partly modelled by lucent shadows, similar to those that express His humanity and humility in the earlier *Supper at Emmaus* (plate 52). As for the Father, the most liquid and dynamic of shadows contribute to the flame-like effulgence into which His face is built, and which is broadened by the radiant strokes across the folds of the blue mantle on his shoulders. As the Father and the Son hold the crown of roses over the ascending Virgin, her well-rounded head becomes the centre of the composition, and her shadowless unblemished features externalize her immaculate nature.

THE LUXURIANT WORLD OF THE FABLE

Beruete pointed out stylistic analogies among *The Coronation of the Virgin*, *The fable of Arachne* and *Venus at her mirror* (plates 124, 127, and 130), which he concluded had been painted by Velázquez 'towards the end of his career' in the late 1650's.[1] This conclusion, accepted by most scholars at least for *The fable of Arachne* and *Venus at her mirror*, has been disproved by the discovery that the latter was inventoried in a Madrid private collection on 1 June 1651, when Velázquez had not yet returned from his second Italian journey. Some writers, clinging to a residuum of the disproved conclusion, have suggested that Velázquez may have painted *Venus at her mirror* in the course of his second Italian journey and dispatched it to Madrid, where it was inventoried before his return. It would be surprising if Palomino, who was remarkably well informed about the paintings executed by the Master during that journey, should have failed to mention so important a composition. In the present state of our knowledge, it rather appears that both *Venus at her mirror* and *The fable of Arachne* belong in a group,

[1] *Velázquez*, pp. 108–12. For a fuller discussion of the matter, see López-Rey, *Velázquez: A Catalogue Raisonné*, nos. 23, 56, 64, and 591.

which also includes *The Coronation of the Virgin* and *A woman as a sibyl*, datable to the mid- or late 1640's, before November 1648, when Velázquez set out from Madrid for Italy (plates 130, 127, 124, and 132).

The Coronation of the Virgin and *Venus at her mirror* resemble each other in a 'certain preponderance of purple tones', as Beruete observed.[1] In the mythological composition, Velázquez has harmonized red and blue, the curtain and Cupid's sash, by means of lavender-pink hues, the ribbon looped over the mirror frame.

Till recently, *Venus at her mirror*, though damaged by old rips, rubbing, spotty repaints and, in 1914, by a suffragette's knife, could be recognized at once as a masterpiece (plate 130). One could readily grasp the masterful contrasts of smooth and rough impasto, essential to Velázquez's intent. One could also discern what was incidental to his way of painting, the *pentimenti*, tentative shapes that he quickly painted over and which, with time, became noticeable to the naked eye, without, however, marring his achievement.

The painting was drastically cleaned and implausibly restored in 1965. The old repaints and the engrained brownish varnish were removed; at the same time, though, some of the tentative contours that Velázquez had purposely painted over were brought to light all too plainly. Such is the case with the figure of Cupid, particularly his right hand and left foot, and with Venus's profile, shoulders, right arm and left foot. As for her torso and the reflection of her face in the mirror, both were rather thoroughly redone. As a result, the painting now appears messily sketched in some areas and overworked in others.

The reddish cheeks of the nude goddess have been stressed both in the profile view of her head and in its frontal reflection in the mirror. This mirror reflection, originally thinly painted and long recorded as 'worn',[2] has been intensified into a sort of close-up. Some loose strokes about the base of the neck have been emphasized to the point that they now cut off the live flow of the contour, disturbing the rhythm of the reclining head. As for the mirror itself, the *pentimenti* in its top and left side have become a little too conspicuous and, as a consequence, the frame appears to be out of shape.

The light blue touches that originally enlivened the blackish sheet on the bed have been substantially increased and extended over most of it. It is perhaps not irrelevant to mention here that a seventeenth-century Spanish actress created a scandal when it became known that she used black taffeta sheets on her bed.[3]

In Velázquez's *Venus at her mirror*, the flowing shape of the goddess, her back turned to the viewer, weighed down a leaden grey drapery with some bluish reflections; her face was softly reflected in the black-framed mirror held by Cupid, and the blue of his sash, the red of the curtain and the lavender ribbons on the mirror frame acted as foils to her pale flesh tones. The Master centred the composition about the mirror, which, tilted away from the face of Venus, underscored the curtained space of the bed. Nothing like this space, exuberant with vivacities of textures and hues, could be found in any other painting of the same subject. Only in epi-

---

[1] *Velázquez*, London, 1906, p. 112.

[2] Neil Maclaren, *National Gallery Catalogues, The Spanish School*, London, 1952, pp. 75–8.

[3] Felipe Picatoste, *Estudios sobre la grandeza y decadencia de España*, III, *El siglo XVII*, Madrid, 1887, p. 121.

thalamia of the time, such as Marino's, could one find a Venus-like image immersed in so sensuous an atmosphere.[1]

The reflection of the face of the chestnut-haired goddess in the tilted mirror corresponded quite closely with that of the Virgin in *The Coronation* (plates 134 and 135); even now, both have the same oval shape and their features are identical point by point. The head of the Virgin, however, is spotlessly luminous and her tresses accent the impeccable balance of her features. Rather differently, Venus's face was, and to a considerable extent still remains, adumbrated in shadow, which, together with the irregular frame provided by the untidy hair, alters the harmony of its oval shape and the symmetry of its features. Obviously, Velázquez worked in both cases, and, for that matter, in *The fable of Arachne* and *A woman as a sibyl* (plates 131 and 132), from the same model, the same sketch, or just the same idea of a beautiful young woman. Yet, he put on canvas two different images, one of divine and the other of earthly beauty.

VELÁZQUEZ'S NATURALISM

In discussing *The fable of Arachne*, commonly known as *The spinners*, one must, unfortunately, begin by saying that this masterpiece is in a precarious state of preservation; in fact, the pigment has been flaking off in some spots for years. It must also be noted that one-sided views of Velázquez's naturalism, held in succession for almost two centuries, have led to regarding this work as just a genre composition (plates 127 and 128).

Within the last two decades, the painting has yielded its true subject to discerning observation, corroborated by documentary evidence to the effect that it was, indeed, originally known as *The fable of Arachne*.[2] It has also been documented, somewhat unnecessarily, that the Master was acquainted with this subject: at the time of his death, his library included two copies of Ovid's *Metamorphoses* — one in Italian, the other in Spanish — where the contest between Pallas and Arachne is related.

The first known mention of Velázquez's *The fable of Arachne* is of 1664, four years after his death. It was then in the collection of Don Pedro de Arce in Madrid, and Pedro de Villafranca, a painter and engraver familiar with Velázquez's paintings, appraised it as a work by the Master at five hundred ducats, considerably higher than any other painting in the collection, which included the names of other outstanding Spanish and Italian masters. Nothing more is known about it till 1772, when it was described as representing a tapestry workshop in the inventory of the Madrid Royal Palace. In 1664, the size of the painting was given as approximately 1·67 m. in height and more than 2·5 m. in width. The canvas inventoried in 1772 was roughly 2·1 m. in height and 2·92 m. in width. These measurements correspond closely

---

[1] See Giambattista Marino, *Epitalami*, Venice, 1646.

[2] Diego Angulo Iñiguez, 'Las Hilanderas', *Archivo Español de Arte*, vol. 21, January–March 1948, pp. 1–19, and María Luisa Caturla, 'El coleccionista madrileño don Pedro de Arce, que poseyó "Las Hilanderas", de Velázquez', *Archivo Español de Arte*, vol. 21, October–December 1948, pp. 292–304.

with those of the painting which was transferred from the Madrid Royal Palace to the Prado Museum in 1819: 2·2 m. in height, and 2·90 m. in width.

It has always been noticeable that *The fable of Arachne* at the Prado has been enlarged by the addition of strips at the top, bottom and both sides of the canvas. The size of the added strips, measured without removing the canvas from its frame, is as follows: top, 48·5 cm.; right side, 18·7 cm.; left side, 19·8 cm.; the one at the bottom varies from 2·6 cm. at its lowest point (right) to 7·85 cm. at its highest (left). It may be, of course, that the original canvas was cut off at one point or another when the additions were made. Even if we make allowances for this possibility, the size of the canvas without the added strips — 1·69 m. in height and 2·5 m. in width — is remarkably close to that of Velázquez's *The fable of Arachne* inventoried in 1664. Moreover, as Beruete observed, the preparation of the added strips is thinner than that of the original canvas, and the whole painting was extensively restored long ago. The available evidence points to the conclusion that *The fable of Arachne* at the Prado is the one which belonged to Don Pedro de Arce, and that it was enlarged by a hand other than Velázquez's sometime between 1664 and 1772. As explained before, most scholars have convincingly held that *The fable of Arachne* and *Venus at her mirror* are executed in much the same manner and that, consequently, both were probably painted in the same period, which, in the present state of our knowledge, means 1644–8.[1]

Coming now to the subject, as told in Ovid's *Metamorphoses*, Arachne, a low-born weaver, had achieved so great a reputation that Lydian women came from distant parts to admire her work. She became so proud of her success that she boasted of having a skill superior to that of Pallas Athena, the goddess of the arts and crafts. On hearing of this, Pallas came, disguised as an old woman, to admonish her not to defy the gods. Arachne, however, repeated her daring words, whereupon Pallas discarded her disguise, showing herself in armour and helmet, and took up the challenge. A contest was arranged and Pallas wove a set of six tapestries depicting the fate of mortals who had dared the power of the gods. Arachne chose as subjects six stories of mortals who had allured and subjected the gods, beginning with Europa and the Bull. Pallas won, and punished Arachne by transforming her into a spider.

So much for Ovid's narrative. As for Velázquez's work, ignoring the additions (plate 128), it represents the dark-hued interior of a weaver's workshop, with skeins, balls and tufts of wool scattered here and there, and a lit-up alcove in the background.[2] To the right of the workshop,

[1] In my catalogue of Velázquez works I mistakenly stated that *The fable of Arachne* had been damaged in the fire that gutted the Madrid Royal Palace on 24–7 December 1734 (*Velázquez*, London, 1963, no. 56). The error originated with Enrique Lafuente Ferrari, who in the 1940's, when he was keeper of the historical and art collections at the Madrid Royal Palace, wrote that this work 'suffered considerably in the fire of 1734' (*Velázquez*, London, 1943, no. CXVII, and *Velázquez*, Barcelona, 1944, p. 170). Lafuente's statement was accepted as factual by other scholars, including me. Before 1963, I had not been able to check the list of 1192 paintings rescued from the fire, drawn up in 1735, against every one of the partial lists compiled in later years, according to the temporary location of the paintings. Thanks to the courtesy of the staff of the Archive of the Royal Palace, I have now been able to do so, and can state that none of the extant lists includes *The fable of Arachne*.

[2] Velázquez made changes, of course, in the process of execution, and so did the unknown painter who enlarged the composition. A few of those changes have always been noticeable to the naked eye; others have recently been revealed by the use of x-rays or infra-red light. For instance, the Master painted out the full face of a woman which he

a girl in a white blouse and greenish-blue skirt is winding yarn as another young woman brings a basket to her side. To the left, a weaver in a white kerchief and brown costume works at a spinning wheel; though she is bundled up like an old woman, the youthfulness of her figure is revealed by the shapely leg. Obviously she is Pallas, engaged in her contest with Arachne, the girl in the white blouse.

Set slightly back from the two rivals, there is a woman carding tufts of wool that she picks up from the floor; her figure, a deep-shadowed blob of white, brown and red, underlines the luminosity of the alcove behind, two steps above the workshop. Another moment of the contest is depicted in the lit-up space of this alcove, whose rear wall is covered with a tapestry of *The rape of Europa*. Three ladies clad in seventeenth-century costumes — one in rose, another in blue, and the third in yellow — stand there. The one in rose looks into the workshop, while the others look at Pallas, in armour and helmet, and Arachne, now wearing a red sash over her dress — white blouse and olive green skirt — which, classical-looking though it is, recalls the one she is seen wearing in the workshop.

A diagonal shaft of light fuses the space of the alcove with the composition woven into the tapestry hanging on the rear wall: Titian's *The Rape of Europa*. To Velázquez, Titian was the greatest of the Italian painters. The Venetian master's *The Rape of Europa*, now at the Gardner Museum, Boston, was at the Madrid Royal Palace in Velázquez's day (plate 126). Rubens copied it there in 1628-9 (Prado, no. 1693), as other painters had done before or were to do later. Mazo, Velázquez's son-in-law, was one of them. Velázquez must certainly have expected so well-known a composition to be readily identified by his contemporaries when he included it in *The fable of Arachne*.

The rediscovery of the subject of this Velázquez work has led to various iconographical interpretations.[1] It seems clear that the girl winding the skein is Arachne, depicted also in the background scene, and that Pallas is represented twice too, disguised as an old woman in the workshop and wearing helmet and armour in the alcove. As for the three ladies in seventeenth-century dresses, it has been suggested that they stand for the Lydian admirers of Arachne. Another interpretation, based on sixteenth-century allegories of Pallas as the goddess of the Arts, holds that the lady in yellow near what roughly looks like a viola da gamba, to the left, personifies Music, while Arachne herself stands for Painting, and the other two ladies for Architecture and Sculpture. The viola da gamba has also been understood to symbolize Music as the antidote to the spider's poison, or Harmony, the latter interpretation being based on Ripa's *Iconologia* — which was also in Velázquez's library.

The interpretation of the background scene as Pallas Athena surrounded by the personifications of the four Fine Arts has led to considering the contrast between the shadowy workshop and the luminous alcove as a pictorial paraphrase of the mannerist belief, expressed in sixteenth-

had originally placed in the space between the sitting Arachne and the girl at her back. This discovery is due to Gonzalo Menéndez Pidal, co-author with Diego Angulo Iñiguez of ' "Las hilanderas" de Velázquez — Radio-grafías y fotografías en infrarrojo', *Archivo Español de Arte*, January–March, 1965, pp. 1–12.

[1] Angulo Iñiguez, art. cit.; Tolnay, 'Velázquez's "Las Hilanderas" ', *Gazette des Beaux-Arts*, vol. 35, January 1949, pp. 21–38; and Gerstenberg, *Diego Velázquez*, pp. 232–9.

century treatises, on the superiority of the Fine Arts over craftsmanship. It has even been argued that the painting contains 'in a nutshell' the art theory that Velázquez did not put in writing, and that the myth of Arachne was 'so to speak, inserted *a posteriori* into the fundamental theme' of the composition.[1]

Were we to search for clues to the meaning of Velázquez's painting in his library, our choice of possible interpretations might be considerably broadened, even more so if we made the assumption that his mind docilely adhered to whatever he read. It is, for instance, possible that the Spanish translation of the *Metamorphoses* that he owned was Sánchez de Viana's, regarded as authoritative at the time. In the commentaries with which Viana accompanied his translation, it was explained that the fable of Arachne signified the bitterness which fills an artist when he sees his work unjustly criticized.[2] Pérez de Moya, in his *Filosofía secreta*, of which Velázquez had a copy in his library, interpreted the fable of Arachne in a like manner.[3] It is within the realm of conjecture that Velázquez, who might have read Viana's text even if he did not own the book and who certainly was acquainted with Pérez de Moya's, had had some disappointing experience which reminded him of their interpretation of the Ovid passage, and that this played some part in his choice of subject for a work which, from all we know, was not painted for the King. Even if it turned out that so flimsy an hypothesis corresponded to fact, the interpretation of the painting would have to be based on the composition itself.

Some of the pictorial facts in *The fable of Arachne* have been a puzzle to scholars. Are the figures of Pallas and Arachne in the alcove woven into the background tapestry or standing before it? The answer has been provided by the observation that Arachne casts a shadow, however slight, on the floor, and that consequently neither her figure nor that of Pallas can be regarded as woven into the tapestry. Even so, as indicated above, Velázquez does not make very explicit the spatial relations among the tapestry, the figures of Pallas and Arachne, and those of the three ladies.[4] Indeed, the shaft of light that comes in obliquely from the left blends the space of the alcove with that of the tapestry and sweeps the view of the floor out of perspective certainty. The contrast of this light-hued scene with the dusky tints of the workshop must have been even more vivid in Velázquez's original composition, before it was altered by another hand intent on making the rendition of space plausible by a rather trivial architectural device — which resulted in the addition of the cross vault and the *oculus*. As for the shaft of light that blends the space of the alcove with that of Titian's composition woven into the tapestry,

[1] Tolnay, art. cit., p. 32.

[2] Pedro Sánchez de Viana, *Anotaciones sobre los quinze libros de las Trāsformaciones de Ouidio. Con la Mithologia de las fabulas y otras cosas*, Valladolid, 1589, fol. 128v. The title page for the translation reads: *Las Transformaciones de Ouidio: Traduzidas del verso Latino, en tercetos, y octauas rimas, Por el Licēciado Viana. En lēgua vulgar Castellana*, Valladolid, 1589. The illustration corresponding to the fable of Arachne depicts the weaver turning from her work, which is being admired by two women, to speak with Pallas, disguised as a sort of hag; a spider's web is partly visible in the upper left, above Arachne's workshop (fol. 92r.).

[3] Juan Pérez de Moya's book was first published in Madrid in 1585; several other editions were printed in the following decades. My reference is to *Filosofía secreta, donde debaxo de historias fabulosas, se contiene mvcha doctrina prouechosa a todos estudios*, Alcalá de Henares, 1611, p. 502.

[4] Cf. Trapier, *Velázquez*, p. 350 and Karl M. Birkmeyer, 'Realism and Realities in the Paintings of Velázquez', *Gazette des Beaux-Arts*, vol. 52, July–August 1958, pp. 63–80.

it obviously comes through the workshop. The window behind the red curtain at the left could be suggested as a naturalistic source for it.

Actually, there are in this, as in most of Velázquez's compositions, several layers of significance. The depiction of the contest between Pallas and Arachne, with the first still in disguise, is certainly a departure from Ovid's text. The ordinary woman into whom Pallas has dissembled herself, and the three workshop helpers have their character traits accented, and their figures modelled in shadows. Not so Arachne, whose face is not visible and whose torso is lit up from somewhere at the left; her opulent figure breaks free from the shadows of the workshop, luminously out-balancing that of Pallas and falling within the rhythm of light marked by the shaft that hits the jambs of the alcove.

It is not possible, at least in the present state of our knowledge, to conclude whether the three ladies in the alcove stand for the Lydian women or, together with Arachne, for the four Arts; nor is it feasible to determine whether the viola da gamba, if it really is a viola da gamba, is meant as a symbol of Music, the attribute of Harmony or the antidote of the spider's poison. It is evident, though, that Arachne is the dominant figure in both the foreground and the background scenes, and that her two representations are integrated into a rhythm of light. The two scenes, dramatically linked by the gesture of the lady looking into the workshop, are, moreover, mortised by live diagonals and contrasts of shadow and light and of tints.

For all the earthliness of the foreground scene, the fingers of both Pallas and Arachne, perspectively set within the frame of the alcove opening, are seen plying the wool sentiently, as sentiently indeed as *St. John* holds the pen and *Martínez Montañés* the modelling tool (plate 28 and colour plate V).

Velázquez, well read as he was in Ovid and his commentators, gave a new turn to the fable of Arachne. He did not present her punishment as other painters and engravers had done in works with most of which he must have been acquainted; rather, he depicted the daring weaver facing Pallas with her, and Titian's work, the demonstrative gesture of her right hand opposed to the threatening one of the goddess. Velázquez made the sky of Titian's composition considerably higher, freed the cupids of their bows and arrows, and stressed by strokes of light and shadow the course of their flight which appears to pass over the figure of Arachne. Light, indeed, blends the space of the tapestry, readily identifiable as a work of art, with that of the alcove, fancied as a live reality, while the dusk tints depicting the workshop frame the whole background scene as a painting within the painting. Velázquez has thus created a work which exalts the flow and might of pictorial naturalism, Arachne's, Titian's, and his own.

TWO MEASURES OF VELÁZQUEZ'S STATURE AT THE COURT

By the end of 1646, one and a half years after Velázquez had portrayed Philip IV in army dress at Fraga, Queen Isabel, who had persuaded the King to lead his armies, was dead and so was the heir to the throne, Baltasar Carlos, in whom many had put their hopes for the Spanish monarchy. Philip's sister, the Infanta María, wife of the Emperor Ferdinand III, had also died in the spring of 1646 at Linz. Velázquez's portraits of all three, as well as of Philip's younger brothers, Fernando and Carlos, both also dead, were in the royal collection.

For some time, Velázquez appears to have painted little for the King. Indeed, from the mid-1640's till 1648, he had time on his hands for executing a number of paintings, including such large compositions as *The fable of Arachne* and *Venus at her mirror*, for private individuals (plates 128 and 130).

Though Philip, after his dismissal of Olivares as chief minister, went on dispensing honours and preferments to Velázquez, the painter encountered for some time ill-will on the part of the bureau from which his salary and fees for paintings were to be drawn. In earlier years he had also had to petition time and again, negotiate, and finally compromise, to arrive at a settlement of back salaries and fees due to him. As contemporary documents show, tardiness in paying the royal servants was then more of a custom than an irregularity.

This time, however, the situation was somewhat different. Even former officials who drew pensions, as well as the recipients of 'alms' — a form of regular royal assistance — were being paid, while Velázquez was advised to wait till money would be available. He felt discriminated against, and said so in the petition which, on 17 May 1647, he addressed to the King, and which led to a clear-cut decision in his favour.

At the time that he wrote that petition his position at the Court had been considerably strengthened. Early in the year, he had been appointed supervisor and accountant for the building of the Octagonal Room in the Alcázar. By taking this important responsibility away from the Superintendent, Don Bartolomé de Legasca, and entrusting it to Velázquez, who was the Assistant Superintendent, the King enhanced the latter's prestige in the royal bureaux, where, as in like precincts then and now, red tape was the only measure of man, any man. Obviously the new chief minister, the Marquis of Carpio, influenced the form — preferments and favourable decisions on litigious matters — which the King's regard for the Master took. Velázquez's prestige must have also been helped by the admiration that the Marquis of Eliche, the son of the chief minister, showed for his art. Indeed, by 1651, Eliche's remarkable collection included four Velázquez paintings, *Venus at her mirror* one of them.

Soon after overcoming the hostility of the bureaucrats, Velázquez found an opportunity to suggest that the King should again send him to Italy. As told by Jusepe Martínez, a friend of the Master, the sovereign, by whose command the Madrid Royal Palace was being refurbished, asked Velázquez to look for painters from among whom the best should be chosen to paint pictures to adorn a new gallery. Velázquez answered that Philip should not be satisfied to have paintings which were within the reach of everyone, and requested leave to go to Venice and Rome where he would secure for the King the best available works by Titian, Paolo Veronese, Bassano, Raphael, and others like them, as well as antique statues, or moulds of them to be cast in Spain, which would be needed to decorate the rooms on the ground floor.[1] Philip agreed, and in November 1648 the administrative machinery was set in motion for Velázquez's second Italian journey; on the 22nd a dispatch was sent to the Spanish Ambassador in Venice instructing him to assist the Court painter in the task of finding suitable paintings for the King.

Changes were then being anticipated at the Court. The marriage of Philip, then forty-three,

[1] Jusepe Martínez, *Diálogos practicables del Arte de la Pintura*, pp. 118–19.

to his thirteen-year-old niece Mariana of Austria, who a few years earlier had been destined to marry the now dead Baltasar Carlos, had been decided on, and the Duke of Nájera was about to leave, at the head of other royal envoys, for Trent where they were to meet the King's bride and escort her to Spain. Philip granted two thousand ducats to Velázquez for his travelling expenses, and ordered that he should journey with the Duke and his suite to Italy, and be given the carriage to which he was entitled by reason of his office, as well as 'a mule to carry several paintings'. It is not known what these paintings were, by whom, or for whom intended. It is doubtful, but not wholly improbable, that they were to be presented to the future Queen, since Velázquez, though travelling with Nájera, was not part of his suite, nor did he go to Trent.

Not long before leaving for Italy, probably sometime in 1648, Velázquez painted the earliest extant portrait of the Infanta María Teresa, then about ten years old (plate 145). The thought occurs that this portrait might have been intended to acquaint the future Queen with the likeness of Philip's only surviving child.

Even if that was not the case, it is more than probable that word of Velázquez's fame reached Mariana before she set foot on Spanish soil. On 21 December 1647, shortly after her betrothal to Philip IV, a masked ball was held at the Royal Palace in Madrid to celebrate her thirteenth birthday. According to a rhymed account of this fête written by the courtier Gabriel de Bocángel, the nine-year-old Infanta María Teresa opened the dance at the head of seventeen ladies and *meninas* or maids of honour; then the ladies and *meninas*, singly, in pairs or in quadrilles, performed other dances before the King, the grandees and the Court dignitaries.

Since Bocángel's poem, published in 1648, was dedicated to Mariana, one may confidently assume that a copy of it was sent to her at Vienna. The name of Velázquez shines in one of the stanzas, where two ladies are depicted as so beautiful, graceful and statuesque that they appear to be 'now miracles by Velázquez, then reliefs by Phidias':

> *Milagros ya de Velázquez,*
> *Y ya relieves de Fidias.*[1]

In the autumn of 1649, soon after her arrival at Madrid, Mariana, the new Queen, sat to Mazo for a portrait. It was doubtless explained to her that the great Velázquez, whose master-pieces, including several portraits of the King, decorated the royal chambers, was absent from the Court.

ITALY AGAIN: THE MASTER'S SUCCESS

Some members of the royal mission started from Madrid on 16 November 1648; the Duke of Nájera left two days later, but still a week before the King's command ordering Velázquez to accompany him. The Master may, nevertheless, have left with either group, for in those years of absolute monarchy, when bureaucracy became full-blown, it was as usual for a royal decree

[1] Gabriel Bocángel y Unzueta, *Piedra cándida con que en real y festiva máscara nvmera los felícissimos años de la Serenissima, y Augustissima Señora Archiduquesa María Ana de Austria, Reina de las Españas, el Rey N. S. Don Felipe IIII*, Madrid, 1648, fol. 10r.

to formalize what was already under way as to order what would never, or only partly and belatedly, be complied with. It is also possible that Velázquez set out from Madrid for Málaga, his port of embarkation, by himself, taking with him his assistant, Juan Pareja, who was to be his travelling companion.

The Duke arrived at Málaga on 7 December. It still took six weeks — then not too long a wait — to make ready the ships, load the cargo, and gather together all who were to sail with the assembled fleet. On 21 January 1649 they set sail and, after a good many stops at ports along the Spanish coast, on 11 March they reached Genoa, where Velázquez parted company with the Duke and started on his way to Venice.

He arrived on 21 April, as the Spanish Ambassador, the Marquis de la Fuente, hastened to report, explaining that the painter was staying at his house, seeing as many paintings as he reasonably could. According to Palomino, Velázquez bought at that time Veronese's *Venus and Adonis* and several works by Tintoretto, including a group of scenes from the Old Testament which formed the decoration of a ceiling, and a sketch for *The Paradise*, all of them now at the Prado Museum (nos. 386, 388, 389, 393–6, 398, and 492).[1] However, it appears that it was rather in 1651, when he was back in Venice, that Velázquez acquired '*el model del Tentoreto*' for *The Paradise*, as Mario Boschini recalled in a poem published in 1660.[2]

Velázquez's stay at Venice in 1649 was very likely short, for three days after his arrival the Spanish Ambassador described him as wishing to set out for Modena where, he had been advised, he could find 'something very much to his purpose'. The reference probably was to Correggio's *Night*, then in the collection of the Duke of Modena, which he was set on buying.

It was another work by Correggio, however, that induced him to go first to Parma where, Palomino states, he went to see a cupola fresco decoration by that artist — very likely the *Assumption of the Virgin* in the Cathedral rather than the not so widely known *Christ in Glory* in the Church of San Giovanni Evangelista, though whichever it was that made him take to the road, once he was there he must have seen both.

Then, provided with letters of introduction from the Spanish Ambassador at Venice, he arrived in Modena. The Duke, Francesco d'Este, had been in Madrid in the autumn of 1638,

---

[1] For this and all the following references to Palomino's account of Velázquez's second Italian journey, see *El Museo Pictórico*, pp. 910–17.

[2] *La carta del navegar pitoresco*, Venice, 1660, pp. 56–8. According to a letter to Philip IV's chief minister, Don Luis Méndez de Haro, written from Venice on 12 July 1653 by the Marquis de la Fuente, Velázquez had left with him at an unspecified date some notes about paintings which were available in Venice, one of them being 'a *Glory* by Tintoretto' which Velázquez had seen at an unnamed dealer's 'en Casa del formento'. The Marquis had now learned that a dealer named Muti, who lived at 'el Rio de San Casan' had a *Glory* by Tintoretto; he had been unable to see it, and wondered whether it could be the one mentioned in Velázquez's notes. The picture to which the Marquis referred as being in Venice in 1653 was between 2·92 and 3·34 m. in height, and about 5 m. in width ('6 *baras de largo y tres y media o cuatro de alto*'). Obviously, it could be neither the one at the Prado (no. 398, height 1·68 m.; width 5·44 m.) nor the one at the Louvre (no. 1496, height 1·43 m.; width 3·62 m.). It may be that Velázquez, after leaving his notes with the Marquis de la Fuente bought in 1651, as Boschini says, *The Paradise*, or *Glory*, by Tintoretto now at the Prado. Surely, nothing said in the Marquis de la Fuente's letter warrants the conclusion that the *Glory* by Tintoretto seen years earlier by Velázquez at Venice was still there in 1653. Since not even the catalogue of the Prado Museum has mentioned it, I should point out that *The Paradise* by Tintoretto now there was inventoried in 1700 at the Madrid Royal Palace, under no. 553, as 'damaged'.

and while there he sat for Velázquez who undertook to paint his portrait, on which he was still at work in March 1639, according to a dispatch from Count Fulvio Testi, the Duke's Minister in Madrid. This dispatch contains what was probably the current estimate of Velázquez as a painter: like other 'famous men', he hardly ever got around to finishing a work, and never told the truth as to when that would be; he was also expensive, but, as a portrait painter, he was not inferior to any of the most renowned among either the 'ancients or the moderns'.

It is not known whether the portrait of Francesco d'Este to which Count Fulvio Testi referred was ever finished. Obviously, it must have been, or been intended to be, larger than the bust portrait now at the Modena Gallery, in which the Duke is seen wearing the Golden Fleece, awarded to him by Philip IV in October 1638. Indeed, this portrait looks like a fragment of a larger composition, though it has been suggested that it may be a study from life (plate 118).

The Duke had another Velázquez work, a miniature, now lost. Soon after his visit to the Spanish Court, Philip IV had sent him a jewel in the shape of an imperial eagle, on the reverse of which there was 'a little portrait of the King done by Velázquez, and so like and so beautiful that it is an astonishing thing' — to let Count Fulvio Testi speak again.

Velázquez left Modena for Bologna and, after a probable stop at Florence, arrived at Rome by the end of May 1649; there he stayed for a short while before proceeding to Naples. He carried a letter from the King for the Spanish Viceroy there, the Count of Oñate, instructing him to give the artist eight thousand *reales* — the balance, roughly one-third, of the two thousand ducats granted to him for travelling expenses.

The precise date of Velázquez's arrival in Naples is unknown, and so is that of his departure. He seems to have been busy, as he later was in Rome, commissioning moulds from antique sculptures to be sent to Madrid, where they were to be cast in plaster or bronze. Some of the latter were used for the decoration of the Octagonal Room at the Royal Palace, the refurbishing of which had, as we know, been entrusted to Velázquez.

Back in Rome by 10 July, he went on selecting antique sculptures, shipped some of the moulds to Spain, and commissioned Giuliano Fanelli and Alessandro Algardi to do the casting of others. Contrary to what Palomino wrote he was not in Rome as Ambassador Extraordinary to the Pope, for no mention of such a mission was made by any of the witnesses who, six or seven years later, endeavoured to recall every honour bestowed on him or high position in which he had served in order to facilitate his admittance into the Order of Santiago. Indeed, Cardinal Alonso de la Cueva (1572?–1655), an old diplomatic hand, whose work at the Sacred College left him time to help the Spanish Ambassador to the Pope, was convinced that Velázquez had no legitimate business in Rome. In letters to his brother, the Marquis of Bedmar, the old Spanish Cardinal, who had held important appointments under both Philip III and Philip IV, referred to the Master as 'a certain Velázquez, Usher of the King's Chamber', who claimed to have been commissioned by the King to look for works of art in Italy, and whose activities were nothing but a 'swindle', a sour remark that reveals some sort of resentment against the Master.

Much as it may have displeased Cardinal de la Cueva, deference was shown to Velázquez at the Papal Court, where Prince Ludovisi, and Cardinals Pamphili and Francesco Barberini[1] as well as others, honoured him with their courtesies. Pietro da Cortona was one of the artists whom he visited. Philip IV wanted him to come to Spain to undertake some fresco decorations, and there is documentary evidence that at one time, early in 1650, the monarch understood that Cortona would be sailing with Velázquez on the latter's return to Spain — which, as it turned out, was not the case. Palomino also mentioned Bernini, Poussin and Mattia Preti, among the artists that the Spanish Master had contact with in Rome. He must also have come to know Salvatore Rosa, if the discussion between the two reported by Boschini, to which I shall presently refer, reflects an actual thrashing out of their divergent views on painting.

There are points concerning Velázquez's travels in Italy on which Palomino is not reliable. It has, for instance, been shown that when he enumerated the works of art that Velázquez wanted to see in Bologna, he just followed Vincencio Carducho's description, which was already outdated in 1633 when it was published. This accounts for such errors as the anomaly of depicting Velázquez as desirous of seeing the statue of Julius II which had gone into the making of a cannon in 1511.[2] It is plain that, in this case, Palomino was filling in his narrative with stock stories, as he now and then does throughout his book when describing cities or, to cite another instance, when praising the true-to-life likeness of a good portrait, which is almost invariably said to have been mistaken for the person of the sitter in flesh and blood. Yet Palomino's account of the works that Velázquez painted in Rome has a ring of authenticity, and many of its essential points have been substantiated by documentary evidence. He himself acknowledged that he had had at hand 'some notes on Velázquez's life' gathered by the Master's pupil, Juan de Alfaro.

Alfaro was born in 1643 at Cordoba, where he was apprenticed for a very short time, seemingly a matter of days, to Antonio del Castillo, and then sent by his parents to Madrid, where he entered Velázquez's workshop. After attaining a measure of distinction, he returned to his native city when he was not yet twenty.[3] He must have been at least ten years old when he was apprenticed to Castillo, and consequently he could not have entered Velázquez's workshop before 1653. The information that he gathered about the Master, and which he later passed on to Palomino (1655–1726), is particularly detailed when it comes to works, portraits all of them, executed during the journey from which Velázquez had returned in 1651.

Of those portraits, Alfaro, as well as Palomino, could have seen only the one of Pareja and

---

[1] Palomino mentions Antonio instead of Francesco Barberini. However, according to Francis Haskell, Antonio Barberini 'did not return from France until 1653, long after the departure of Velázquez, and Palomino must be confusing Antonio with Francesco' (*Patrons and Painters*, London, 1963, p. 60, n. 5). In the same footnote, Haskell misquotes Palomino as saying that 'when in Rome Velázquez painted a portrait of Cardinal Antonio Barberini'. Palomino simply says that the Cardinal was among those who honoured the painter with their courtesies, and makes no allusion to any portrait in that context (*Museo pictórico*, p. 912).

[2] Trapier, *Velázquez*, p. 298.

[3] Palomino, *El Museo pictórico*, pp. 999–1002. Juan de Alfaro was born on 16 March 1643 at Cordoba, and died on 7 December 1680 at Madrid. I owe this information to Don José Valverde Madrid, who has discovered several documents bearing on Alfaro, some of which he has summarized in an article published in the newspaper *Informaciones*, Cordoba, 4 November 1965.

the replica of that of Innocent X which Velázquez brought with him to Spain. The rest remained in Italy, and there is no indication that any of them has ever been in Spain. Palomino's statement that Velázquez painted all those portraits 'with long-handled brushes, and in Titian's vigorous manner' sounds like an echo of talk in Velázquez's workshop that Alfaro had likely heard from Pareja, if not from the Master himself; it has, indeed, the ring of a painter's emphatic account of a pictorial feat in which craftsmanship and artistic achievement elucidate each other.

In Palomino's statement, Titian is made the touchstone for Velázquez's art. According to Martínez, Titian's was the first name on Velázquez's lips when he suggested to the King that he be sent to Italy to buy paintings. Neither Martínez nor Palomino was, of course, quoting Velázquez *verbatim*. Yet, since Martínez and Alfaro — Palomino's acknowledged source — were pupils and enthusiasts of Velázquez, their admiration for the Venetian master would have been at least coloured by that expressed by Velázquez himself — who, in *The fable of Arachne*, had, in a sense, made of Titian the very embodiment of Painting.

Certainly, during his stay at Rome — from early in July 1649 till the end of November of the following year, at the most — he gave the full measure of his art, painting many portraits, particularly that of his Holiness Innocent X. Other members of the Pope's household, from his domineering sister-in-law, Olimpia Maldachini, to his barber (plate 141), also sat for him, as well as a woman painter by the name of Flaminia Triunfi, of whom the only thing known today is that the Spanish Master put her likeness on canvas. Neither this portrait nor that of Olimpia Maldachini has come down to us.

It is not known through whom it was arranged that the Pontiff should sit to Velázquez. For the painter of Philip IV, it must have been a challenge to portray Innocent X who, in appearance, was rather unsightly and, in taste, truly discerning, as shown by his patronage of Bernini. It is, however, known that, when it was decided that he should portray the Pontiff, Velázquez, who had been for some time out of practice, felt the need to prepare himself by painting 'a head from life', and asked his assistant to sit for it (plate 140).

Andrie Smidt, a Flemish painter then in Rome, who went to live in Madrid after Velázquez's death, recalled that the portrait of Pareja was exhibited at the Pantheon on St. Joseph's day, 19 March 1650, where it was unreservedly admired by all painters, whatever their nationality; he also thought that it was on account of this that Velázquez was made '*Académico romano*' in that year.[1] Actually, Velázquez's admission into the Academy of St. Luke was recorded in January 1650, and he was admitted into the 'Congregazione dei Virtuosi al Pantheon', a religious brotherhood of painters, just a few weeks later, on 13 February. For all we know, the portrait of Pareja may have been painted at any time between early July 1649, when Velázquez returned to Rome, and 19 March the following year, when it was exhibited by the 'Virtuosi al Pantheon' on the day of their patron saint. Consequently, it may well have determined the admission of Velázquez to either, or both, associations of painters before it was publicly shown.

As for the portrait of the Pope, it made an even greater impact on the Roman painters of those and later days. Many copies, some with variations, most of only the bust, were made

[1] Palomino, *El Museo Pictórico*, p. 913.

after it. Pietro Martire Neri (1591–1661), who apparently was then in Velázquez's circle at Rome, copied it at least twice (plate 142); he also executed a portrait of *Cristoforo Segni*, major-domo to the Pope, presumably after a sketch by the Master which has not been preserved (plate 167).[1]

Velázquez himself must have been pleased with his portrait of the Pope for he took a copy to Spain with him (plate 143). His Holiness expressed his pleasure by sending him as a present a gold medal with his own portrait in middle relief. These two facts, reported by Palomino, have been corroborated by the inventory of the Master's possessions drawn up at the time of his death; listed there were 'a portrait of the Pope Innocent X', and not one, but two gold medals with the likeness of that Pontiff — one with a Roman obelisk, which must have been Bernini's at Piazza Navona, and the other with a cross and two angles on the reverse. Moreover, Innocent X encouraged Velázquez's desire to be admitted into one of the three Spanish military orders.

While he was painting portrait after portrait, and doubtless enjoying it, for he was free not to undertake them, Philip IV was putting pressure on him to return to the Court. The King urged his Ambassador in Rome to make sure that Velázquez proceeded expeditiously with the task of acquiring works of art, warning against the painter's dilatory disposition, which might lead him to stay in Rome longer than necessary; he should be back in Madrid no later than May or early in June, wrote the sovereign on 17 February 1650. To secure this, Philip instructed the Count of Oñate, his Viceroy in Naples, to provide Velázquez with the money necessary for his passage. Yet, according to a later dispatch, sent from Madrid on 21 June 1650, the Master was expected to go to Venice again.

He was back in Modena on 12 December 1650, evidently to keep the promise he had made to Francesco d'Este to visit him again. As it happened, the Duke was absent and his secretary, Gemignano Poggi, a timorous character, created a seriocomic situation: much as he wanted to oblige the renowned visitor, he was reluctant to let him into the ducal gallery for fear that he might carry off some of the paintings. So, he lodged him in the Commenda, and took him on a tour of the nearby Palazzo Sassuolo, decorated with frescoes which could not easily be removed. While looking at those frescoes, Velázquez mentioned to Poggi that Agostino Mitelli and Michele Colonna, two of the artists who had worked on them, were to sail with him from Genoa within a few days, though it was in fact not until 1658 that the two fresco painters went to Spain.

Boschini, in the poem already mentioned, provides the only information we have concerning Velázquez's whereabouts from mid-December 1650, when he was at Modena, till the following June when he landed at Barcelona. According to Boschini, Velázquez was in Venice in 1651, probably shortly after his stay at Modena, and was acclaimed as the painter of the portrait of *Innocent X*, painted in Rome 'with the true Venetian stroke', a replica of which, presumably the one that later he took to Madrid, was shown and admired at Venice. During the time that he spent there looking for old masters' works for his King, Velázquez was full of praise for the great Venetian painters, Titian and Tintoretto above all. To him, the latter's *Paradise* at the Sala del Gran Consiglio was in itself enough to make a painter immortal.

[1] See López-Rey, *Velázquez: A Catalogue Raisonné*, nos. 444, 445, and 474.

Paintings by old masters were hard to find, and Velázquez 'only bought five': two by Titian, another two by Veronese, and the 'model' for Tintoretto's *Paradise*. Then he returned to Rome to take care of matters pertaining also to the service of the King. As Boschini has it, it was there, after his return from Venice, that Velázquez, in answer to a challenging question from Salvatore Rosa, said, with a ceremonious bow, that, to tell the truth freely and candidly, Raphael did not please him at all, and that when it came to good and beautiful painting, Venice was first and Titian her standard bearer — or, as Boschini put it in his rhymed account of Velázquez's reply:

> *. . . Rafael (a dirue el vero;*
> *Piasendome esser libero, e sinciero)*
> *Stago per dir, che nol me piase niente.*
>
> *.   .   .   .   .*
>
> *.   .   .   .   .*
>
> *A Venetia se troua el bon, e'l belo:*
> *Mi dago el primo liogo a quel penelo:*
> *Tician xè quel, che porta la bandiera.*

Of Velázquez's return journey, we only know, from Palomino, that he arrived by ship at Barcelona in June 1651, and hastened to Madrid. He brought with him 'many paintings by the best masters', as well as the portrait of *Innocent X* with which Philip IV was particularly pleased, as Giulio Rospigliosi, the Nuncio at Madrid, reported early in July. He also brought with him the hope of being made a knight of one of the military orders, an ambition that the Nuncio, on the Pontiff's instructions, undertook to support at the Spanish Court.

THE ROMAN PORTRAITS

According to Palomino, Velázquez, while at Rome, was quite busy selecting and commissioning moulds and casts from antique sculptures and acquiring original pieces for Philip IV; 'without neglecting' this business, however, he completed ten portraits and left several others just sketched in 'though not lacking in likeness to their sitters'. Palomino, whose detailed account includes the names of the sitters for each of the ten completed portraits, does not mention any other work painted by Velázquez during his second Italian journey, at Rome or elsewhere.

Velázquez could not have spent more than seventeen or eighteen months at Rome during the various times that he was there from May 1649 till the spring of 1651. Ten portraits finished, even if most of them were probably half-length, and several others sketched in, even if little more than the sitter's head had been roughed out in each of them, in eighteen months or less, at times when he was busy with other pressing matters, is no small accomplishment for a painter reputed to have had slow working habits. The thought occurs, indeed, that perhaps the Master allowed his reputation for slowness to grow in order to protect himself from unwelcome commissions.

Of the ten completed portraits, five, and a replica of one of them, *Innocent X*, are extant. The only exact date we have bearing on any of them is that of 19 March 1650, when the portrait of Pareja was exhibited at the Pantheon. Since the Master portrayed his assistant as an 'exercise' — to use Palomino's word — to prepare himself for the portrait of the Pope, it is safe to assume that Pareja's portrait was the first he painted. As indicated above, it could have been executed any time between July 1649 and the date just mentioned.

Velázquez showed Pareja turned three-quarters to the right, his head, raised and boldly highlighted, set off by the whiteness of the broad — and broadly painted — scalloped collar (plate 140); the copperish flesh tones of the face are framed by bushy black hair, beard and moustache, and accented by the strong reddish stroke which models the lobe of the ear. The vivid head stands out against a subtle harmony of greens: the greenish-grey background, lightly brushed in; the green doublet, fluidly painted, with highlights bringing vivacities of green out of the darker sleeves. A blackish shoulder belt runs across the chest in a rhythm opposite to that of the lifted, black-haired head, heightening the roundness of the figure and the live quiet of the composition, as does the roughed-in hand which holds the folds of the green cape hanging from his left shoulder.

Sketchy strokes around the figure carry the fluidity of the contour deep into space. Hence — as, for instance, in *Philip IV in army dress* (plate 109) — atmospheric space and the nature of its rendition are simultaneously enhanced as Pareja's copperish flesh tones and the blackness of his hair stand out against a harmony of greens.

His hand thus practised, Velázquez undertook the portrait of *Innocent X* (plate 144). He achieved an astounding masterpiece; he, indeed, brushed on the canvas both a striking human likeness and an absolute harmony of reds, yellows and whites. *Innocent X*, wearing a white alb and red biretta and mozzetta, broadly highlighted into scarlet, sits in an armchair which the yellow of its golden galloons and finials sets off from the red that curtains the whole background. His robust carriage is accented by the searching look in his blue-grey eyes and the bold highlights on the purplish face. There is a most tenuous shade of green in the varying greys of his hair, moustache and beard, as well as on the yellow of the armchair's galloon to his left. The collar, painted in a slightly greyish white with the edges and wrinkles highlighted in sheer white, lets through a pale glow from the red underneath, while yellowish and bluish-grey tints enliven the white of the alb and of the paper in the Pope's hand. The hands are modelled with yellow lights and purplish touches — the latter being somewhat more vivid in the right hand, where the stone in the pastoral ring gives off a blackish gleam.

The sense of depth is mainly achieved by a variety of red hues which flow into each other: the lit-up folds of the red backdrop; the red chair; the deeper red of the shadow of the Pope's head on the back of the chair; the flashing scarlet stroke in the red mozzetta that outlines the sitter's right shoulder. The outlines are quite fluid everywhere, and the pigments are laid on thinly, particularly in the face, but for the heavy impasto used to brush in the highlights.

Though the sitter's features have been made vivid, his ugliness has not been stressed. It is, indeed, a marvellous likeness in reds, yellows and whites, in which papal splendour appears, as it were, knit into Innocent X's character traits and vigorous carriage. Certainly, Velázquez embodied in it the sense of earthly power, as he had done in his portraits of Olivares and as he never did when portraying the person of his King.

For subtlety in the depiction of human clay, the portrait supposed to be of *Monsignore Michelangelo*, barber to the Pope, is one of Velázquez's outstanding works (plate 141). As in the portrait of *Pareja*, the background is of a greenish grey lightly brushed in, and the head is also thinly painted, with impasto used for the highlights on the face, the black hair and the edges of the transparent white collar on the black costume. The outlines are broad, and that of the right shoulder is made the more fluid by a stroke of white which, vivid and thick about the neck, thins to a tenuous glimmer as it slopes down. Strong highlights on the forehead, nose, upper lip and neck accent the glints and flecks of impasto which give vivacity to his features. It is not surprising that, before the identification of the rascally-looking sitter was suggested, he was assumed to be a buffoon, even though he is not clowning, or dwarfish, or otherwise misshapen. Indeed, whatever the nature and ways of the barber to the Pope may have been, Velázquez achieved in this portrait, presumed to be of him, the very image of the earthly — and he did so by just the use of paint and brush.

Camillo Astalli was created a Cardinal on 19 September 1650. Consequently, Velázquez must have portrayed him wearing the red mozzetta and biretta either within the next ten or twelve weeks, before the painter started on his way to Modena, or in the early part of 1651, when he returned from Venice to Rome.

Like the portraits of *Pareja* and of the so-called *Monsignore Michelangelo*, that of *Cardinal Astalli* has a greenish-grey background and is thinly painted but for the impasto that highlights the sitter's roseate flesh tints, which harmonizes with the light red of the mozzetta and the biretta smartly worn at an angle (plate 138). Broad strokes of a green pigment, darker than the background, outline the biretta at the top and right side; they are probably *pentimenti* since they are brushed over the red of the once larger cap. These strokes, the ones that broaden the sitter's left shoulder, and the sketchy white collar which lets through the red of the mozzetta contribute to the rendition of atmospheric depth and to the accentuation of the pictorial reality of the portrait, which, in execution, is much the same as the other portraits painted by Velázquez in Rome, and not unlike some of his earlier works.

The highlights on Astalli's rosy face and black hair bring animation to his features. Yet somewhat differently from the portrait of *Monsignore Michelangelo*, a light, which leaves the side of the face and the underchin in shadow, smooths the flecks of pigment used for the flesh tones into as even a surface as that of the creaseless mozzetta. Long before the sitter was properly identified, Beruete spoke of him as having a 'good carriage and a touch of levity'.[1] What we know today of Cardinal Astalli would tend to substantiate that view — which is to the credit of both the painter and the critic.

We are acquainted through written sources with the character of Innocent X, know something about Cardinal Astalli's, and nothing about either Pareja's or Monsignore Michelangelo's. Yet, neither our understanding nor our enjoyment of any of these portraits hinges on any knowledge we may have, or lack, about its sitter. The character traits of each of them are

[1] *Velázquez*, p. 70.

expressive in themselves. Whether identifiable or not, their likenesses have been made vivid in a compelling pictorial world — the world of Velázquez's naturalism.

THE RETURN TO THE COURT: CHAMBERLAIN AND PAINTER

Philip's probable wish to have a portrait of his new Queen, Mariana, by Velázquez, plus the need he felt to refurbish the old Alcázar, may have been responsible for his urging the quick return of the Master to the Court. Yet Velázquez managed to delay for a full year, and it was probably not till some time after his arrival in Madrid in June 1651 that he could portray the Queen, who was then about to give birth to her first child.

The royal baby, the Infanta Margarita, was born on 12 July, and Mariana was ill for several months afterwards. Velázquez consequently could hardly have portrayed her before 1652. From then on, he and his assistants painted a large number of portraits of the Queen, the marriageable Infanta María Teresa, and the little Infanta Margarita — quite a few of which, as well as others of the King, were sent to foreign Courts.

Velázquez was all the busier after being granted the office of Chamberlain of the Royal Palace. There had been six applicants upon whose qualifications a six-member board passed. Though none of the board members recommended Velázquez in the first place, it was he whom Philip appointed to the coveted position on 16 February 1652.

He was sworn in three weeks later on 8 March. His new office brought him a handsome salary and the right to a large apartment in the Treasure House, which was connected by a passageway with the Royal Palace where he had had his workshop for years. As to his new duties, they included looking after the decoration and furnishings of the royal residences, which had to be readied in succession as the Court moved from Madrid to Aranjuez, and then to the Escorial, and from there to the Pardo, and back to Madrid, throughout the year, as well as making arrangements for the King and his suite whenever he journeyed. All this entailed, of course, frequent and extended absenses from Madrid. He had likewise to supervise the arrangements and decoration required for state affairs or for some less solemn festivities. However, he had assistants who took care of the routine chores, leaving him time free to paint.

For a long time he was busy with the refurbishing of several chambers in the Madrid Royal Palace, for which he had acquired in Italy moulds from antique sculptures, on whose casting he had also to keep an eye. He painted, moreover, four large mythological compositions for one of the new chambers, the Hall of Mirrors. It was a time when, though the Spanish monarchy and treasury were steadily sinking, a tasteful effort was being made to give new splendour to the forlorn Court, where the new young Queen made it possible to hope again for a male heir to the throne, and the marriageable age of the young Infanta allowed thought of some venturous alliance.

In neither of the two palace interiors which he painted in those years, *The Royal Family* and *Prince Felipe Próspero* (plate 152 and colour plate VI), did Velázquez depict the kind of splendid décor which, as Chamberlain of the Palace, he was bringing to the royal chambers. Indeed, both interiors are rather plain and shadowy but for the luminous area where the royal sitter stands. Well read in architecture though he was, Velázquez never depended on architectural motifs for grandeur of pictorial composition. Nor did he ever emphasize wall décor or other room ornaments in his portraits. The only work which might be regarded as something of an exception in this regard is the portrait of the Infanta Margarita painted in 1659 (plate 159). In this painting — which cannot really be considered an 'interior' since there is no depiction of architectural space strictly speaking — there is, in the background, a huge clock on the face of which one could originally see, according to an eighteenth-century account, the chariot of the Sun circling round the numerals of the hours.

Even in earlier years, however, Velázquez's assistants had occasionally let ornament play an important compositional function and brought a depiction of architectural décor into royal portraits entrusted to them at the workshop. Such, for instance, is the case with the portraits of Philip IV, Prince Baltasar Carlos, or Queen Isabel, executed at various dates from the 1630's to the 1650's (plate 166). A sharper departure from the Master's sense of composition is to be found in Mazo's portrait of *Queen Mariana*, painted in 1666, long after Velázquez's death (plate 171). Not much later, in the late 1660's and again in the early 1670's, Carreño de Miranda would portray Queen Mariana, as well as Charles II — her and Philip IV's sickly son and last monarch of his dynasty — in that famous Hall of Mirrors, in works where the vivid depiction of the ornaments and mirror reflections are one with the portrayal of the royal sitter (Prado, nos. 642 and 644, and Staatliche Museen, Berlin, no. 407). By comparison with Velázquez, Carreño appears to have shifted the emphasis from the portrayal of the person of the King to that of the power and grandeur of the absolute monarch — which was current in the European painting of the seventeenth century.

The old Royal Palace, or Alcázar, at Madrid, was gutted by fire in the following century, and over five hundred paintings, including quite a few by Velázquez, were lost with it. Only one of the four he had painted for the Hall of Mirrors was saved. Luckily, however, most of his royal portraits of the 1650's, including his most extraordinary work, *The Royal Family*, could be rescued or were safe elsewhere.

VELÁZQUEZ'S WORKSHOP

So little is known of the make-up of Velázquez's workshop either at Seville or at Madrid that one must presume that the names of most of his pupils and assistants are buried in the dust of archives, perhaps not undeservedly. As for those names which have come down to us, except for a few, there is little of substance to add to them.

It is recorded that in 1620 Velázquez signed up Diego de Melgar, then thirteen or fourteen years old, as an apprentice for a period of six years. The Master left Seville for Madrid three years later, and there is no indication as to whether or not he took Melgar with him.

No old copy of any of the religious paintings executed by Velázquez in Seville is extant or has even been mentioned. As for the portraits that he painted there, a copy of only one of them has come down to us: a half-length, executed by an unknown painter, after one of the two full-length portraits of *Mother Jerónima de la Fuente* which Velázquez painted and dated in 1620.[1]

There are, however, enough copies or replicas of his *bodegones* to conclude that the Master had followers or imitators, some of whom may have been his pupils, perhaps even before he left Seville for Madrid, where his Sevillian *bodegones* were admired and imitated. Yet, in their extant copies or replicas of his early works one misses the fluid handling of light, shade and hue by which Velázquez achieved his rendition of both texture and aerial space. Instead, one finds a sharp contrast of light and shade which is more Caravaggesque than Velázquez-like, that is, more in keeping with the 'modernism' which Velázquez had left behind even as a young man, but which remained ingrained in other painters of his day, including some of his followers (plate 19). Occurrences of this sort are not unusual at times which may be described as plateaus of modernism.

Diego de Melgar and the nameless followers of young Velázquez naturally awake our curiosity. As for their works, the task of trying to individualize them would require the discovery of new data in order to arrive at conclusive results, which would most likely be of slight historical relevance and remain peripheral to the study of Velázquez's art.

Soon after his appointment as painter to the King, the Master was given the use of a workshop in one of the buildings within the compound of the Royal Palace, as well as an apartment in one of the houses that the King owned in the city.[2] As we shall see, later he was allowed to use as a workshop some rooms of the apartment that Prince Baltasar Carlos had occupied in the Royal Palace till his death in 1646. As for his residence, he moved it to the rooms which in 1655 the King assigned to him in the *Casa del Tesoro*, another building within the royal compound.

Most of the Master's pupils at Madrid were of gentle birth, like Don Diego de Lucena, who probably entered the workshop in the mid-1620's, for he died in middle age in the 1650's; he was admired for his portraits, none of which is known today. Francisco de Burgos Mantilla, born about 1609, was nine years old when he moved from his native Burgos to Madrid, where he was a pupil first of Pedro de las Cuevas (d. 1644), and then of Velázquez; he was active and successful in Madrid as a portrait painter in 1648, according to Lázaro Díez del Valle, to whom we also owe the information that he endeavoured to imitate Velázquez's manner in his works,[3] none of which has come down to us with his name.

Don Nicolás de Villacis (1616–94) studied with Velázquez in the years 1632–6; he then

---

[1] In my *Velázquez: A Catalogue Raisonné*, London, 1963, no. 579, I expressed no opinion on the attribution of this half-length portrait to Velázquez which I then knew only from a photograph. Now that I have seen it, I would catalogue it as a copy of good quality.

[2] Francisco Íñiguez Almech, 'La Casa del Tesoro, Velázquez y las obras reales', *Varia velazqueña*, I, pp. 649–82.

[3] Díez del Valle's text is included in F. J. Sánchez Cantón, *Fuentes literarias para la historia del arte español*, Madrid, 1933, II, p. 372. For other data on Burgos Mantilla, see his testimony concerning Velázquez's qualifications for admission in the Order of Santiago, given on 24 December 1658.

went to Italy, and returned to his native Murcia in 1650. A few extant works have been attributed to him, though actually we know little, if anything, about his style.

Francisco de Palacios, who reportedly died at the age of thirty-six in 1676, was among the Velázquez's pupils who distinguished themselves mainly as portrait painters. If the dates we have concerning him are right, he could not have been a pupil of Velázquez before 1651, when the Master returned from Italy. Nor could he be the Francisco Palacios who in 1648 signed two still-lifes, a type of composition that, incidentally, Velázquez is not known to have painted at any time (Vienna, Harrach Museum).

Most of the information that we have about Lucena, Villacis and Palacios was gathered by Antonio Palomino, a painter and writer on art who, as we know, had been closely associated with Juan de Alfaro, another pupil of Velázquez.[1] According to Palomino, Alfaro was allowed, because of his status as Velázquez's pupil, to make copies of great masters' works, such as Titian's and Rubens's, at the Royal Palace. He excelled particularly in copying Van Dyck, whose manner soon had a greater impact than Velázquez's on his works. Alfaro, however, remained an enthusiastic admirer of Velázquez, at whose death, in 1660, he composed, with the help of his brother, Dr. Enrique Vaca de Alfaro, a Latin epitaph which Palomino printed in his life of Velázquez.

Juan de Pareja was Velázquez's assistant but not his pupil in any meaningful sense of the word.[2] He was born, apparently of Moorish descent, about 1610 at Seville, where, as he stated in 1630, he was a professional painter, even though he was then planning to go to Madrid for four months of further study with his brother, Jusepe, also a painter. There is no indication of when he became assistant to Velázquez, whom he accompanied in that capacity on his Italian journey of 1648–51. His extant dated works, none of which shows true affinity to Velázquez's style, were executed between 1658 and 1669, the year before his death. Awkwardly composed and somewhat rudimentary in execution, they reveal no more than a competent knowledge of the painter's craft. Probably, Velázquez entrusted him mainly with menial tasks, such as grinding and mixing pigments, preparing varnishes, fixing canvases on stretchers and priming them.

Velázquez's workshop, where Philip IV often came to watch him painting, or perhaps just for a chat, was by no means a professional painters' precinct. Great and lesser writers who praised his art, such as Quevedo, Gracián, García de Salcedo Coronel, Gabriel de Bocángel, Manuel de Gallegos, and Manuel de Faria y Sousa, most of whom were also courtiers, are likely to have been there at one time or another. There must also have been among the occasional or frequent visitors at least a sprinkling of courtiers who, in the fashion of the time — not too different from our own in this respect — amused themselves by practicing the art of painting. Two such individuals were the Count of Siruela, a renowned diplomat who died in 1651, and Don Tomás de Aguiar, a gentleman who by 1657 had achieved some

[1] *El museo pictórico*, pp. 867–8, 984, 999–1004, and 1046–7. Cf. J. C. López Jiménez, 'D. Nicolás de Villacis, discípulo de Velázquez', *Boletín del Seminario de Estudios de Arte y Arqueología*, Valladolid, 1964, pp. 195–210.

[2] On Pareja, see Palomino, *op. cit.*, pp. 960–1, and Juan Antonio Gaya Nuño, 'Revisiones sexcentistas: Juan de Pareja', *Archivo Español de Arte*, 1957, pp. 271–85.

reputation for the portraits that he painted from life.[1] The head portraits of both, Aguiar and Siruela, presumably by Velázquez, were in his workshop when he died; they are at present lost or unidentified.

One of Velázquez's duties was to make sure that his assistants or other painters, such as Mazo, kept up with the demand for replicas or copies of his portraits of members of the royal family, or for that matter of the Count-Duke of Olivares, whose painter he also was. Copies of other portraits were commissioned by the sitters, their families or institutions with which they were associated — which explains, for instance, the sizeable number of copies that we have of the portrait of *Cardinal Borja*, the original of which has not been convincingly identified.[2]

The copyists, of course, were not necessarily Velázquez's assistants or protegees. The portrait of *Philip IV in army dress*, now at the Frick Collection (plate 109), painted by the Master at Fraga in June 1644, was immediately sent by the King to the Queen. The Catalans who resided in Madrid requested permission to display it during their celebration of the recapture of Lérida, at the church of St. Martin, where many people came to see it. Within a few days, copies, two of which have come down to us, were made of it.[3]

In the bust-length replica of his *Innocent X*, Velázquez painted little more than the sitter's head; the rest is plainly by another hand (plate 143). Assistants sometimes completed a portrait began by the Master. An instance of this is the three-quarter length of *Queen Isabel*, sent to Vienna in 1632, in which the head is by Velázquez, while the lesser work of assistants is noticeable nearly everywhere else in the painting (plate 161). Likewise, in the portrait of *Prince Baltasar Carlos*, of about 1639, now also at the Vienna Museum, only the head appears to be by the Master's hand, though he may have sketched the whole composition (plate 160).

Some assistants were obviously given a free hand to devise new compositions, which, mediocrity being what it has always been, was readily achieved by borrowing compositional elements from other works by the Master. For example, the full-length of *Queen Isabel* sent to England in 1639[4] reproduces the head of the portrait sent to Vienna in 1632, mentioned in the preceding paragraph, and includes particulars, such as the barking dog and the somewhat disarranged rug, taken from *Joseph's bloody coat*, from where also seems to derive the device of the background open-view (plates 166, 58, and 161).

THE COIN OF IMITATION

Velázquez's followers, when he was a young man, saw in him mainly a painter of *bodegones*; from the mid 1620's on, particularly after his return from Italy in 1631, his impact on other painters of the time, including some who were older than he, was chiefly noticeable in portrait-painting.

---

[1] As recorded by Lázaro Díez del Valle (see Sánchez Cantón, *op. cit.*, II, pp. 334 and 339).

[2] In my *catalogue raisonné* of Velázquez's works, published in 1963, I included six extant versions of this portrait, none of which can, in my view, be conclusively attributed to the Master (nos. 462–7). Since then Velázquez's name has been claimed for one more portrait of Cardinal Borja, known to me only from a photograph; it is reported to measure 0·615 m. in height and 0·495 in width, and to be at Munich in private hands.

[3] See López-Rey, *Velázquez: A Catalogue Raisonné*, nos. 255–6.   [4] See page 172.

Except for *Bacchus*, *Democritus*, and *Supper at Emmaus*, all painted at Madrid before Velázquez's departure for Italy in 1629, and *Christ on the Cross*, most likely executed in 1631 or 1632, shortly after his return to Spain, none of his religious, mythological or historical compositions appears to have been copied in his time (plates 57, 55, 52, and 53). At least, no copy is extant that may be regarded as of the period, and none has ever been recorded as executed by any of his contemporaries, not even by those of his pupils or followers, such as Alfaro or Martínez del Mazo, whose practice it was to copy paintings by other masters in the royal collections.

However, Velázquez's *The forge of Vulcan* had an impact on Carducho, who, as we know, was intent on including naturalist images in the classic design of his compositions. He was particularly successful in doing so in *Saint Bruno declining the archbishop's mitre offered by Pope Urban II*, dated 1632 (plate 11). In this painting, one of Carducho's best, a suffusing light creates a sort of atmospheric environment for the three secondary figures at the left and for the archbishop's vestments placed at the centre, while the main figures are distinctly set against the background. The male profile to the left certainly recalls, both in its outline and in its modelling, that of Apollo in *The forge of Vulcan*, which had been in Madrid since 1631 (plates 12 and 62).[1]

Velázquez made a good many drawings from Michelangelo's and Raphael's frescoes at the Vatican in 1629–30. Yet, no deep or lasting impact of either Raphael's or Michelangelo's art is discernible in his works. As we know from his words and works, Titian was the painter whom he admired above all others; however, this admiration did not lead to imitation. There is, indeed, no evidence that Velázquez ever copied any of the Venetian master's works, except for *The Rape of Europa*, then at the Royal Palace in Madrid, which he sketched with lusty changes in *The fable of Arachne* shortly before he left for Italy in 1648 (plate 125).

Perhaps Velázquez had come to realize during his first Italian journey that, contrary to Pacheco's views, copying was not really a way to commune with another artist's work, much less to arrive at a personal creation, and in consequence he discouraged others from copying his works. It might also be that from the 1630's on Velázquez's large compositions appeared to other painters too overpowering to be imitated.

There is a painting by Velázquez, a life-size *White horse*, which some of his followers appropriated in their works as if it had discovered, or abrogated, for them the live reality that it portrayed (plate 84). It is probably one of the three paintings of riderless horses, each of a different colour — the other two being grey or chestnut — which were in Velázquez's workshop at his death. The painting has suffered from cleaning and restoration, but the design that masterfully builds the shape of the horse into space remains alive.

One unspirited copy of this *White horse* is known today (Madrid, private collection). It is likely that others were made in the Master's time and afterwards. At least, it is recorded that,

---

[1] However, in the profile painted by Carducho, the eye, linearly defined, is not Velázquez-like. The head of the bearded old man in Carducho's work is also sharply drawn, but otherwise it recalls two of Velázquez's paintings of about 1619–20: the half-length *Saint Paul*, at the Museo de Arte de Cataluña, Barcelona (plate 54), and a similar head, somewhat rubbed and darkened, in the Countess of Saltes' collection, Madrid (see López-Rey, *Velázquez. A Catalogue Raisonné*, nos. 34 and 35, plates 19 and 20).

as late as 1760, a promising young painter — who, as it happened, did not fulfil his promise — won a reward from the Spanish Royal Academy of Fine Arts for having copied 'the horse of Velázquez' and other paintings which were at the then recently founded Academy.[1]

Apart from the colour, Velázquez's *White horse* is quite close in shape, pose and live design to the chestnut mount in his equestrian portrait of the *Count-Duke of Olivares*, painted about 1634-5 (plate 77). In the small replica that Mazo painted of this portrait, probably in the mid-1630's, there are two obvious changes, both showing familiarity with, and dependence on, other works by the Master: the horse is white as in the painting where Velázquez represented it without a rider, and the precipice over which the horse curvets in the original has been replaced by a slope somewhat similar to that in Velázquez's equestrian portrait of *Philip IV* (plates 84, 85 and 75).

Mazo also included Velázquez's white horse, riderless, in *The stag hunt at Aranjuez*, in the Prado (plate 173). It appears again, dappled in brown and white, as the mount of the Duke of Feria in *The taking of Brisach*, painted about 1634-5 by Jusepe Leonardo for the Great Hall of the Buen Retiro Palace (plate 174).

As we know, the impact of Velázquez's portrait of *Innocent X* on Italian and Spanish painters of the time was of very high moment. No fewer than thirteen copies, executed either after the original three-quarter length or after the Master's own bust-length replica, have come down to us. Some of them are, of course, copies of copies. Such appears to be the case with the short bust at the National Gallery of Art, Washington, D.C., in which, to mention only one telling difference, the eyes of Innocent X are brown with a little touch of grey rather than blue-grey as Velázquez painted them.

Pietro Martire Neri, who, as indicated above, appears to have been close to Velázquez in 1650 at Rome, signed two copies of the Master's likeness of Innocent X. In one of them, he enlarged the composition to a full-length double portrait of *Innocent X with a prelate* (plate 142). Curiously, he copied the figure of the Pope from Velázquez's original without, however, attempting to imitate the Master's modelling of the face, while he endeavoured to achieve a Velázquez-like modelling in the head of the other sitter, the standing prelate.

From the mid-1620's till some time after Velázquez's death, Spanish portrait-painting was to a very large extent under his spell. It was as if he had cast afresh for the benefit of his fellow painters the reality of the individual. As for the sitters, social affectation probably played some part in their desire or willingness to appear on canvas with a Velázquez-like dignity of carriage.

By comparison with Velázquez's originals, the extant portraits from his workshop or by his followers often seem garish, and almost invariably make the sitter look relatively small in a space which is either pictorially jejune or too contrived. Naturally, most of them are mediocre; a few, however, are executed with a sense of emulation, making use of brilliant accents which add weight to the naturalism of the pictorial image.

The Master must have been aware of the gap between his work and that of his gifted assistants or followers, especially evident in their replicas of his portraits of the King. He

---

[1] *Distribución de los premios concedidos por el Rey N. S. a los discípulos de las tres nobles artes hecha por la Real Academia de S. Fernando en la junta general de 28 de Agosto de 1760*, Madrid, p. 18. The young painter's name was Ginés de Aguirre.

probably was also aware that, as in like cases, the imitation and emulation of his works were the small coin of the admiration paid to him.

LIFE, FASHION, AND PAINTING

It was most probably soon after his return to Madrid that Velázquez painted a new likeness of the Infanta María Teresa, whom he had portrayed some three years earlier (plate 145). Only the head of this likeness of the Infanta has come down to us (plate 146): now she has the lower lip considerably more developed in the manner characteristic of her Habsburg family; her left eye is more sharply almond-shaped, while the underlid of the right one still bulges out, and the outswelling of her temple is somewhat more marked.

María Teresa was about ten years old when Velázquez painted her earliest extant portrait (plate 145) and just a few months over fourteen when he painted the latest of those which have come down to us. The teenager's features were obviously taking new shapes under the eyes of her portraitist, who, between the sitting for one portrait and that for another, saw a somewhat different presence which he fashioned into a new pictorial likeness.

The case was similar, though not quite the same, with the portraits of the Queen, who was just four years older than her blood cousin, María Teresa. Velázquez had what might have been a harder, but certainly turned out to be a more rewarding, task with the Infanta Margarita — whom he portrayed from the time when she was a couple of years old up to when she was eight. If, while at Rome, the Master had enjoyed painting as the Pope and members of the Papal Court sat for him, back in Madrid he obviously continued to delight in his work as the Queen and the Infantas came to have their likenesses put on canvas by him.

A portrait of the Infanta María Teresa by Velázquez and a workshop replica of it left Madrid on 22 February 1653 as presents from the Spanish King, one for the Emperor Ferdinand III, at Vienna, and the other for the Duke Leopold Wilhelm, at Brussels. The original, now at the Vienna Museum, must consequently have been painted late in 1652 or early in 1653; unfortunately, it has been cut down, more notably at the bottom (plate 147).

It is likely that Velázquez portrayed the Infanta María Teresa at least once more, at the time when her marriage to Louis XIV of France, which took place on 9 June 1660, was being arranged. However, the Vienna portrait, of 1652 or early 1653, is the latest we have of her by the Master's hand. In it, Velázquez fashioned the likeness of the Infanta into the subtlest harmony of white, silver and pink against a greenish-blue background. Everything, the voluminous and richly decorated headdress, the pleated tulle yoke, the bodice tight over the stiff corsage, and the ample farthingale on which ribbons and watches rest, is keyed to the make-believe rouge and pearly tones on the Infanta's face. Such make-up and such a costume were a Spanish fashion which French ladies of the time found hideous. In more recent times, Velázquez has been pitied for having to portray faces which looked so lifeless and cumbersome costumes which made the sitter's figure and pose quite unnatural. However, if the paintings themselves may be taken as evidence, it would rather seem that the Master enjoyed painting such portraits.

In the one of María Teresa (plate 147), he opposed the artificial tones of her make-up to the live pink and ivory hues of her broadly painted hands. Yet it is the face, rouged and pearly, that keys up the whole composition: the yoke-like collar of pink tulle, the light chestnut headdress decorated with a white plume and silver and rose ribbons, the strands of pearls which cast brownish shadows on the silver-tinselled grey-white costume, the rose ribbons which lie on the farthingale or those which adorn the Infanta's wrists. Lit up by a silvery light, she stands against the greenish-blue of a cloth-covered table and the background curtain, made into a vivid pictorial presence without putting the emphasis on the particulars of fashion in a manner that Velázquez's imitators generally failed to achieve.

The Infanta Margarita does not look more than two years old in what obviously is the earliest Velázquez portrait of her which has come down to us, which is consequently datable to the middle of 1653 (plate 150). As he had done more than twenty years earlier in the portrait of the sixteen-month-old Prince Baltasar Carlos (plate 68), Velázquez represented the sitter standing on a dais covered by a rug — here patterned in blue, red and light ochre. At the right of the Infanta there is what looks like a table covered with a blue cloth, whose ample folds come to the foreground and blend, at the other end, with those of the greenish-blue drapery which opens into the background shadows. This background opening marks a fluid diagonal which runs across the composition to the very foreground, where it sets off the figure of the Infanta. Her roundish face, rosy and ivory, is framed by her flaxen hair; she is dressed in a pink and silver costume decorated with black lace and gold jewellery, and stands against the greenish-blue curtain and blackish and ochre shadows, her right hand resting on the blue table-cloth on which lies a white rose by a crystal glass containing a pink rose, a blue iris, and other flowers of yellow or light-blue hues — which keys up the whole colour scheme of the composition.

In this portrait, Margarita's neck is short and her chin roundish, which probably corresponded to her true appearance. However, in Velázquez's later portraits of her, shadows and lights elongate the neck and make the jaw look somewhat pointed, though in none has the chin quite the same shape as in the others nor, for that matter, have the eyes. Some of Velázquez's assistants, however, went on executing portraits where the Infanta's jaw is roundish and her neck short. The Master's concern to shade off Margarita's round chin and to elongate her neck recalls similar changes in the likenesses that he painted of Philip IV after 1624.

Late in 1652 or early in 1653 Velázquez completed his first portrait of the nineteen-year-old Queen Mariana (plate 149). She is seen full-length, dressed in the same fashion as the Infanta, wearing a silver-braided black costume decorated with red ribbons and gold chains and bracelets, completed with a large gold brooch pinned to the stiff bodice. Her pose is almost identical with that of María Teresa: her right hand rests on the back of a chair, reddish purple like the overhanging curtain and the cloth-covered table in the background, which brings about a pervasive harmony of reds and black. The sense of depth is stressed by the shadow of the farthingale on the foreground; moreover the golden yellows of a clock shine in the background as do the like hues of the jewels on the Queen's costume and headdress, making the more vivid the depiction of aerial space.

This likeness of Mariana, with her rouged face made smallish under a heavy headdress, her bust encased in a tight bodice, and the rest of her figure, including the feet, lost to the eye in the stiff fullness of the farthingale, has given to some the 'impression of doll-like immobility',[1] and led to the suggestion that the fashion of his time resulted in some sort of handicap for Velázquez who, nevertheless, did his best to do justice to the splendid attire of his royal sitter. Rather, it would seem that the Master took pleasure in underscoring the pictorial nature of his work by keying the likeness of the sitter to the make-believe appearance of her face.

If a parallel between Velázquez's painting and the literature of his day were permissible, without implying its being either necessary or conclusive, one could suggest that his vivid depiction of his sitters' artificial flesh tones as such, and the image of both human likeness and sheer pictorial presence that he thus impels simultaneously, bring to mind the play-within-the-play which, on the stage of the time, intensified, again simultaneously, both the true-to-life and the theatrical nature of the action being played.

It cannot be overemphasized, however, that such parallels between literature and other arts, helpful as they are for setting our understanding of an artist, or just one work, within the flow of the time, ought not to be understood as proving, or even suggesting, influence of one art on the other. Nor are they to be taken as evidence of the existence of a foreordained, or otherwise fixed, plan to which artists of the same period worked. They are no more than coincidences helpful for describing rather than circumscribing the current of creative life at a given point of historical time.

THE MASTER'S LAST PORTRAIT OF THE KING

As Philip, newly married but with no male issue, seemed to be bringing to a close the days of his dynasty in Spain, other European Courts eyed with inquietude, hope, or impatience, the immediate future of the Spanish throne. As an understandable result, manners being what they were, many requests were made for portraits of Philip, by then a rather infirm person, his young Queen, his marriageable daughter, and the little Infanta who had disappointed the Spaniards' hopes for a male heir to the throne. Hence the sizeable number of portraits of the sovereigns and the two Infantas which have come down to us.

The image of the King is reflected, together with that of the Queen, in a mirror in the background of the large group-portrait, *The Royal Family*, finished by Velázquez in 1656 (plates 152 and 156). Only one other likeness of Philip IV — a bust portrait — unquestionably painted by the Master in the 1650's has come down to us (plate 151). Also extant are three workshop portraits of the King with significant variations from the Master's, and at least five which differ more markedly from his one extant composition.

In addition to these fine versions, there are others of mediocre quality, executed by Velázquez's less gifted assistants or by some of the hack painters then active at Madrid; some were, it would seem, painted after the Master's death, in the last five years of Philip's life, and a few are obviously the work of much later copyists or imitators.

---

[1] Cf. Beruete, *Velázquez*, p. 103; Trapier, *Velázquez*, p. 324.

As Chamberlain, Velázquez had time-consuming obligations, besides those of Court painter. It is, for instance, more than likely that he had to lend a hand in the elaborate plans which were made for the solemn reburial of Philip IV's ancestors and first wife, Isabel, in the new Pantheon at the Escorial. At the conclusion of the reburial, on 18 March 1654, Philip, who had viewed the remains of his ancestors — the Emperor Charles V one of them — and his first wife, was a sorrowful man, fearful of death, and tormented by the uncertainty of eternal salvation.[1]

After that memorable occasion, Velázquez undertook the large composition, *The Royal Family*, which must have occupied him for a long while. Once this work was completed, he turned his energies to four large mythological compositions for the Hall of Mirrors at the Palace.

Though, as indicated above, Philip was by then rather infirm in appearance, Velázquez represented him in a portrait of the early 1650's as untouched by age or illness (plate 151). The light which, as in earlier portraits by the Master's hand, laves the face of the King, elongates his well-turned neck, as only the thinnest of shadows are used for the modelling of the whole. The costume, a black doublet and cloak, is just roughed in by bold strokes and subtle highlights which impart a statuary fullness to the bust.

An *antequem* date for this portrait of *Philip IV* is provided by an engraving based on it, made by Pedro de Villafranca in 1655 (plate 153). There are, however, a few differences between Velázquez's painting and Villafranca's engraving. For one thing, in the latter, the King is clad in armour rather than in a doublet, though the white collar, which protrudes beyond his hair, is identical with that in the painting; secondly, contrary to the painting, the curls at the right of Philip's head are arranged in regular waves. These are, of course, slight variations. Of greater significance is the fact that Villafranca has hinted at a double chin in place of the elongated and well-rounded neck depicted by Velázquez. As it happens, every bust portrait of Philip IV datable from the mid-1650's on differs in this from Velázquez's original, as well as in lesser details. Every one of them, indeed, represents Philip with a double chin, often quite flabby, which makes his neck shortish and contributes to his ageing appearance.

Doubtless the likeness of Philip as an aged man corresponded to the truth of his physique more closely than the one painted by Velázquez. The large number of such portraits which have come down to us indicates that the likeness they embodied was the one preferred by those familiar with the appearance of Philip. It might even be that Philip himself, who was by then self-reproachful and well aware of his shortcomings as a King and of his many other weaknesses, also preferred the portraits in which the flaws of his human nature were depicted.

The bust portrait at the Prado Museum is the only extant one of the King undisputedly painted by Velázquez after his return from Italy in 1651. From then on, for whatever reasons, he let other painters in his circle, including his assistants, paint likeness after likeness of the

---

[1] See Francisco de los Santos, *Descripción breve del Monasterio de S. Lorenzo el Real del Escorial*, Madrid, 1657, fols. 155ff. For Philip's sentiments, see his letters of 25 March and 20 April 1654 (*Cartas de la venerable Madre Sor María de Agreda y del Señor Rey Don Felipe IV*, ed. by Francisco Silvela, Madrid, 1888, vol. II, pp. 289-90, and 293-4).

ageing Philip which seemingly conformed to the taste of nearly everybody, though not to his own.

Velázquez's name has been claimed at one time or another, though always with reservations, for a few of the bust portraits of the aged Philip. Two of them, one in Vienna and the other in London are rather fine, particularly the latter (plate 162). Today it is only the London picture which is still regarded by some as being, at least in part, by the Master, who would have painted the head, while the dress and the golden chain would be by an assistant. It should be noted that the shoulder braid in Philip's doublet and the chain with the Golden Fleece appear in this and in almost every one of the derivative portraits of Philip, though not in Velázquez's original. In the latter, the highlights which fully model the bust make it questionable that a gold chain was to be painted on, with all the changes, particularly as to highlights, that would have entailed. In some of the derivative pictures the chain is seen without the Golden Fleece hanging from it, most likely as a result of the canvas having been cut down.

Even Beruete, who did include the London portrait among the Master's works, pointed out that, though it is 'a picture of admirable effect', its execution does not entirely agree with that of Velázquez's last works. The colouring, particularly that of the hair, is lifeless; a sort of indistinctness in the filmy texture of the pigments contributes, moreover, to the lack of the in-the-round quality in the bust of the King. The lack of spatial depth is, indeed, the most telling difference between this and Velázquez's work.

The portrait of Philip IV, of which the London picture is the finest extant version, was also reproduced in an engraving made in 1657 by Pedro de Villafranca (plate 154). This suggests that the likeness of the King with a double chin, first engraved by Villafranca in 1655, had gained currency two years later.

Velázquez himself might have arrived at the point of fashioning the self-reproachful and shaken Philip into an elderly figure. However, there is no painting unquestionably by Velázquez's hand nor other evidence which can give substance to such a surmise. All indicates that it was rather one of the painters in the Master's circle who turned his portrayal of the King as a quasi-divine person into the likeness of an ageing man.

THE MASTER AND THE FOLLOWER

There is reason to infer that Mazo was the painter in Velázquez's circle who, in the 1650's, originated the version of the bust portrait of Philip IV in which, contrary to the Master's original, the sitter's natural characteristics are accented. A bust portrait of the ageing King hangs prominently on the wall of *The family of the artist*, at the Vienna Museum (plate 169). In this group portrait, a painter is seen working, though not from life, on a portrait of the Infanta Margarita, which resembles, even to the green colour of the dress, a copy, now in the Budapest Museum, of the likeness that Velázquez painted of her in 1659.

According to a convincing and generally accepted view, *The family of the artist* was painted by Mazo; it portrays his family, and he is the painter seen at work in the background. That the family depicted is Mazo's appears to be supported by the fact that the coat of arms in the upper left corner displays a mallet (*mazo*) held by a hand in armour. It has been suggested that the room represented is the same depicted in *The fable of Arachne*, seen from another point.[1] It should be added that the bust of a woman seen below the portrait of the King seems to be one in marble, from the second century A.D., then at the Royal Palace, where Mazo had his workshop, at least after Velázquez's death (plates 163 and 164).[2] Still more important is that, in composition and execution, the painting coincides with Mazo's works, and so does the extant colour sketch for the figure of one of the boys, at the centre (plate 165).

The portrait of the King in the background of *The family of the artist* corresponds quite closely in appearance, proportions and modelling to the likeness of the ageing Philip in the London National Gallery (plates 162 and 163). Hence, it would seem that it was Mazo who originated the variant of Velázquez's portrait of *Philip IV*, of which the London picture is the finest though not necessarily the earliest example, that gained acceptance in the mid-1650's; if so, it may be that his success prompted him to display that likeness of the King in the picture of his own workshop, probably after Velázquez's death, when he became Court painter. In that capacity, he went on painting portraits of the King and of the Infanta Margarita till the mid-1660's, when both he and Philip IV died.

Even if this picture of Mazo's workshop had been painted by another artist, the prominence given in it to the bust portrait of Philip IV as an ageing man would lead to the inference that Mazo was regarded as the originator, or at least as the outstanding painter of this true-to-life image of the King.

The earliest known document concerning Mazo is the entry in the registry of the church of Santiago, at Madrid, which tells of his marriage in 1633 to Francisca Velázquez. The date of his mother's birth, 26 June 1596, together with that of his marriage, suggests that he was born in the early or mid-1610's.

It is documented that Velázquez furthered his son-in-law's career with a steady hand, securing palace appointments for him and his children.[3] In the early 1640's, Mazo became master of drawing and painting to Prince Baltasar Carlos, who in 1645 was godfather to his fifth child. The Prince died the following year, at the age of sixteen, but Philip IV decreed that the perquisites that Mazo had been receiving be continued, and kept employing him as a painter.

While contemporary writers on art, as well as administrative documents of the time, including petitions to the King signed by Mazo himself, often refer to him as Velázquez's son-in-law, none mentions him as his pupil, and there is, indeed, no indication that he was, before his marriage, in that or any other professional capacity at the Master's workshop. Nor is there any

---

[1] Francisco Iñiguez Almech, 'La Casa del Tesoro, Velázquez y las obras reales', *Varia velazqueña*, I, pp. 649–82.

[2] It is now at the Prado Museum, catalogued as 'Domitia Lucilla (?)'; its height is 0·62 m. See A. Blanco, *Museo del Prado, Catálogo de la escultura*, Madrid, 1957, p. 80, no. 114–E.

[3] See the personal file of *MAZO, Juan Bautista* at the Archive of the Madrid Royal Palace. Most, though not all, of the documents in this file as well as others pertaining to Mazo, have been included, in the documentary section of *Varia velazqueña*, Madrid, 1960, II, pp. 235–410. Many of them have been extracted or quoted in Juan Antonio Gaya Nuño's article, 'Juan Bautista del Mazo, el gran discípulo de Velázquez', published in vol. I of the same publication (pp. 471–81), and in other articles written as a sequel to the third centenary of Velázquez's death.

evidence that he later became an assistant to Velázquez, a status which would hardly have been helpful for his advancement at the Court. At the same time, it is true that he came closer than any other painter to Velázquez's manner, though not so close as the misattributions of works of one to the other has led to believe. As his contemporaries noted and his signed or fully documented works plainly show, Mazo had a personality of his own, however much he, in fact, owed to Velázquez's style.

Jusepe Martínez (1601–82), a friend of Velázquez, praised Mazo for his mastery in painting small figures,[1] certainly a cardinal compositional element in both his hunting pictures and his city views, such as that of *Saragossa* (plate 168), which Martínez, a native and resident of the city, most likely saw in 1646 when Mazo was at work on it.

In 1657, Lázaro Díez del Valle, an enthusiastic admirer of Velázquez, wrote that Mazo painted admirably hunting subjects and views of cities, of which he cited those of Pamplona and Saragossa, executed at Philip IV's command. Díez del Valle also praised Mazo for his portraits of Philip IV and Queen Mariana, emphasizing one of the latter which was displayed at one of the gates of Madrid shortly after her arrival, in the autumn of 1649, at the Spanish Court.[2] Since Velázquez had left Madrid for Italy the year before and did not return till June 1651, Mazo's portrait of Queen Mariana, which, according to Díez del Valle, was of surprising naturalism and marvellous execution and one of the first of the new Queen to be publicly shown, must have been very much his own work, close though it may have been to Velázquez's style.

Martínez praised Mazo also for his copies after Titian, and it is known that he copied many works by Rubens, Jordaens, and other Flemish or Italian masters, particularly for Prince Baltasar Carlos. Such copies must have cut down considerably the time available for his original work. So, obviously did the replicas after Velázquez's royal portraits which he painted, though in these he felt free to follow his own bent for brilliancy of execution and true-to-life naturalism.

Mazo's palette is rather like Velázquez's, except for a penchant that he often shows for stressing blue or bluish tints. Of greater import as a departure from the Master's style is Mazo's way of shaping men and things by highlights which flash the pictorial image, as it were, toward the surface of the painting, even from the background. As a counterbalance, an explicit, even emphatic, perspective design marks out the spatial confines of the composition, making it look squarish. A further departure from Velázquez is Mazo's luxuriant depiction of detail or incident, which he achieves with brilliant, depthless strokes, whether on the figure of a sitter, a curtain, a wall, a floor, the surface of a river, or plain grounds. These stylistic traits ought not to be understood merely in a negative sense, as failures to be Velázquez-like; they actually reveal Mazo's own personality. Such traits are, indeed, as manifest in *The view of Saragossa*, of 1647 (Prado, plate 168), as in the portrait of *Queen Mariana*, of 1666 (London, National Gallery, plate 171), to cite his earliest and latest extant dated works. They are

[1] *Discursos practicables del nobilísimo arte de la pintura*, ed. Valentín Carderera, Madrid, 1866, p. 119.

[2] The text is included in F. J. Sánchez Cantón, *Fuentes literarias para la historia del arte español*, Madrid, 1933, II, p. 374.

manifest, too, in the portrait of *Infanta Margarita* (Prado, plate 170), most likely painted about 1664–65, where the background curtains build the space behind the glimmering figure of the Infanta as if they were stage flats — which is quite unlike Velázquez, as a comparison with his portrait of *Queen Mariana*, of about 1652–53, also at the Prado, makes evident (plate 149).[1]

VELÁZQUEZ AT WORK IN HIS WORLD

The painting of *The royal family*, commonly known as *Las meninas*, has always been regarded as an unsurpassable masterpiece (plate 152). According to Palomino, it 'was finished' in 1656, and, while Velázquez was painting it, the King, the Queen, and the Infantas María Teresa and Margarita often came to watch him at work. Some forty years later, in the 1690's, a new Court painter, the deft and quick Luca Giordano, paused before the old masterpiece long enough to proclaim it 'the theology of Painting'.[2]

Palomino's account of this work is quite detailed, and the truth of it has been verified by documentary evidence in most respects. He identified by name and occupation nearly every person, and even the room, represented in the large group-portraits. The location is the main chamber of the apartment which Prince Baltasar Carlos had occupied in the Royal Palace till his death, in 1646. Some time later, Velázquez begun to use it as a workshop; he was still using it as both a workshop and a sort of office for the paper work which, as Chamberlain of the Palace, he had to do, in 1660, when he died.[3]

[1] The Prado portrait, in which the Infanta Margarita, born in 1650, appears to be between fourteen and sixteen years old, could not have been painted before 1664, at least four years after Velázquez's death. In it, the features of the Infanta are markedly different from those in the portrait painted by Velázquez in 1659 (plates 159, 170). She, indeed, looks much the same as in another portrait, at the Vienna Museum, in which she is wearing a brooch with he imperial double eagle, the gift of her bridegroom, the Emperor Leopold, to whom she was betrothed in 1664 and whom she married two years later. This portrait is painted in a manner close to Mazo's, and I once suggested that it was 'most likely' that he had executed it (*Velázquez: A Catalogue Raisonné*, no. 410). However, a recent re-examination of its brushwork has convinced me that it was executed after Mazo's original by a less dexterous hand.

The Prado *Infanta Margarita* has for years been attributed to Velázquez in the Museum's catalogues, formerly with the contention that the sitter was really the older Infanta María Teresa, now with the qualification that the Master left it unfinished and that, after his death, Mazo completed it, painting the 'face, neck and hands', to quote from the 1963 edition (p. 738, no. 1192). The suggestion that Velázquez started the portrait by painting the background curtains and the sitter's dress is incredible. Surely, he was no itinerant painter. For a full discussion of the matter, see López-Rey, *Velázquez: A Catalogue Raisonné*, nos. 409–10.

[2] Palomino, *El Museo pictórico*, pp. 920–2. The title *La familia* does not occur in the 17th-century royal inventories as I, like other scholars, had mistakenly believed. (*Velázquez: A Catalogue Raisonné of his Oeuvre*, no. 229.) Still, there is some reason to believe that, as stated in the Prado catalogue, that was the name by which the painting was then known, for in the list of pictures rescued from the fire that gutted the Madrid Royal Palace on 24–7 December 1734, compiled four days later, it was registered as *The family of Philip IV*.

[3] Cf. F. J. Sánchez Cantón, *Las meninas y sus personajes*, Barcelona, 1952, and Yves Bottineau, 'L'Alcázar de Madrid et l'inventaire de 1686', *Bulletin Hispanique*, October–December, 1958, pp. 450–83. See also '*Certificación de las alhajas que se hallan en el cuarto del Príncipe tocantes a S. M. por muerte de Diego Velázquez . . .*', drawn up on 10 August 1660, and '*Relación de las Pinturas que ay en el Obrador del Pintor de Cámara de Palacio oy 10 de Agosto de 1694*', both in the Archive of the Madrid Royal Palace (the first is included in *Varia velazqueña*, II, pp. 388–9; the second has hitherto remained, as far as I know, unnoticed).

In his cited article, Bottineau has shown that Palomino's identification of the room depicted in *The royal family* as one in the '*cuarto del Príncipe*' is right, contrary to the views held by Francisco Iñiguez Almech in *Casas reales y*

Mazo, painter to the late Baltasar Carlos, had executed the forty paintings which decorated the chamber; thirty-five of them were copies after Rubens or other Flemish painters, and only five — small canvases representing a wild boar and some dogs — were original. All were still there in 1694, when Luca Giordano was given the key to the chamber, by then part of what was officially known as 'the Court painter's workshop'.

In the painting, the painter himself is seen at the easel; the mirror on the rear wall reflects the half-length figures of Philip IV and Queen Mariana standing under a red curtain. The Infanta Margarita is in the centre, attended by two *meninas*, or maids of honour, Doña Isabel de Velasco and Doña María Sarmiento, who curtsy as the latter offers her mistress a drink of water in a *búcaro* — a reddish earthen vessel — on a tray. In the right foreground stand a female dwarf, Mari-Bárbola, and a midget, Nicolás de Pertusato, who playfully puts his foot on the back of the mastiff resting on the floor. Linked to this large group there is another formed by Doña Marcela de Ulloa, *guardamujer de las damas de la Reina* — attendant to the ladies-in-waiting — and an unidentified *guardadamas*, or escort to the same ladies. In the background, the *aposentador*, or Palace marshal, to the Queen, Don José Nieto Velázquez, stands on the steps leading into the room from the lit-up door.

Philip IV's children by his first wife, Queen Isabel, were dead, except for the eighteen-year-old Infanta María Teresa, whose likeness does not appear in the painting. Philip had married the new Queen in 1649, and the Infanta Margarita, born on 12 July 1651, was then their only child; her apparent age in the painting confirms that this could not have been executed substantially earlier or later than 1656, as reported by Palomino.

The descriptions and interpretations of this work have nearly always been keyed to the flaxen-haired Infanta, comely in her white dress with touches of black and pink, or to the group that she forms with her attendants. However, the title *Las meninas*, or *The maids of honour*, did not gain currency till the early part of the nineteenth century, and it was not till 1843, the time of sentimental realism, that it entered the catalogue of the Prado Museum.[1]

jardines de Felipe II, Madrid, 1952, pp. 97–8. The number and apparent dimensions of the pictures above and between the windows on the side wall of Velázquez's composition correspond with the data provided by the 1686 inventory about the paintings that decorated a like wall of the main chamber of the '*cuarto del Príncipe*'. As for the pictures of *Pallas and Arachne* and *Apollo and Marsyas*, they too appear to correspond in size with the paintings of the same subjects which, according to the cited inventory, hung side by side on another wall of the same chamber.

[1] The earliest such description occurs in the inventory of the Madrid Royal Palace drawn up in 1666 by Mazo, who did not mention that the composition included a self-portrait of Velázquez. However, the inventories of 1686 and 1700 recorded that the Master had 'portrayed himself' in the painting; in 1747, soon after the damage suffered by the painting in the fire of 1734 had been repaired, it was described as representing the Infanta Margarita, 'when Velázquez portrayed her', according to the restorers, or 'being portrayed by Velázquez', as the compiler of another list put it. The latter phrase was repeated in the inventory of 1772, and four years later by Anthony Raphael Mengs (*Obras*, 2nd ed., Madrid, 1797, p. 222). In the inventory of 1794, drawn up by Goya and two other Court painters, the painting was merely designated by the old title, *The family of Philip IV*. Such differences in the description of a work of art are common and of little factual consequence, though not without interest. Nor can one attach factual significance to the differences in the measurements of the painting, up to half a *vara* in height and half a *vara* in width, reported in the various lists and inventories, for such measurements often were rough estimates made by eye, which might or might not include the frame, and were further clouded by the lack of any absolute uniformity as to the dimension of the *vara*.

George Kubler has published a hitherto unknown description of *The royal family*, which occurs in *Antiguidade da*

There is another portrait of the *Infanta Margarita* by Velázquez that most probably was also painted in 1656 (plate 148). She is wearing a white costume decorated with red rosettes and black lace, standing on a rug, patterned in reds, ochres, blue and black, against a reddish ochre background, enlivened by a red curtain. This is the only portrait in which the Master stressed the curls of Margarita's hair. Fashion, of course, would suffice to explain such change, as well as the fact that her hair is parted on the right rather than on the left. What matters, however, is that the two likenesses of Margarita painted by Velázquez about 1656 are different pictorially, which is not surprising since he really was a creative painter. In *The royal family*, the face of the Infanta appears elongated by thin shadows and by the luminous strokes which make her hair weightless and shape her figure into a lucent image, the like of which the Master never painted again.

In his discussion of the self-portrait of 'Velázquez painting' in *The royal family*, Palomino explained that the red cross of Santiago on the Master's doublet had been added, by command of Philip IV, after his death. It is, indeed, a fact that Velázquez did not become a knight of the Order of Santiago till 28 November 1659, less than one year before he died.

The fifty-seven-year-old painter represented himself without a wrinkle on his pensive face, his dark chestnut hair flowing down to his shoulders. The face is almost identical with that in the other Velázquez's self-portrait which has come down to us, a head that appears to be a fragment of a larger composition; unfortunately, this painting is in so poor a state of preservation that it is hard to suggest a date for it, though one may surmise that it was painted in the late 1640's or early in the following decade (plates 136 and 157).

Palomino called attention to the paintings decorating the walls of the room depicted in *The royal family*, saying that one could see, if only dimly, that they were subjects from Ovid's *Metamorphosis* painted by Rubens. He obviously had in mind the two canvases hanging high

Arte da Pintura, written by the Portuguese painter Felix da Costa (1639–1712) before 1696 ('Three remarks on The Meninas', *The Art Bulletin*, June, 1966, pp. 212–14. Kubler has also edited Costa's treatise, *The Antiquity of the Art of Painting*, New Haven and London, 1967). Costa, who states that the painting 'adorns a room of the royal palace at Madrid', says that Velázquez had portrayed himself 'in a cape bearing the cross of Santiago', 'with his glance upon' Margarita, whose hair is being dressed by 'kneeling ladies-in-waiting'. The only painting of this subject listed in the seventeenth and eighteenth century inventories of the Madrid Royal Palace is the one now at the Prado, in which Velázquez wears no cape and is not glancing at the Infanta, nor is the Infanta having her hair dressed. Kubler has suggested that 'Costa must have been looking at a lost drawing or canvas prior to the state we now see' in the Prado painting. The main difficulty with this hypothesis, acknowledged by Kubler, is that Costa begins his description with an elaborate discussion of the cross of Santiago, which he believes was painted by Velázquez himself, and which, as we know, could not have been painted till at least a few years after the painting was completed. Since there is no positive indication that Costa was ever in Spain, it may well be that his inaccurate idea of the composition of *The royal family* sprang from his recollection of an oral description, which might have been provided, among others, by his brother and fellow painter, Bras d'Almeida (1649–1707), who had been in Spain before 1677.

In 1690, the Count of Monterrey bought a picture, not attributed to any particular painter, which apparently was a copy of *The royal family*, described as representing the Infanta Margarita and 'Velázquez painting a dog lying on the floor'. As I have suggested elsewhere, this may have been the picture which was regarded as an original sketch by Velázquez late in the eighteenth and early in the nineteenth century and which is actually a fairly faithful copy of the painting now at the Prado, including, of course, the cross of Santiago (*Velázquez: A Catalogue Raisonné of his Oeuvre*, no. 230, plate 232).

on the rear wall, over the mirror, the only ones whose subjects are recognizable. In fact, their originals were Rubens's *Pallas and Arachne* and Jordaens's *Apollo and Marsyas*. As we know, Mazo's copies of these two paintings hung side by side on the same wall in the chamber portrayed by Velázquez.

During the last two decades or so, the Velázquez' self-portrait has been linked to the two mythological pictures seen dimly in the background of the composition. It has been argued that, since these pictures, *Pallas and Arachne* and *Apollo and Marsyas*, 'symbolize the victory of divine art over human craftsmanship, or the victory of true art over unskilfulness', they ought to be taken as 'commentaries which explain the inspired attitude' in which Velázquez depicted himself, in 'a moment of suspense', concentrating 'on the inner image' which the sixteenth-century mannerists called *disegno interno* as distinct from *disegno esterno*, the latter being definable as the putting on canvas of the artist's inner image. As has been remarked, this interpretation 'takes Velázquez out of his own age and places him in the Cinquecento'.[1] It, moreover, casts a creative painter in the implausible role of a scholiast.

Velázquez, when in his teens, was acquainted with mannerist theory and practice at Pacheco's workshop, as can be gathered from the latter's *Arte de la Pintura*, and even from one or two of Velázquez's earliest works. However, as Pacheco's account of his apprentice days reveal, and as most of his youthful works show, it took Velázquez little time to reject mannerist ideas as lifeless, which they certainly were by then.

This is not to imply that Velázquez, who years earlier had painted *The fable of Arachne*, was unaware of, or indifferent to, the symbolic meaning of the two pictures over the mirror on whose surface he portrayed the King and the Queen as reflected images. He was doubtless as aware of that symbolism as he was also of the current concept that exalted the true-to-life likeness of a portrait by comparing it with the image of the sitter reflected in a mirror. Yet, it would be meaningless to reduce the significance of Velázquez's masterpiece to an illustration of either of these ideas, or both, which were part of the small coin current at the time.

Van Eyck's portrait of *Arnolfini and his wife*, of 1434, where the images of persons not otherwise included in the composition are reflected in a background mirror, was in the Spanish royal collection in Velázquez's time (plate 7). There can be no doubt that Velázquez knew it, and hence he might have had it in mind at one time or another during the composition of *The royal family*. Nor can there be any doubt that the composition of this work is essentially different from Van Eyck's, where the convex mirror on the rear wall reflects, not only the two men coming in through a door at the opposite end of the room, but also, and equally distinctly, the other three walls and the back view of the two sitters, none of whom is related by action or gesture to the space lying out of the picture frame (plate 7). Grouped together, indeed, they centre about themselves the space of the interior, which the reflection in the mirror makes the more definite. This has little in common with *The royal family*, the closest and most meaningful antecedent to which is to be found within Velázquez's own *oeuvre*, in his *Christ in*

[1] Cf. Charles de Tolnay, 'Velázquez's "Las Hilanderas" and "Las Meninas"', *Gazette des Beaux-Arts*, vol. 35, 1949, pp. 21–38, and Karl M. Birkmeyer, 'Realism and Realities in the Painting of Velázquez', *Gazette des Beaux-Arts*, vol. 52, 1958, pp. 63–80.

the house of Martha and Mary, painted almost forty years earlier, in Seville, before he could have seen the Arnolfini portrait at Madrid (plate 5).

Radiographs of *The royal family* have shown that Velázquez introduced several changes in the process of composition which, as we know, was often one with that of execution (plate 155). He made slight changes in most of the figures, and altered his own pose. He had sketched himself at first with his head bent to his right rather than to his left as he appears in the painting; there is no indication, however, that he depicted himself at any time looking at the Infanta or at any other of the figures in the group behind which he stands. As for the figures in this group — the Infanta, the two *meninas* and the two dwarfs — no major change is noticeable in any of them. A highlighted shape revealed by the X-rays between the figure of the painter and the edge of the canvas he is painting on might be the head of a wimpled woman, perhaps that of Doña Marcela de Ulloa who, stands at the opposite side in the finished painting, forming a group with a man, who like herself, is an attendant to the ladies-in-waiting.

As Velázquez completed it, the group portrait has three foci: the figure of the Infanta Margarita is the most luminous; the likeness of the Master himself is another; and the third is provided by the half-length images of the King and the Queen in the mirror on the rear wall. He built the composition on live diagonals, anchoring it, as it were, on the two which intersect at about the spot where the Infanta stands, and encompass at one end the shining mirror and the lit-up doorway and at the other the expanse of light which fans out in the foreground. The interlocking of these luminous areas is the more vivid as the middle distance is cut off by the shadows which spread across the floor. The depth of the chamber is stressed by the alternation of window jambs and picture frames on the right-hand wall, the stretcher of the large canvas on the left foreground, and the perspective sequence of the empty lamp hooks on the ceiling, which mark as central the spot in the rear wall where the King and the Queen are seen reflected in the mirror. In no other painting has Velázquez rendered space in so architectural a manner as in this, the only work in which he has depicted a ceiling. Neither is there any other composition of his which is so vividly keyed to the space lying out of the picture frame.

The Infanta, one of her *meninas*, the girl dwarf, the courtier in the rear doorway, and the painter himself are looking, each from a different point, into the space outside the field of the composition, where the sovereigns supposedly stand. At the same time the viewer's attention is compelled to the half-length images of the King and the Queen reflected in the background — again a painting, fancied as a reality, within the painting. Thus, an interplay of variable distances to and from an outer focal point is established which spans, and hence underlines, the chasm between the realm of painting and the realm of reality.

It has been pointed out in various ways that there is no other canvas that Velázquez brushed in more broadly or accented with sharper strokes; it has also been noted that 'the unusual disproportion' between the height of the canvas and the figures leaves a large space above their heads, which contributes both to the truthfulness and the airiness of the composition.[1] Certainly

[1] Beruete, *Velázquez*, p. 117.

VELÁZQUEZ' WORK AND WORLD

Velázquez has harmonized roughened-out shapes and striking vivacities of touch with a sharply delineated perspective setting in a manner which makes vivid at one and the same time the world around him and his depiction of it. He has portrayed himself, his brush in his right hand, a palette and a mahlstick in the other,[1] and the key of his office of Chamberlain at his belt, at work on a canvas. His face and his hands are lit up as he stands in the area of shadow which fills most of the composition. As a foil to this self-contained figure, there are, at the other side, the shadowed shapes of two Court attendants engaged in conversation.

The painting that Velázquez portrayed himself working on is not shown. Instead, the back is depicted, the stark structure of the stretcher and the easel and the coarse texture of the canvas, its uneven edge lit up along the upright board, sharply rendered. As somewhat of a contrast, the artist's right hand is luminously modelled, the fingers tapering to the point where they hold the slender brush, unerringly shaped by strokes of light. The poise of the hand as he holds the brush in readiness between the palette and the canvas is coupled with the expression in his eyes — one of sentient contemplation of the scene towards which he is gazing.

Several scholars have speculated whether the Master represented himself portraying the Infanta, who is being offered a drink of water, or the King and the Queen whose images are mirrored in the background, or, as the large size of the canvas would suggest, painting the very composition in which he included his own likeness with those of the royal persons. Whatever the particular subject, which it is idle to try to identify, he evidently portrayed himself in the act of putting on canvas a composition drawn from the life eddying about him at the Royal Palace.

The vast ceiling, without decoration but for the two empty lamp hooks, underlines the bareness of the chamber, unfurnished, and unadorned except for the pictures and the mirror on the walls — a state which could hardly have been the actual case with Velázquez's workshop. This bareness, further emphasized by the stark view of the upright canvas on which the Master is seen at work, sets off the radiant and richly textured group of the Infanta and her entourage, and makes the whole into a world of painting, where the narratives of the ancient myths of art are dimly seen in the distance, and the painted images, more vivid than a mirror's, people the empty space of the room, or, for that matter, the blank canvas.

There is in *The royal family* a starry interplay of ambivalences, with one slant spanning the gulf between the realm of painting and the realm of reality, another underscoring both the Infanta's regal bearing and her childish charm, a third offering a luminous view of Philip's forlorn Court, and yet another making vivid at one and the same time the compass of Velázquez's world — his circumstance — and the might of his brushstroke.

VELÁZQUEZ KNIGHTED

The hope of being knighted must have entered Velázquez's mind rather early, not later than his first Italian journey. In 1632, Pacheco punctually noted that in that year he had learned

---

[1] Some scholars have remarked that the palette in Velázquez's hand is too small; it is not smaller than the one in the *Self-portrait* by Pedro de Moya (1610–74), at the Museum of Bordeaux. Obviously, so small a palette was not unusual in the seventeenth century.

from his son-in-law that the King of France, aware of Giuseppe d'Arpino's dissatisfaction with the none-too-prominent order of which he was a knight, had appointed him to a more prestigious one, sending him his new robes, a gold chain and a sword. Pacheco rounded off the paragraph which contains this piece of information — the last bit in chapter VII of *Arte de la Pintura* — with the statement that the Pope had bestowed the mantle of the Order of Christ on the Spaniard Jusepe Ribera. Pacheco, moreover, chose to open the following chapter, concerned in the main with an account of Velázquez's life, with a short narrative of the successes of Diego de Romulo Cincinato — a now obscure Spanish painter — knighted in 1625 by the Pope, and Peter Paul Rubens, who, though already a knight, was knighted again by Charles I of England.[1] Long as he lived, Pacheco did not see his son-in-law knighted. Back in Rome in 1650, Velázquez, after his success with the portrait of Innocent X, secured, as mentioned above, the Pope's support for his desire to be made a knight of one of the Spanish military orders.

For the Master, the 1650's were marked by events of sorrow and joy which underscored the fullness, success and melancholy of his last years. On 5 November 1652, his seventh and last grandchild was born. Not much later, its mother, Velázquez's only remaining child, died. On 3 November 1654, Inés de Silva Velázquez, his granddaughter, married Dr. Onofrio de Lefranchi, who received an appointment as magistrate to the Court of Justice of his native Naples, granted expressly by Philip IV as a dowry for the Master's granddaughter. Lefranchi died in 1657 at Naples, and Velázquez had to send Mazo there, apparently to expedite the recovery of Inés's dowry. The King helped with the expenses of Mazo's journey out of the royal 'secret funds', appointed him assistant to the Chamberlain of the Royal Palace, that is, to Velázquez, and authorized him to pass on to his son Gaspar the position of Usher of the Chamber which twenty-four years earlier Velázquez had passed to his son-in-law as dowry for his daughter, Gaspar's mother. Velázquez's patriarchal contentment must have been broken when his two-and-a-half-year-old great-grandson, Jerónimo Lefranchi, who was living under his roof, died on 27 March 1658. Within three months of the melancholy event, Philip IV appointed Velázquez to the Order of Santiago, decreeing that the inquiry required for the investiture be promptly opened.

Two great masters, Velázquez's friends since his youth, were then at Madrid. Alonso Cano (1601–67), for a while Velázquez's fellow apprentice at Pacheco's workshop, had been at the Court for some time, engaged in litigation with the canons of the Cathedral of Granada, who had deprived him of the prebendary which he had held for several years; thanks to the King's support, a decision had recently been rendered in his favour. Francisco de Zurbarán (1598–1664) had just arrived in Madrid, where, as it turned out, he stayed till his death. At Seville, his reputation, as well as his income, had been declining for some time, rather understandably for he had let his towering personality be lessened by the steady and mediocre output of his workshop, which he ran with little concern for true values. At Madrid, he was to display again a sense of artistic integrity, though too late for him to win back his old prestige.

As it happened, the rising star of Sevillian painting, Bartolomé Esteban Murillo (1617–82) had also arrived at Madrid for a visit a few months earlier, and he was probably still there when

[1] Pacheco, *Arte de la Pintura*, vol. I, pp. 149–54.

the appointment of Velázquez to the Order of Santiago, a milestone in the painters' struggle for social status, became known.

In compliance with the rules of the Order, an inquiry was opened in Tuy, Verín, Vigo and other Spanish places near Portugal, as well as in Seville and Madrid, to determine whether Velázquez's ancestry was free from any Jewish or Moorish strain, and whether he descended from the nobility on both his paternal and his maternal side. One hundred and forty-odd witnesses came forward to testify in the affirmative. Several of them were aristocrats, such as the Marquis of Malpica, who, putting aside old rivalries, described himself as Velázquez's colleague in the royal service. Among the fellow artists were Zurbarán, Cano, Nardi, and Burgos Mantilla, as well as Juan Carreño de Miranda (1619–71) and Sebastián de Herrera Barnuevo (1614–85) from the younger generation.

Another point to be proved was that Velázquez had never had a shop of any sort or practiced any menial craft or occupation. Luckily, the rules of the Order, as revised in 1653, stated that only those painters who practiced their art as a trade should be regarded as engaged in a menial occupation.[1] Velázquez's friends took full advantage of this loophole. Reading their testimonies in the light of what we know of his life, it is obvious that many of them, including Cano who some months earlier had been ordained as a priest, were so bent on securing the knighthood for Velázquez that, though they were under oath, they felt free to stretch, or even to disregard, the truth. They affirmed, for instance, that the Master had not studied his art under another painter, or had ever had a workshop in the professional sense, not even at Seville, or sold any of his paintings, and that, in fact, he had always painted either for his own pleasure or for that of the King.

The stumbling block was the nobility of Velázquez's ancestors, which could not be substantiated, particularly on his mother's side. Early in April 1659, the outcome was still unpromising. At that point, however, the King decided to take a short cut through the maze of red tape and instructed his ambassador at Rome to request from the Pontiff, then Alexander VII, the issuance of a brief exempting Velázquez from the proof of nobility. The Pope complied promptly with the royal request, and on 28 November 1659, Philip invested his favourite painter with the Order of Santiago, thus fulfilling the Master's high hope.

Earlier, in 1657, Baltasar Gracián, a writer widely admired for his subtlety, had depicted the heroes of his allegorical novel, *El criticón*, setting out for the Isle of Immortality in a sloop of everlasting cedar, whose golden oars were like feathers and whose sails looked like canvases painted by either the ancient Timantes or 'the modern Velázquez'.[2]

THE HALL OF MIRRORS

The weariness which had pervaded the ageing Spanish monarchy for years and which Quevedo, an early admirer of Velázquez, had keenly expressed in 1643, when he was

---

[1] *Regla, y establecimientos, de la Orden y Cavalleria del glorioso Apostol Santiago, Patrón de las Españas, con la historia del origen y principio de ella*, Madrid, 1655, fol. 57 v.

[2] Third part, last chapter (or *crisi*).

released from a long imprisonment after Olivares's downfall, became more and more evident throughout the 1650's with Philip's own increasing penury and lack of purpose. Yet the splendid refurbishing of the Royal Palace went on.

On 22 October 1659, the Duke of Gramont, who had come to the Spanish Court as ambassador to request the hand of the Infanta María Teresa for Louis XIV, admired the paintings hanging in the chamber where he was received by Philip IV, and expressed the wish of seeing the rest of the royal collection. Velázquez took him on a tour of the Palace, where the new Hall of Mirrors had just been completed.[1]

The Master had designed and supervised the refurbishing of this hall, which derived its new name from the Venetian mirrors prominent in Velázquez's overall decorative scheme. The subject of the whole fresco ceiling decoration, divided into five sections, was the fable of Pandora; the painting of the various scenes had been entrusted to Agostino Mitelli and Michele Colonna, whom Velázquez had engaged to come to Spain years earlier, and to the younger Spaniards, Juan Carreño de Miranda and Francisco Rizi de Guevara (1608–85), who assisted them. On the walls hung oil paintings, all in black frames, by Titian, Tintoretto, Veronese, Rubens, José de Ribera, and Velázquez; most of them were mythological compositions, though there were several biblical subjects too. Four focal points were provided by large portraits of the monarchs from the reigning Spanish dynasty: Titian's *Charles V at the battle of Mühlberg* (plate 78) and *Philip II after the battle of Lepanto* (Prado, no. 431), Velázquez's *Philip III and the expulsion of the Moriscos from Spain*, and Rubens' *Philip IV equestrian with the allegorical figures of Faith and Divine Justice*.

The mythological compositions painted by Velázquez for the Hall of Mirrors were *Apollo flaying Marsyas*, *Mercury and Argus*, *Venus and Adonis*, and *Psyche and Cupid*. Three of them, as well as the portraits of Philip III and Philip IV mentioned above, were destroyed in the fire that gutted the Palace in 1734. Rescuers, however, succeeded in cutting *Mercury and Argus* out of its frame; like its lost companion piece, *Apollo flaying Marsyas*, it hung in a narrow space above a large window, which explains the somewhat unusual proportions of the canvas, the height of which was originally one-third of its width. Sometime between 1746 and 1772, narrow strips were added at the bottom and the sides of the canvas, and a substantially larger one at the top, with the result that the height, originally about 0·835 m., was increased by half to its present 1·27 m. (plate 158).

For all the monumentality of the figures, which gives depth and breadth to the composition, Velázquez has once more stressed the denseness of the world of the fable in *Mercury and Argus*, broadly brushed-in. As dark tints make both Argus and Mercury almost faceless, the highlights on their bodies accent the murderous treachery of the action depicted. Argus, in black and grey rags, is weighted down by sleep in the shadow of the cave, as Mercury, wrapped in a red and dull-yellow cloth, steals in on his knees, while the earthen reddish blob of Io, the heifer, quietly outlines itself against both the shadows of the cave and the distant cloudy sky.

[1] Palomino, *El Museo Pictórico*, p. 929.

THE LAST WORKS

The last years of Velázquez's life were a time of melancholy dismay for many a perceptive Spaniard. Philip IV, after the solemn reburial of his ancestors in the Pantheon of the Escorial, had become even more painfully aware of his inadequacies as a king, and watched more helplessly than ever the threatening march of world events. Reverses of every kind — military, diplomatic, commercial — only compounded by the self-righteous thought and actions with which they were met, had been for over two decades steadily narrowing the approaches of the Spanish monarchy to the present and to the future.

The French proposal for the marriage of Louis XIV with his cousin María Teresa, which the Infanta contemplated with cheerfulness, had been looked upon with distrust by many Spaniards who feared that it might result in the political union of France and Spain under a French king. It was only after the birth of Prince Felipe Próspero, on 20 November 1657, that those fears were allayed, and the marriage of the French king and the Spanish Infanta was agreed upon. In the event, even this prudently delayed action proved precipitate. The heir to the throne, on whom the hopes for the continuity of the Spanish monarchy were pinned, was a sickly child from birth, and despite the great care taken to protect him against both infectious diseases and the evil eye, he died before reaching his fourth birthday, little more than a year after the marriage of his half-sister and the King of France.

In 1659, Philip commanded Velázquez to paint the portraits of Felipe Próspero and his sister, the Infanta Margarita, for Emperor Leopold I, whom she was to marry years later. These two paintings, still extant, together with a lost miniature portrait of Queen Mariana, were, as far as it is known, the last works painted by Velázquez.

Margarita was then eight years old, and Felipe Próspero about two, somewhat younger than Velázquez's great-grandson had been on his death the year before. The portrait of the *Infanta Margarita* was altered into an oval shape in the eighteenth century (plate 159). Though now skilfully restored, it lacks the sense of depth that it must have had originally when the chariot of the Sun could be distinctly seen circling around the numerals of the hours on the face of the huge clock in the background. Still, the blue-clad Infanta appears encompassed by the ochre hues of the clock and the sideboard on which it stands and those of the fur muff she holds in her hand. For pervasive harmony of colour, this portrait must have been — and to a considerable extent still is — an outstanding work. Everything is keyed to the Infanta's blue eyes and pearly face, faintly rouged, and framed by the pale gold of her hair and necklace: the gold and faded red of the hanging on the wall, the golden yellow of the *passementerie* gimp across her bust and of the gilt-bronze lions on the sideboard, the silver trimmings on the blue velvet costume, and the greenish touches which lighten this blue, harmonizing it with the tint that suffuses her white collar, undersleeves, and wrist cuffs.

As for *Prince Felipe Próspero* (colour plate VI), Velázquez represented him wearing a silver-banded rose dress under a transparent white pinafore against which a pomander ball, to prevent infection, and several amulets to ward off the evil eye, are conspicuous. He does not appear to be

143

quite two years old; indeed, he looks scarcely older than the sixteen months that Baltasar Carlos was when, twenty-eight years earlier, the Master portrayed him — at a time when the Monarchy appeared still as a living idea and a boundless reality to sensitive Spaniards.

In that earlier portrait of *Baltasar Carlos* (plate 68), Velázquez included the figure of a dwarf, whose shape and gesture are a foil to the majestic bearing and pose of the Prince, who towers over his surroundings. In the painting of Felipe Próspero, a playful little dog — one which, according to Palomino, was very dear to Velázquez[1] — brings a note of warmth into the composition where the frail figure of the Prince is seen against a looming space. The purplish hues dominant in either portrait are about all that the two works have in common.

A rug, red and brown on light blue, marks out a rectangle where the Prince stands by a short-legged armchair set at a diagonal to the full-size stool at his back. He rests a hand on the gold-braided armchair, where the dog is curled, and his silver and rose cap lies casually on the silver-tasselled cushion which builds up the height of the stool — a compositional scheme which emphasizes the stature of the Prince child without dwarfing him. The live diagonal rhythm is furthered by the perspective relation between the lit-up purplish drapery hanging from above in the foreground and the one shadowed forth near the half-lighted doorway at the rear.

The bloodless face of the blue-eyed Felipe Próspero is modelled with greyish tints, which also tinge the top of the white pinafore, where the rose shoulder bow is set off by a vivid blue shadow; the Prince, in his white, silver and rose dress, looks all the paler as highlights silver his straw-coloured hair. The cheerless half-light coming from the distant doorway adumbrates a high floor line and accents the vertical lines of a wainscoted door against whose bottom panels the head of the Prince is perspectively set. Thus, the vastness of the chamber is stressed, and the shadowy space is made to loom over the Prince child, whose melancholy shape and comely bearing are enhanced by the brilliancy and casualness of his immediate surroundings. It is a somewhat dramatic portrait, painted with as much warmth as sentience, the first royal portrait in which Velázquez embodied a dismal sentiment. As it happened, it was one of his very last works.

LAST SERVICE TO THE KING, AND DEATH

From October 1659 till the following Spring, Velázquez, as Chamberlain of the Palace, was busy with the arrangements for the Spanish section of the building erected on the Isle of Pheasants, off Fuenterrabía, in the North of Spain, close to France, where peace between the two countries was to be formalized and the Infanta María Teresa given in marriage to Louis XIV. After deciding on the decoration and choosing the tapestries for the Spanish rooms, Velázquez left Madrid on 8 April 1660, two weeks ahead of the King, to attend to one of his duties, the preparation of lodgings for the royal party along the route to Fuenterrabía. He was accorded the use of a travelling litter for the journey, which he made in twenty-four days, accompanied by a crew of workers riding on mules.

On 7 June Velázquez, wearing a gold chain from which hung the diamond-studded badge

[1] *El museo pictórico*, p. 929.

VI. Velázquez, Prince Felipe Próspero. 1659. *Vienna, Kunsthistorisches Museum*

of the Order of Santiago, was one of the magnificently dressed courtiers present at the great hall when Philip led the Infanta from the Spanish section — decorated with a series of tapestries of the Apocalypse — to the French side, decked with hangings from the series of Scipio and Hannibal. The following day, he started on his way back to Madrid, this time with the royal party. He arrived home on the 26th, much to the relief of his family and friends, for rumours of his death had circulated at the Court. He felt 'weary of travelling by night and working by day, but in good health', as he wrote to Diego Valentín Díaz, a fellow painter whom he had just seen at Valladolid during a five-day stop on the return trip, to whom he also told that Queen Mariana and Prince Felipe Próspero, who had stayed at the Court, looked 'very pretty'.

Routine matters were awaiting him at the Palace, and he had to busy himself with payments due to others for services rendered or small purchases made in the course of the royal journey. On 1 July, he went to a bullfight, as he did on occasion; it turned out to be a rather simple affair, without horsemen, which made him and other courtiers think of the more elaborate one they had watched with the King a few days earlier at Valladolid.

On 31 July he had been for the whole morning attending the King at the Palace when he felt fatigued and feverish, and had to retire to his apartments. Philip sent two of his doctors to care for him and, on hearing that there was little or no hope of recovery, he asked the Patriarch of the Indies, Archbishop Don Alfonso Pérez de Guzmán, to assist his dying painter.

Death came to Velázquez on Friday, 6 August 1660. His body, clothed in the robes of the Order of Santiago, lay in state in his bedroom, where an altar was erected, till the following night when he was buried in the church of San Juan Bautista at solemn services attended by titled aristocrats and royal servants. His wife, who survived him by only seven days, was also buried there. Nothing remains of either their tomb or the church of San Juan Bautista.

A few years later, Louis XIV had a series of tapestries made, under the direction of his favourite painter, Charles Lebrun, to commemorate his marriage to María Teresa. One of them represents the meeting of the French and the Spanish kings in the grand hall at the Isle of the Pheasants, each surrounded by his Court, and depicting the Spaniards and the French as quite different in costume and bearing from each other (plate 172). Lebrun portrayed Philip in a graceful stance though aged and somewhat stoop-shouldered; as for the Infanta, he made her figure stand out rather ungracefully by the use of a perspective which emphasizes the bulk and stiffness of her farthingale. To the student of Velázquez, Philip IV and the Infanta María Teresa appear miscast in Lebrun's somewhat anecdotal portrayal of courtly pomp, a world alien to that of sheer monarchical sentiment into which the Spanish master had fashioned his royal sitters.

Like other truly great masters, Velázquez was more a creator than a recorder of his epoch, and it is so that his work — where he gave sentient shape to the divine persons, the King, the aristocrat, the dwarf, the artist, and plain men and women, and religious belief, mythological scenes and man-made events — lives, unique and communing, in the continuum of historical time, and hence, in our present.

BIBLIOGRAPHIC REGISTER

The following list includes only the publications cited in the preceding pages.

AINAUD, J., 'Ribalta y Caravaggio', *Anales y Boletín de los Museos de Arte de Barcelona*, July–Dec. 1947. *See p. 24, n. 2; p. 37, n. 2.*

ALEMÁN, Mateo, *Guzmán de Alfarache* (first published, Madrid, 1599), edited by Samuel Gil y Gaya, Madrid, 1965. *See p. 87, n. 3.*

ALLENDE-SALAZAR, Juan (ed.), *Velázquez. Des Meisters Gemälde*, vol. VI of *Klassiker der Kunst*, 4th ed., Berlin and Leipzig, 1925. *See p. 12, n. 3, p. 87, n. 4.*

—— in the catalogue of the exhibition, *From Greco to Goya*, held at the gallery of Tomás Harris Ltd., London, 1938. *See p. 12, n. 3.*

ANGULO IÑIGUEZ, Diego, *Velázquez: Como compuso sus principales cuadros*, Madrid, 1947. *See p. 102, n. 2.*

—— 'Las Hilanderas', *Archivo Español de Arte*, vol. 21, Madrid, Jan.–March 1948. *See p. 105, n. 2; p. 107, n. 1.*

—— 'La cuerna de venado, cuadro de Velázquez', *Reales Sitios*, vol. 4, Madrid, 1967. *See p. 51, n. 1.*

See also MENÉNDEZ PIDAL, Gonzalo.

ARETINO, Pietro, *Lettere*, Paris, 1609. *See p. 73, n. 1.*

ASENSIO, José María, *Francisco de Pacheco: sus obras artísticas y literarias*, Seville, 1886. *See p. 23, n. 4; p. 31, n. 4.*

ASTRANA MARÍN, Luis, *see* QUEVEDO.

BACK-VEGA, Emmerich and Christa, 'A lost masterpiece by Caravaggio', *The Art Bulletin*, New York, March 1958. *See p. 37, n. 2.*

BARRY, G., *The Siege of Breda*, Louvain, 1627. *See p. 76, n. 1.*

BAXANDAL, David, 'A dated Velázquez bodegón', *The Burlington Magazine*, vol. 99, London, 1957. *See p. 28, n. 1.*

BEROQUI, Pedro, *El Museo del Prado*, Madrid [1933]. *See p. 65, n. 3 and p. 81, n. 1.*

—— *Ticiano en el Museo del Prado*, Madrid, 1946. *See p. 59, n. 1.*

BERUETE, Aureliano de, *Velázquez*, Paris, 1898; English edition, revised by the author, London, n.d. [1906]; German edition, newly revised by the author, Berlin, 1909. *See p. 12, n. 2; p. 28, n. 1; p. 35, n. 1; p. 58, n. 1; p. 61, n. 2; p. 63, n. 1; p. 71, n. 1; p. 87, n. 4; p. 93, n. 2; p. 103, n. 1; p. 104, n. 1; p. 119, n. 1; p. 129, n. 1; p. 138, n. 1.* (Unless otherwise indicated, references are to the English edition.)

—— *El Velázquez de Parma*, Madrid, 1911. *See p. 12, n. 2; p. 96, n. 1.*

BIRKMEYER, Karl, 'Realism and Realities in the Paintings of Velázquez', *Gazette des Beaux-Arts*, vol. 52, Paris, July–Aug. 1958. *See p. 108, n. 4; and p. 137, n. 1.*

BLANCO, A., *Museo del Prado, Catálogo de la escultura*, Madrid, 1957. *See p. 132, n. 2.*

BLECUA, José Manuel, *see* QUEVEDO.

BOCÁNGEL Y UNZUETA, Gabriel de, *La Lira de las Musas*, Madrid [1637]. *See p. 93, n. 1.*

—— *Piedra cándida*, etc., Madrid, 1648. *See p. 111, n. 1.*

BOSCHINI, Mario, *La carta del navegar pitoresco*, Venice, 1660. *See p. 112, n. 2.*

BOTTINEAU, Yves, 'L'Alcázar de Madrid et l'inventaire de 1686', *Bulletin Hispanique*, Bordeaux, Oct.–Dec. 1958. *See p. 134, n. 3.*

—— 'Felipe V y el Buen Retiro', *Archivo Español de Arte*, vol. 31, Madrid, 1958. *See p. 65, n. 1.*

BRAHAM, Allan, 'A second dated bodegón by Velázquez', *The Burlington Magazine*, vol. 107, London, 1965. *See p. 28, n. 1.*

CAMÓN AZNAR, José, *Velázquez*, Madrid, 1964. *See p. 13, n. 4; p. 62, n. 2.*

CARDERERA Y SOLANO, Valentin, *see* MARTÍNEZ.

CARDUCHO, Vincencio, *Diálogos de la Pintura*, Madrid, 1633. *See p. 37, n. 3; p. 46, ns. 1 and 2.*

CATURLA, María Luisa, *Pinturas, frondas y fuentes del Buen Retiro*, Madrid, 1947. *See p. 65, n. 1.*

—— 'El coleccionista madrileño don Pedro de Arce, que poseyó "Las Hilanderas" de Velázquez', *Archivo Español de Arte*, vol. 21, Madrid, Oct.–Dec. 1948. *See p. 105, n. 2.*

—— *Un pintor gallego en la corte de Felipe IV: Antonio Puga*, Santiago de Compostela, 1952. *See p. 65, n. 1.*

—— 'Cartas de pago de los doce cuadros de batalles para el Salón de Reinos del Buen Retiro', *Archivo Español de Arte*, vol. 33, Madrid, 1960. *See p. 65, n. 1; p. 66, n. 1.*

CEÁN BERMÚDEZ, Juan Agustín, *Diálogo sobre el Arte de la Pintura*, Seville, 1819. *See p. 29, n. 1.*

CEDERLOF, Olle, 'Kallorna till "Las Lanzas"', *Konsthistorisk tidskrift*, vol. 26, Stockholm, 1957. *See p. 80, n. 3.*

CESPEDES Y MENESES, Gonzalo de, *Historia de Don Felipe IIII, Rey de las Españas*, Barcelona, 1634. *See p. 75, n. 1.*

CONNOISSEUR, THE, July, 1964. *See p. 40, n. 1.*

COROMINAS, J., *Diccionario crítico y etimológico de la lengua castellana*, Madrid, 1954. *See p. 87, n. 3.*

CORREA CALDERÓN, E., *see* GRACIÁN.

COSTA, Felix da, *The Antiquity of the Art of Painting*, edited by George Kubler, New Haven and London, 1967. *See pp. 135–6, n. 1.*

COTARELO Y MORI, Emilio, *Ensayo sobre la vida y obras de D. Pedro Calderón de la Barca*, Madrid, 1924. *See p. 76, n. 2.*

COVARRUVIAS I LEYVA, Diego de, *Elogios al Palacio Real de Buen Retiro escritos por algunos ingenios de España . . .* Madrid, 1635. Limited edition Valencia, 1949. *See p. 67, n. 1; p. 68, n. 1; p. 69, n. 1.*

CRUZADA VILLAAMIL, Gregorio, *Anales de la vida y de las obras de Diego de Silva Velázquez*, Madrid, 1885. *See p. 48, n. 2; p. 74, n. 1.*

DOLCE, Lodovico, *L'Aretino*, Venice, 1557. *See p. 25.*

FARAT, Honoré, *Persigny: Un ministre de Napoleon III, 1808–1872*, Paris, 1957. *See pp. 87–9, n. 4.*

FICHTER, William L., 'Una poesía contemporánea inédita sobre las bodas de Velázquez', *Varia velazqueña*, vol. I, Madrid, 1960. *See p. 27, n. 2.*

FRANCIS, Henry S., 'Velázquez: Portrait of the jester Calabazas', *The Bulletin of the Cleveland Museum of Art*, 1965. *See p. 87, n. 2.*

GARCÍA FIGAR, Fray Antonio, O. P., 'Fray Juan Bautista Maino, pintor español', *Goya*, Madrid, July–Aug. 1958. *See p. 37, n. 4.*

GAYA NUÑO, Juan Antonio, 'Revisiones sexcentistas: Juan de Pareja', *Archivo Español de Arte*, Madrid, 1957. *See p. 123, n. 2.*

—— 'Juan Bautista del Mazo, el gran discípulo de Velázquez', *Varia velazqueña*, vol. I, Madrid, 1960. *See p. 132, n. 3.*

GERSTENBERG, Kurt, *Diego Velázquez*, Munich and Berlin, 1957. *See p. 33, n. 1; p. 58, n. 1; p. 60, n. 2; p. 85, n. 2; p. 107, n. 1.*

GRACIÁN, Baltasar, *El político* (edited by E. Correa Calderón, foreword by E. Tierno Galván), Madrid, 1961. *See p. 73, n. 2.*

—— *El criticón*, III, Madrid, 1657 (Critical edition by M. Romera Navarro, Philadelphia, 1938). *See p. 141, n. 2.*

HASKELL, Francis, *Patrons and Painters*, London, 1963. *See p. 48, n. 2; p. 114, n. 1.*

HETZER, Theodor, *Tizian, Geschichte seines Farbe*, Frankfurt a/M, 1948. *See p. 25, n. 1.*

HILBORN, Harry Warren, *A Chronology of the Plays of D. Pedro Calderón de la Barca*, Toronto, 1938. *See p. 76, n. 2.*

HUGO, Herman, *The Siege of Breda* [Brussels?] 1627. *See p. 76, n. 1; p. 79, n. 1.*

IÑIGUEZ ALMECH, Francisco, *Casas reales y jardines de Felipe II*, Madrid, 1952. *See p. 134, n. 3.*

—— 'La Casa del Tesoro, Velázquez y las obras reales', *Varia velazqueña*, vol I, Madrid, 1960. *See p. 122, n. 2; p. 132, n. 1.*

JORDAN, William B., 'Juan van der Hamen y León: a Madrilenian Still-life Painter', *Marsyas*, New York, 1964–5 [printed 1966]. *See p. 38, n. 1.*

KUBLER, George, 'Vicente Carducho's allegories of Painting', *The Art Bulletin*, New York, Dec. 1965. *See p. 46, n. 1.*

—— 'Three remarks on The Meninas', *The Art Bulletin*, New York, June 1966. *See p. 136, n. 1. See also* COSTA.

LAFUENTE FERRARI, Enrique, *Velázquez*, London, 1953. *See p. 13, n. 2, n. 6; p. 74, n. 1; p. 93, n. 2; p. 106, n. 1.*

—— *Velázquez*, Barcelona, 1944. *See p. 13, n. 2; p. 93, n. 2; p. 106, n. 1.*

—— 'Velázquez y Felipe IV', *Mundo Hispánico*, Madrid, 1961. *See p. 13, n. 2.*

LÓPEZ JIMÉNEZ, José Crisanto, 'D. Nicolás de Villacis, discípulo de Velázquez', *Boletín del Seminario de Estudios de Arte y Arqueología*, Valladolid, 1964. *See p. 123, n. 1.*

LÓPEZ JIMÉNEZ, José, *see* PANTORBA.

LÓPEZ MARTINEZ, Celestino, *Desde Jerónimo Hernández hasta Martínez Montañés*, Seville, 1929. *See p. 21, n. 3.*

LÓPEZ NAVÍO, José, 'Velázquez tasa los cuadros de su protector D. Juan de Fonseca', *Archivo Español de Arte*, Madrid, Jan.–March 1961. *See p. 45, n. 1.*

BIBLIOGRAPHIC REGISTER

LÓPEZ-REY, José, 'Idea de la imitación barroca', *Hispanic Review*, vol. XI, Philadelphia, July 1943. *See p. 73, n. 1.*

—— 'A Pseudo Velázquez: the Picture of a Dwarf with a Dog', *Gazette des Beaux-Arts*, Paris, Oct.–Dec. 1950 [printed 1959]. *See p. 15, n. 2.*

—— 'A Head of Philip IV by Velázquez in a Rubens Allegorical Composition', *Gazette des Beaux-Arts*, Paris, Jan. 1959. *See p. 98, n. 1.*

—— 'Nombres y nombradía de Velázquez', *Goya*, Madrid, July–Oct. 1960. *See p. 20, n. 2.*

—— 'Pincelada e imagen en Velázquez', *Varia velazqueña*, vol. I, Madrid, 1960. *See p. 15, n. 3; p. 32, n. 2.*

—— *Velázquez: A Catalogue Raisonné of his Oeuvre*, London, 1963. *See p. 11, n. 1; p. 12, n. 1; p. 13, n. 6; p. 14, n. 1; p. 15, ns. 1 and 2; p. 19, n. 1; p. 28, n. 1; p. 30, n. 1; p. 31, n. 1; p. 33, n. 2; p. 43, n. 1; pp. 47–8, n. 1; p. 51, n. 1; p. 53, n. 1; p. 57, n. 1; pp. 87–9, n. 4; p. 103, n. 1; p. 106, n. 1; p. 116, n. 1; p. 122, n. 1; p. 124, n. 3; p. 125, n. 1; p. 134, ns. 1 and 2; pp. 135–6, n. 1.*

—— 'Maino y Velázquez: Dos retratos de Felipe IV en el Metropolitan Museum of Art de Nueva York', *Colóquio*, Lisbon, Oct. 1963. *See p. 42, n. 1.*

—— 'A portrait of Philip IV by Juan Bautista Maino', *The Art Bulletin*, New York, Dec. 1963. *See p. 42, n. 1.*

—— foreword to catalogue of exhibition *The Golden Age of Spanish Still-Life Painting*, Newark, N.J., 1964. *See p. 38, n. 1.*

—— 'An unpublished Zurburán: The surrender of Seville', *Apollo*, London, 1965. *See p. 80, n. 1.*

—— 'Sobre la atribución de un retrato de Felipe IV a Gaspar de Crayer', *Archivo Español de Arte*, Madrid, April–Sept. 1966. *See p. 42, n. 1.*

—— 'Velázquez's *Calabazas* with a portrait and a pinwheel', *Gazette des Beaux-Arts*, Paris, Oct. 1967. *See pp. 87–9, n. 4.*

LOZOYA, Marqués de, *La Rendición de Breda*, Barcelona, 1953. *See p. 75, n. 1.*

MACLAREN, Neil, *National Gallery Catalogues, The Spanish School*, London, 1952. *See p. 104, n. 2.*

MAHON, Denis, *Studies in Seicento Art and Theory*, London, 1947. *See p. 54, n. 1.*

MANCINI, Giulio, *Considerazioni sulla Pittura*, edited by Adriana Marucchi, Rome, 1956. *See p. 24, n. 1.*

MARAÑÓN, G., *El Conde-Duque de Olivares*, Madrid, 1952. *See p. 74, n. 1.*

MARINO, Giambattista, *Epitalami*, Venice, 1646. *See p. 105, n. 1.*

—— *La Galería del Cavalier Marino distinta in putture & sculture*, Venice, 1620. *See p. 86, ns. 1, 4.*

MARTÍNEZ, Jusepe, *Discursos practicables del nobilísimo arte de la pintura*, edited by Valentín Carderera y Solano, Madrid, 1866. *See p. 37, ns. 1 and 4; p. 80, n. 2; p. 96, n. 2; p. 110, n. 1; p. 133, n. 1.*

MAYER, August L., *Kleine Velázquez-studien*, Munich, 1913. *See p. 13, n. 1.*

—— 'Velázquez und die niederländischen Küchenstücke', *Kunstchronic und Kunstmarkt*, 3 Jan. 1919. *See p. 33, n. 1.*

MAYER, August, L., *Diego Velázquez*, Berlin and Leipzig, 1924. *See p. 13, n. 1; p. 33, n. 1.*

—— *Velázquez. A Catalogue Raisonné of the Pictures and Drawings*, London, 1936. *See p. 13, n. 1; p. 87, n. 4.*

—— *Velázquez*, Paris, 1940. *See p. 13, n. 1.*

MENÉNDEZ PIDAL, Gonzalo, and ANGULO IÑIGUEZ, Diego, ' "Las hilanderas" de Velázquez — Radiografías y fotografías en infrarrojo', *Archivo Español de Arte*, Madrid, Jan.–March 1965. *See p. 106, n. 2; p. 107, n. 1.*

MENÉNDEZ PIDAL, Ramón, 'Onomástica inspirada en el culto mariánico', *Cuadernos del Idioma*, vol. I, no. 1, Buenos Aires, 1965. *See p. 31, n. 3.*

MENGS, Anthony Raphael, *Obras*, Madrid, 1797 (1st edn., Madrid, 1780). The paper here referred to was written in 1776. *See p. 135, n. 1.*

MOREAU-NELATON, E., *Manet raconté par lui-meme*, Paris, 1926. *See p. 100, n. 1.*

MORENO VILLA, José, *Velázquez*, Madrid, 1920 (2nd edn., Malaga, 1961). *See p. 58, n. 1; p. 102, n. 2.*

—— *Locos, enanos, negros y niños palaciegos*, Mexico, 1939. *See p. 87, n. 1.*

MULLER, Priscilla E., 'Francisco Pacheco as a Painter', *Marsyas*, vol. X, New York, 1960–1. *See p. 34, n. 1.*

MUSEO DEL PRADO, *Catálogo de las pinturas*, Madrid, 1963. *See p. 12, n. 1; p. 15; p. 38, n. 2; p. 51, n. 1; p. 134, n. 1.*

ORBAAN, Johannes A. F., 'Notes on art in Italy', *Apollo*, London, July 1927. *See pp. 53–4, n. 2.*

OROZCO DÍAZ, Emilio, 'Un aspecto del barroquismo de Velázquez' *Varia velazqueña*, vol. I, Madrid, 1960. *See p. 33, n. 1.*

ORTEGA Y GASSET, José, *Papeles sobre Velázquez y Goya*, Madrid, 1950. *See p. 60, n. 1; p. 77, n. 2.*

PACHECO, Francisco, *Libro de descripción de verdaderos retratos . . .* Seville, n.d. *See p. 23, n. 4; p. 47, n. 1.*

—— *Arte de la Pintura*, edited by F. J. Sánchez Cantón, Madrid, 1956. *See p. 20, n. 1; p. 21, ns. 2 and 4; p. 22, n. 1; p. 23, ns. 1, 2 and 3; p. 24, ns. 3 and 4; p. 25, n. 2; p. 29, n. 1; p. 32, n. 1; p. 34, n. 1; p. 40, n. 1; p. 50, n. 1; p. 53, n. 2; p. 70, ns. 1 and 2; p. 72, n. 1; p. 140, n. 1.*

PALOMINO VELASCO, Antonio, *El Museo Pictórico*, Madrid, 1947 (1st edn., Madrid, 1724). *See p. 21, n. 1; p. 29, n. 1; pp. 53–4, n. 2; p. 112, n. 1; p. 114, ns. 1 and 3; p. 115, n. 1; p. 123, ns. 1 and 2; p. 134, n. 2; p. 142, n. 1; p. 144, n. 1.*

PANTORBA, Bernardino de [José López Jiménez], *La vida y la obra de Velázquez*, Madrid, 1955. *See p. 13, n. 3.*

—— *Sobre un retrato de la Reina Isabel de Borbon*, Madrid, 1960. *See p. 13, n. 3.*

—— *Sobre un retrato perdido de Velázquez*, Madrid, 1960. *See p. 13, n. 3.*

—— *Chiens par Don Diego de Velázquez*, Paris, 1960. *See p. 13, n. 3.*

—— *Velázquez en este momento*, Madrid, 1961. *See p. 13, n. 3.*

—— *Tutta la pittura de Velázquez*, Milan, 1964. *See p. 13, n. 3.*

PÉREZ DE MOYA, Juan, *Filosofía secreta*, Alcalá de Henares, 1611. *See p. 108, n. 3.*

PÉREZ SÁNCHEZ, Alfonso E., *Borgianni, Cavarozzi y Nardi en España*, Madrid, 1964. *See p. 36, n. 1; p. 48, n. 1.*

PIÇAÑO DE PALACIOS, Alvaro, *Discurso primero en confirmación de la purissima concepción de la Virgen María*, Seville, 1615. *See p. 31, n. 2.*

—— *Discurso segundo* etc., Seville, 1616. *See p. 31, n. 2.*

PICATOSTE, Felipe, *Estudios sobre la grandeza y decadencia de España*, III, *El siglo XVII*, Madrid, 1887. *See p. 104, n. 3.*

PICÓN, Jacinto Octavio, *Vida y obras de Don Diego Velázquez*, Madrid, 1899 (2nd edn., Madrid, 1925). *See p. 86, n. 3.*

PONZ, Antonio, *Viaje de España*, edited by C. M. del Rivero, Madrid, 1947. *See pp. 87–89, n. 4.*

QUEVEDO Y VILLEGAS, Francisco de, *Obras completas*, edited by Luis Astrana Marín, Madrid, 1932. *See p. 41, ns. 1 and 3; p. 47, n. 1.*

—— *Obras completas*, edited by José Manuel Blecua, Barcelona, 1963. *See p. 47, n. 1.*

Real Academia de San Fernando, *Distribución de los premios concedidos por el Rey N. S. a los discípulos de las tres nobles artes*, Madrid, 1760. *See p. 126, n. 1.*

Regla, y establecimientos, de la Orden y Cavalleria del glorioso Apostol Santiago, Patrón de las Españas, con la historia del origen y principio de ella, Madrid, 1655. *See p. 141, n. 1.*

RODRÍGUEZ VILLA, Antonio, *Ambrosio Spínola, primer Marqués de los Balbases*, Madrid, 1904. *See pp. 53–4, n. 2.*

ROMERA NAVARRO, M., see Gracián.

RÖTHLISBERGER, Marcel, *Claude Lorrain*, New Haven, 1961. *See p. 102, n. 1.*

SALTILLO, Marqués del, 'Artistas madrileños', *Boletín de la Sociedad Española de Excursiones*, Madrid, 1953. *See p. 38, n. 2.*

SÁNCHEZ CANTÓN, F. J., 'La Librería de Velázquez', *Homenaje a Don Ramón Menéndez Pidal*, vol. III, Madrid, 1925. *See p. 20, n. 3; p. 61, n. 1.*

—— *Fuentes literarias para la historia del arte español*, Madrid, 1933. *See p. 122, n. 3; p. 124, n. 1; p. 133, n. 2.*

—— *Las meninas y sus personajes*, Barcelona, 1952. *See p. 134, n. 3. See also* PACHECO.

SANCHEZ DE VIANA, Pedro, *Anotaciones sobre los quinze libros de las Trásformaciones de Ouidio* etc., Valladolid, 1589. *See p. 108, n. 2.*

SANTOS, Father Francisco de los, *Descripción breve del monasterio de S. Lorenzo el Real del Escorial*, Madrid, 1657. *See p. 41, n. 3; p. 130, n. 1.*

SAXL, F., 'Velázquez and Philip IV', *Lectures*, London, 1957. *See p. 72, n. 2; p. 75, n. 1; p. 79, n. 1.*

—— 'Rembrandt and Classical Antiquity', *Lectures*, London, 1957. *See p. 86, n. 1.*

SILVELA, Francisco (editor), *Cartas de la venerable Madre Sor María de Agreda y del Señor Rey Don Felipe IV*, Madrid, 1888. *See p. 130, n. 1.*

SOBRINO, Alfonso, *Tratado de la Immaculada Concepción*, Seville, 1615. *See p. 31, n. 2.*

SOEHNER, Halldor, 'Die Herkunft der Bodegones de Velázquez', *Varia velazqueña*, vol. I, Madrid, 1960. *See p. 33, n. 1.*

BIBLIOGRAPHIC REGISTER

Soria, Martin S., 'José Leonardo. Velázquez's best disciple', *The Art Quarterly*, Detroit, vol. 13, 1950. *See p. 80, n. 2.*

Tierno Galván, E., *see* Gracián.

Tietze-Conrat, E., *Dwarfs and Jesters in Art*, New York, 1957. *See p. 87, n. 1.*

Tolnay, Charles de, 'Velázquez's "Las Hilanderas" and "Las Meninas"', *Gazette des Beaux-Arts*, vol. 35, Paris, Jan. 1949. *See p. 94, n. 1; p. 107, n. 1; p. 108, n. 1; p. 137, n. 1.*

Tormo, Elias, 'Velázquez, el Salón de los Reinos del Buen Retiro, etc.' *Pintura, escultura y arquitectura en España. Estudios dispersos*, Madrid, 1949. *See p. 65, ns. 1 and 4.*

Trapier, Elisabeth du Gué, 'Velázquez. New Data on a Group of Portraits', *Notes Hispanic*, vol. IV, New York, 1944. *See p. 43, n. 1.*

—— *Velázquez*, New York, 1948. *See p. 23, n. 3; p. 27, n. 1; p. 40, n. 1; p. 74, n. 1; p. 86, n. 3; pp. 87–9, n. 4; p. 93, n. 2; p. 102, n. 2; p. 108, n. 4; p. 114, n. 2; p. 120, n. 1; p. 129, n. 1.*

Unamuno, Miguel de, *Niebla*, Madrid, 1914. *See p. 17, n. 1.*

Valverde Madrid, José, article in the newspaper *Informaciones*, Cordoba, 4 Nov. 1965. *See p. 114, n. 3.*

Waterhouse, Ellis, *Italian Baroque Painting*, London 1962. *See p. 55, n. 1.*

SELECTED BIBLIOGRAPHY

The following is a list of publications which have substantially enlarged, deepened or refined our knowledge of Velázquez's art or which have marked the main divergent approaches to the subject. I have also listed separately the most recent documentary and bibliographical compilations on the matter.

For a full discussion of problems of authenticity, dating or provenance concerning works by Velázquez or from his circle, I refer the reader to my *Velázquez: A Catalogue Raisonné of his Oeuvre*, London, Faber & Faber, 1963.

1855 — STIRLING, William, *Velazquez and his Works*, London; French translation, *Velazquez et ses oeuvres*, Paris, 1865 (with a catalogue of Velázquez's paintings by W. Bürger, pen name of Étienne Joseph Théophile Thoré).

1883 — CURTIS, Charles B., *Velázquez and Murillo*, London and New York.

1885 — CRUZADA VILLAAMIL, Gregorio, *Anales de la vida y de las obras de Diego de Silva Velázquez*, Madrid.

1888 — JUSTI, Karl, *Diego Velazquez und sein Jahrhundert*, Bonn; 2nd ed. revised by the author, Bonn, 1903; 3rd ed., Bonn, 1922; 4th ed. edited by Ludwig Justi, Zurich, 1933; English ed., somewhat abridged and revised by the author, *Diego Velazquez and his Times*, London, 1889; Spanish translation, *Velázquez y su siglo*, Madrid, 1953 (with an appendix, *Después de Justi*, by Juan Antonio Gaya Nuño); Italian translation, *Velazquez e il suo tempo*, Florence, 1958.

1895 — STEVENSON, R. A. M., *The Art of Velasquez*, London; 2nd, revised ed., *Velasquez*, London, 1899; German translation, *Velazquez*, Munich, 1904 (with an introduction by E. F. von Bodenhausen); 3rd ed., with a biographical study of the author by Denys Sutton, and annotated by Theodore Crombie, *Velázquez*, London, 1962.

1898 — BERUETE, Aureliano de, *Velázquez*, Paris; English edition, revised by the author, London, n.d. [1906]; German edition, newly revised by the author, Berlin, 1909.

1913 — MAYER, August L., *Kleine Velazquez-studien*, Munich.

1920 — MORENO VILLA, José, *Velázquez*, Madrid (2nd ed., Malaga, 1961).

1923 — RODRÍGUEZ MARÍN, Francisco, *Francisco Pacheco, maestro de Velázquez*, Madrid (with documents, including the inventory of Velázquez's library drawn up at the time of his death).

1924 — MAYER, August L., *Diego Velázquez*, Berlin and Leipzig.

1925 — ALLENDE-SALAZAR, Juan (ed.), *Velazquez. Des Meisters Gemälde*, vol. VI of *Klassiker der Kunst*, 4th ed., Berlin and Leipzig.

1936 — MAYER, August L., *Velázquez. A Catalogue Raisonné of the Pictures and Drawings*, London.

1947 — ANGULO IÑIGUEZ, Diego, *Velázquez: Cómo compuso sus principales cuadros*, Madrid.

1949 — BORELIUS, Aron, *Études sur Velázquez*, Linköping.

1950 — ORTEGA Y GASSET, José, *Papeles sobre Velázquez y Goya*, Madrid.

1957 — GERSTENBERG, Kurt, *Diego Velázquez*, Munich and Berlin.

1963 — LÓPEZ-REY, José, *Velázquez: A Catalogue Raisonné of his Oeuvre*, London.

1964 — CAMÓN AZNAR, José, *Velázquez*, Madrid.

★ ★ ★

1960 — Instituto Diego Velázquez, *Velázquez: Biografías de los siglos XVII y XVIII. Comentarios a él dedicados en los siglos XVII y XVIII. Su biografía a través de cartas y documentos contemporáneos. Autográfos. Facsimiles de documentos e impresos — Homenaje en el tercer centenario de su muerte*, Madrid.

1960 — Ministerio de Educación Nacional, Dirección General de Bellas Artes, *Varia velazqueña, Homenaje a Velázquez en el III centenario de su muerte. 1660–1960*, vol. II, *Elogios poéticos — Textos y comentarios críticos — Documentos — Cronología*, Madrid.

1963 — GAYA NUÑO, Juan Antonio, *Bibliografía crítica y antológica de Velázquez*, Madrid.

INDEX TO LOCATIONS

155

INDEX TO LOCATIONS

INDEX

INDEX

INDEX

INDEX

MONOCHROME PLATES

MONOCHROME PLATES*

1. Velázquez, Musical trio (0·87 × 1·1 m.). About 1617–18. *West Berlin, Staatliche Museen.*
2. Beuckelaer, Christ in the house of Martha and Mary (1·13 × 1·63 m.). 1565.
   Brussels, Musées Royaux.
3. Velázquez, Head of a girl (21·8 × 16·8 cm.). About 1617–18. *Madrid, private collection.*
4. Velázquez, Study of a head (0·39 × 0·355 m.). About 1618–19. *Hermitage.*
5. Velázquez, Christ in the house of Martha and Mary (0·6 × 1·035 m.). 1618.
   London, National Gallery.
6. Pacheco, St. Sebastian nursed by St. Irene (0·24 × 0·18 m.). 1616.
   Formerly, Alcalá de Guadaira, church of St. Sebastian; destroyed in 1936.
7. Jan van Eyck, Jan Arnolfini and his wife (0·818 × 0·597 m.). 1434.
   London, National Gallery.
8. Eugenio Caxés, The fall of the angels (0·74 × 0·41 m.). 1605.
   Copenhagen, Statens Museum for Kunst.
9. Sánchez Cotán, Still-life (0·69 × 0·89 m.). 1602. *Madrid, Duke of Hernani.*
10. Vincencio Carducho, Colossal head (2·46 × 2·05 m.). *Madrid, Academia de San Fernando.*
11. Vincencio Carducho, St. Bruno declining the archbishop's mitre (3·42 × 3·03 m.). 1632.
    Prado.
12. Vincencio Carducho, detail of painting shown on plate 11.
13. Velázquez, Three men at table (1·07 × 1·01 m.). About 1618. *Hermitage.*
14. Velázquez, Old woman frying eggs (0·99 × 1·169 m.). 1618. *Edinburgh, National Gallery.*
15. Caravaggio, Supper at Emmaus (1·39 × 1·95 m.). About 1598–1600.
    London, National Gallery.
16. Lanchares, Adoration of the shepherds (2·17 × 1·61 m.). 1612. *Madrid, art market.*
17. B. González, St. John the Baptist (1·50 × 0·90 m.). 1621. *Budapest, Hungarian Museum of Fine Arts.*
18. Velázquez, A girl and two men at table (0·96 × 1·12 m.). About 1618–19.
    Budapest, Hungarian Museum of Fine Arts.
19. Velázquez's follower, Three men at table (0·864 × 1·092 m.). *Andover, Hants, Lord Moyne.*
20. Velázquez, Christ at Emmaus (0·558 × 1·18 m.). About 1620–1.
    Blessington (Ireland), Beit Collection.
21. Velázquez, The servant (0·55 × 1·04 m.). About 1620–1. *Chicago, Art Institute.*
22. Velázquez, The waterseller (1·065 × 0·82 m.). About 1619–20.
    London, Wellington Museum.

* The author is grateful to the authorities of the Prado Museum who are completing a thorough check of the recorded sizes of the paintings in their collection and have made available to him the rectified measurements for some of the works reproduced in this book.

23. Velázquez, A man with a goatee (0·4 × 0·36 m.). About 1620. *Prado.*
24. Velázquez, A young man (0·56 × 0·39 m.). About 1618–19. *Prado.*
25. Velázquez, A young girl (15 × 11·7 cm.). About 1622. *Madrid, Biblioteca Nacional.*
26. Velázquez, A young girl (20 × 13·5 cm.). About 1622. *Madrid, Biblioteca Nacional.*
27. Velázquez, The Immaculate Conception (1·346 × 1·016 m.). About 1619.
    London, Frere Collection (on loan at the National Gallery).
28. Velázquez, St. John writing the Apocalypse (1·358 × 1·023 m.). About 1619.
    London, National Gallery.
29. Velázquez, Doña Jerónima de la Fuente (1·6 × 1·1 m.). 1620. *Prado.*
30. The same painting in its present condition.
31. Velázquez, Doña Jerónima de la Fuente (1·6 × 1·06 m.). 1620.
    Madrid, Fernández Araóz Collection.
32. Velázquez, Cristóbal Suárez de Ribera (1·97 × 1·42 m.). About 1618–20.
    Seville, San Hermenegildo.
33. Velázquez, Two young men at table (0·645 × 1·04 m.). About 1622.
    London, Wellington Museum.
34. Juan van der Hamen, Don Francisco de la Cueva (1·17 × 1·05 m.). 1625.
    Madrid, Academia de San Fernando.
35. Juan van der Hamen, Still-life (0·52 × 0·89). 1622. *Prado.*
36. Rubens, Philip IV (1·14 × 0·83 m.). 1628–9. *Hermitage.*
37. Maino, Philip IV (1·981 × 1·181 m.). 1623–4. *New York, Metropolitan Museum.*
38. Villandrando, Philip IV (2·01 × 1·1 m.). 1619–20. *Prado.*
39. Vidal, Philip III (2 × 1·35 m.). 1617(?). *Prado.*
40. Radiograph of part of portrait shown on plate 41.
41. Velázquez, Don Luís de Góngora (0·51 × 0·41 m.). 1622. *Boston, Museum of Fine Arts.*
42. Partial radiograph of portrait hidden under that shown on plate 48.
43. Velázquez, Philip IV (0·608 × 0·473 m.). 1623 or 1624.
    Dallas (U.S.A.), Meadows Museum.
44. Velázquez, Olivares (2·012 × 1·111 m.). 1624. *São Paolo, Museo de Arte.*
45. Velázquez, Philip IV (1·999 × 1·028 m.). 1624. *New York, Metropolitan Museum of Art.*
46. Radiograph of the portrait shown on plate 47.
47. Velázquez, Philip IV in armour (0·57 × 0·44 m.). 1626–8. *Prado.*
48. Velázquez, Philip IV (1·98 × 1·02 m.). 1626–8. *Prado.*
49. Velázquez, Philip IV. 1623. Radiograph of portrait hidden under that shown on plate 48.
50. Velázquez, The Infante Don Carlos (2·09 × 1·26 m.). About 1626. *Prado.*
51. Velázquez, Christ after the flagellation contemplated by the Christian soul (1·65 × 2·06 m.).
    1626–8. *London, National Gallery.*
52. Velázquez, Supper at Emmaus (1·23 × 1·326 m.). 1628–9. *New York, Metropolitan Museum.*
53. Velázquez, Christ on the Cross (2·48 × 1·69 m.). 1631–2. *Prado.*
54. Velázquez, St. Paul (0·98 × 0·78 m.). About 1619–20. *Barcelona, Museo de Arte.*
55. Velázquez, Democritus (0·98 × 0·8 m.). 1628–9. *Rouen, Musée des Beaux-Arts.*

56. Radiograph of painting shown on plate 57.
57. Velázquez, Bacchus (1·65 × 2·27 m.). 1628–9. *Prado.*
58. Velázquez, Joseph's bloody coat (2·23 × 2·5 m.). 1630. *El Escorial, Monasterio.*
59. Velázquez, The forge of Vulcan (2·23 × 2·9 m.). 1630. *Prado.*
60. Velázquez, Study for the head of Apollo (0·36 × 0·25 m.). 1630. *New York, art market.*
61. Radiograph of detail from painting shown on plate 59.
62. Detail of painting shown on plate 59.
63. Velázquez, Don Diego del Corral (2·05 × 1·15 m.). 1631–2. *Prado.*
64. Velázquez, Villa Medici (0·48 × 0·42 m.). 1630. *Prado.*
65. Velázquez, Villa Medici (0·44 × 0·38 m.). 1630. *Prado.*
66. Velázquez, Woman as a sibyl (0·62 × 0·5 m.). 1631–2. *Prado.*
67. Velázquez, The Infanta Doña María (0·58 × 0·44 m.). 1630. *Prado.*
68. Velázquez, Prince Baltasar Carlos with a dwarf (1·36 × 1·04 m.). 1631.
     Boston, Museum of Fine Arts.
69. Velázquez, Queen Isabel (2·03 × 1·14 m.). 1631–2. *Switzerland, private collection.*
70. Velázquez, Prince Baltasar Carlos (1·18 × 0·955 m.). 1632. *London, Wallace Collection.*
71. Velázquez, Doña Antonia de Ipeñarrieta (2·15 × 1·1 m.). 1631–2. *Prado.*
72. Velázquez, Young man (0·895 × 0·695 m.). About 1626. *Munich, Alte Pinakotheck.*
73. Velázquez, Don Juan Mateos (1·08 × 0·895 m.). About 1632.
     Dresden, Staatliche Gemäldesammlungen.
74. Velázquez and other painters, Queen Isabel (2·97 × 3·09 m.). 1628–35. *Prado.*
75. Velázquez, Philip IV (3·01 × 3·18 m.). 1634–5. *Prado.*
76. Velázquez, Prince Baltasar Carlos (2·10 × 1·75 m.). 1634–5. *Prado.*
77. Velázquez, Olivares (3·13 × 2·42 m.). 1634–5. *Prado.*
78. Titian, Charles V at the battle of Mühlberg (3·35 × 2·83 m.). 1548. *Prado.*
79. Rubens, Philip II (3·14 × 2·28 m.). 1628. *Prado.*
80. Detail of painting shown on plate 75.
81. Detail of painting shown on plate 77.
82. Detail of painting shown on plate 75.
83. Velázquez, Head of a stag (0·66 × 0·52 m.). About 1628–9. *Madrid, Vizconde de Baiguer.*
84. Velázquez, A white horse (3·1 × 2·45 m.). About 1634–5. *Madrid, Palacio Real.*
85. Mazo, Olivares (1·25 × 1·015 m.). Mid or late 1630's.
     New York, Metropolitan Museum of Art.
86. Radiograph of painting shown on plate 87.
87. Velázquez, The surrender of Breda (3·07 × 3·70 m.). 1634–5. *Prado.*
88. Detail of painting shown on plate 87.
89. Velázquez, Study of Spínola (26·2 × 16·8 cm.). 1634–5. *Madrid, Biblioteca Nacional.*
90. Maino, The Recapture of Bahia (3·09 × 3·81 m.). 1635. *Prado.*
91. Velázquez, Figure study (26·2 × 16·8 cm.). 1634–5. *Madrid, Biblioteca Nacional.*
92. Rubens, Spínola (1·175 × 0·855 m.). 1627–8. *St. Louis (U.S.A.), City Art Museum.*
93. Detail of painting shown on plate 87.

94. Zurbarán, The surrender of Seville (1·6 × 2·08 m.). 1634. *London, Duke of Westminster.*

95. Jusepe Leonardo, The surrender of Jülich (3·07 × 3·81 m.). 1635. *Prado.*

96. Velázquez, The Infante Don Fernando (1·91 × 1·09 m.). 1632–3. *Prado.*

97. Velázquez, Prince Baltasar Carlos (1·90 × 1·03 m.). 1635–6. *Prado.*

98. Velázquez, Philip IV (1·89 × 1·25 m.). 1632–3. *Prado.*

99. Velázquez's workshop, copy at early stage of portrait shown on plate 98 (2 × 1·2 m.). 1631–2. *Castres, Musée Goya.*

100. Velázquez, Menippus (1·79 × 0·94 m.). 1639–42. *Prado.*

101. Velázquez, Aesop (1·79 × 0·94 m.). 1639–42. *Prado.*

102. Velázquez, Mars (1·82 × 0·97 m.). 1639–42. *Prado.*

103. Velázquez and unknown painter, Don Cristobal de Castañeda (1·98 × 1·21 m.). 1637–40. *Prado.*

104. Velázquez, Calabazas (1·755 × 1·067 m.). 1628–9. *Cleveland Museum of Art, Leonard C. Hanna Jr. Bequest.*

105. Velázquez, Don Juan de Austria (2·1 × 1·23 m.). 1632–3. *Prado.*

106. Velázquez, Calabazas (1·06 × 0.83 m.). 1637–9. *Prado.*

107. Velázquez, Sebastián de Morra (1·07 × 0·82 m.). Mid 1640's. *Prado.*

108. Velázquez, Don Diego de Acedo (1·07 × 0·84 m.). 1644. *Prado.*

109. Velázquez, Philip IV in army dress (1·335 × 0·985 m.). 1644. *New York, Frick Collection.*

110. Velázquez, Francisco Lezcano (1·07 × 0·83 m.). 1643–5. *Prado.*

111. Velázquez's workshop, Philip IV (2·31 × 1·31 m.). 1650's. *Prado.*

112. Velázquez, A bearded man (0·76 × 0·648 m.). Late 1630's. *London, Wellington Museum.*

113. Velázquez, Young lady (0·712 × 0·47 m.). Mid 1630's. *Chatsworth, Duke of Devonshire.*

114. Velázquez, Lady with a fan (0·928 × 0·685 m.). Mid 1630's. *London, Wallace Collection.*

115. Radiograph of painting shown on plate 108.

116. Partial radiograph of painting shown on plate 149.

117. Velázquez, A knight of Santiago (0·665 × 0·56 m.). Late 1640's. *Dresden, Staatliche Gemäldesammlungen.*

118. Velázquez, Francesco II d'Este (0·68 × 0·51 m.). 1638. *Modena, Pinacoteca.*

119. Unknown painter and Velázquez, Philip IV, equestrian (3·39 × 2·67 m.). About 1645. *Uffizi.*

120. Detail of painting shown on plate 119.

121. Velázquez, Cardinal Borja (18·6 × 11·7 cm.). 1643–5. *Madrid, Real Academia de San Fernando.*

122. Velázquez, Hand of an ecclesiastic (0·25 × 0·27 m.). 1630's. *Madrid, Palacio Real.*

123. Velázquez, St. Anthony and St. Paul (2·60 × 1·92 m.). Mid or late 1630's. *Prado.*

124. Velázquez, The Coronation of the Virgin (1·79 × 1·35 m.). About 1644. *Prado.*

125. Detail of painting shown on plate 127.

126. Titian, The rape of Europa (1·76 × 2·06 m.). 1562. *Boston, Isabella Stewart Gardner Museum.*

127. Velázquez, The fable of Arachne (with later additions) (2·2 × 2·90 m.). 1644–8. *Prado*.
128. The same painting without later additions (approximately 1·67 × 2·5 m.).
129. Partial radiograph of painting shown on plate 127.
130. Velázquez, Venus at her mirror (1·225 × 1·77 m.). 1644–8. *London, National Gallery*.
131. Detail of painting shown on plate 127.
132. Velázquez, Woman as a sibyl (0·64 × 0·58 m.). 1644–8. *New York, private collection*.
133. Velázquez, The Needlewoman (0·74 × 0·6 m.). Mid 1630's–early 1640's.
    Washington, D.C., National Gallery.
134. Detail of painting shown on plate 130.
135. Detail of painting shown on plate 124.
136. Velázquez, Self-portrait (0·455 × 0·38 m.). Late 1640's or early 1650's.
    Valencia, Museo Provincial.
137. Velázquez, A girl (0·515 × 0·41 m.). Early 1640's.
    New York, The Hispanic Society of America.
138. Velázquez, Cardinal Astalli (0·61 × 0·485 m.). 1650–1.
    New York, The Hispanic Society of America.
139. Velázquez, Monsignor Camillo Massimi (0·736 × 0·585 m.). 1650.
    Wimborne, Bankes Collection.
140. Velázquez, Juan de Pareja (0·82 × 0·698 m.). 1649–50. *Longford Castle, Earl of Radnor.*
141. Velázquez, So-called Barber to the Pope (0·483 × 0·444 m.). 1650.
    New York, private collection.
142. Neri, Innocent X with a prelate (2·13 × 1·67 m.). *El Escorial, Monasterio.*
143. Velázquez and assistant, Innocent X (0·78 × 0·68 m.). 1650.
    London, Wellington Museum.
144. Velázquez, Innocent X (1·4 × 1·2 m.). 1650. *Rome, Galleria Doria-Pamphili.*
145. Velázquez, The Infanta María Teresa (0·48 × 0·37 m.). About 1648.
    New York, Robert Lehman.
146. Velázquez, The Infanta María Teresa (0·444 × 0·4 m.). 1651.
    New York, Metropolitan Museum, Bache Collection.
147. Velázquez, The Infanta María Teresa (1·27 × 0·99 m.). 1652–3.
    Vienna, Kunsthistorisches Museum.
148. Velázquez, The Infanta Margarita (1·05 × 0·88 m.). About 1656.
    Vienna, Kunsthistorisches Museum.
149. Velázquez, Queen Mariana (2·35 × 1·32 m.). 1652–3. *Prado*.
150. Velázquez, The Infanta Margarita (1·28 × 0·995 m.). 1653.
    Vienna, Kunsthistorisches Museum.
151. Velázquez, Philip IV (0·69 × 0·56 m.). 1652–3. *Prado*.
152. Velázquez, The Royal Family (3·18 × 2·76 m.). 1656. *Prado*.
153. Pedro de Villafranca, Philip IV (28·1 × 17·7 cm.). 1655.
    From *Regla, y establecimientos, de la Orden y Cavalleria del glorioso Apostol Santiago*, Madrid, 1655.

154. Pedro de Villafranca, Philip IV (26 × 17·1 cm.). 1657.
   From Francisco de los Santos, *Descripción breve del monasterio de S. Lorenzo el Real del Escorial*, Madrid, 1657.
155. Partial radiograph of painting shown on plate 152.
156. Detail of painting shown on plate 152.
157. Detail of painting shown on plate 152.
158. Velázquez, Mercury and Argus (1·28 × 2·5 m.; the height was 0·835 m. originally). About 1659. *Prado.*
159. Velázquez, The Infanta Margarita (1·27 × 1·07 m.). 1659.
   Vienna, Kunsthistorisches Museum.
160. Velázquez and assistant, Prince Baltasar Carlos (1·285 × 0·995 m.). About 1639.
   Vienna, Kunsthistorisches Museum.
161. Velázquez and assistant, Queen Isabel (1·285 × 0·99 m.). 1632.
   Vienna, Kunsthistorisches Museum.
162. Mazo, Philip IV (0·641 × 0·537 m.). Mid-1650's. *London, National Gallery.*
163. Detail from painting shown on plate 169.
164. Roman bust (height 0·62 m.). Mid-II century. *Prado.*
165. Mazo, Sketch for boy in The family of the artist (0·518 × 0·263 m.). 1660–1.
   Dulwich College Picture Gallery.
166. Velázquez's assistant, Queen Isabel (2·56 × 1·45 m.). 1639*. *Hampton Court.*
167. Neri, Cristoforo Segni (1·14 × 0·92 m.). *Swiss private collection.*
168. Mazo, View of Saragossa (1·81 × 3·33 m.). 1647. *Prado.*
169. Mazo, The family of the artist (1·50 × 1·72 m.). About 1660–1.
   Vienna, Kunsthistorisches Museum.
170. Mazo, The Infanta Margarita (2·05 × 1·47 m.). About 1664–5. *Prado.*
171. Mazo, Queen Mariana (1·97 × 1·46 m.). 1666. *London, National Gallery.*
172. Charles Lebrun (tapestry after original by him, cartoon by Mathieu père). Meeting of Philip IV and Louis XIV on the Isle of Pheasants (5·15 × 6·97 m.).
   Versailles Museum.
173. Mazo, The stag hunt at Aranjuez (2·49 × 1·87 m.). *Prado.*
174. Jusepe Leonardo, The taking of Brisach (3·04 × 3·6 m.). About 1635. *Prado.*

* Not 1638, as formerly believed. See Enriqueta Harris, 'Velazquez and Charles I' in *Journal of the Warburg and Courtauld Institutes*, vol. XXX, London, 1967 (published 1968), pp. 414–20.

Plate 1. Velázquez, Musical trio. About 1617–18. *West Berlin, Staatliche Museen*

Plate 2. Beuckelaer, Christ in the house of Martha and Mary. 1565.
Brussels, Musées Royaux

Plate 3. Velázquez, Head of a girl. About 1617–18. *Madrid, private collection*

Plate 4. Velázquez, Study of a head. About 1618–19. *Hermitage*

Plate 5. Velázquez, Christ in the house of Martha and Mary. 1618. *London, National Gallery*

Plate 6. Pacheco, St. Sebastian nursed by
St. Irene. 1616. *Formerly, Alcalá de Guadaira,
church of St. Sebastian*

Plate 8. Eugenio Caxés, The fall of the
angels. 1605. *Copenhagen, Statens Museum
for Kunst*

Plate 7. Jan van Eyck, Jan Arnolfini and
his wife. 1434. *London, National Gallery*

Plate 9. Sánchez Cotán, Still-life. 1602.
Madrid, Duke of Hernani

Plate 10. Vincencio Carducho, Colossal head. *Madrid, Academia de San Fernando*

Plate 11. Vincencio Carducho, St. Bruno declining the archbishop's mitre. 1632. *Prado*

Plate 12. Vincencio Carducho, St. Bruno declining the archbishop's mitre (detail). 1632. *Prado*

Plate 13. Velázquez, Three men at table. About 1618. *Hermitage*

Plate 14. Velázquez, Old woman frying eggs. 1618. *Edinburgh, National Gallery*

Plate 15. Caravaggio, Supper at Emmaus. About 1598–1600. *London, National Gallery*

Plate 16. Lanchares, Adoration of the
shepherds. 1612. *Madrid, art market*

Plate 17. B. González,
St. John the Baptist. 1621.
Budapest, Museum of Fine Arts

Plate 18. Velázquez, A girl and two men at table. About 1618–19
Budapest, Hungarian Museum

Plate 19. Velázquez's follower, Three men at table.
Andover, Hants, Lord Moyne

Plate 20. Velázquez, Christ at Emmaus. About 1620–1. *Blessington (Ireland), Beit Collection*

Plate 21. Velázquez, The servant. About 1620–1. *Chicago, Art Institute*

Plate 22. Velázquez, The waterseller. About 1619–20. *London, Wellington Museum*

Plate 23. Velázquez, A man with a goatee.
About 1620. *Prado*

Plate 24. Velázquez, A young man.
About 1618–19. *Prado*

Plate 25. Velázquez, A young girl. About 1622.
Madrid, Biblioteca Nacional

Plate 26. Velázquez, A young girl.
About 1622. *Madrid, Biblioteca Nacional*

Plate 27. Velázquez, The Immaculate Conception. About 1619.
London, Frere Collection (on loan at the National Gallery)

Plate 28. Velázquez, St. John writing the Apocalypse. About 1619. *London, National Gallery*

Plate 29 (in its original state).
Plate 30 (in its present altered condition).
Velázquez, Doña Jerónima de la Fuente, 1620. *Prado*

Plate 32. Velázquez, Cristóbal Suárez de Ribera.
About 1618–20. *Seville, San Hermenegildo*

Plate 31. Velázquez, Doña Jerónima de la Fuente. 1620.
Madrid, Fernández Araoz Collection

Plate 33. Velázquez, Two young men at table. 1620–1.
London, Wellington Museum

Plate 34. Juan van der Hamen, Don Francisco
de la Cueva. 1625. *Madrid, Academia de San
Fernando*

Plate 35. Juan van der Hamen, Still-life. 1622. *Prado*

Plate 36. Rubens, Philip IV.
1628–9. *Hermitage*

Plate 37. Maino, Philip IV.
1623–4. *New York,
Metropolitan Museum*

Plate 38. Villandrando,
Philip IV. 1619–20. *Prado*

Plate 39. Vidal, Philip III.
1617 (?) *Prado*

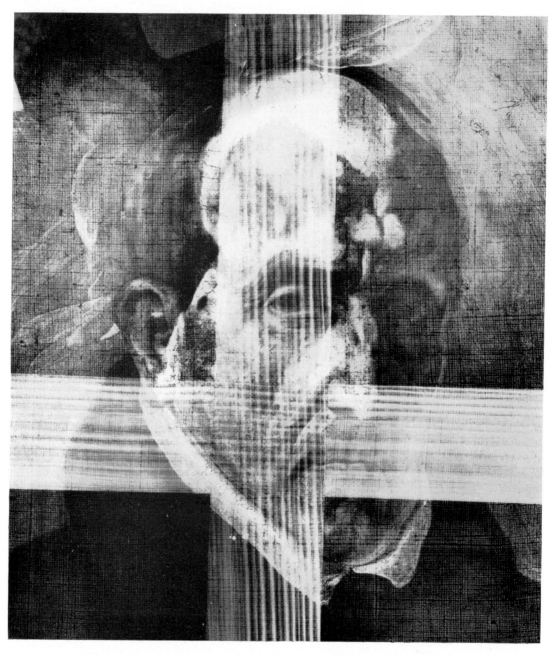

Plate 40. Partial radiograph of Velázquez's portrait of Góngora
(reproduced on opposite page), showing laurel wreath

Plate 41. Velázquez, Don Luís de Góngora, 1622. *Boston, Museum of Fine Arts*

Plate 42. Velázquez, Philip IV. 1623. *Prado*. Partial radiograph of the portrait hidden under that reproduced on plate 48

Plate 43. Velázquez, Philip IV. 1623 or 1624. *Dallas (U.S.A.), Meadows Museum*

Plate 44. Velázquez, Olivares. 1624. *São Paolo, Museo de Arte*

Plate 45. Velázquez, Philip IV. 1624.
New York, Metropolitan Museum of Art

Plate 46. Velázquez, Philip IV in armour. About 1625. *Prado.*
Radiograph of the portrait hidden under that reproduced on plate 47

Plate 47. Velázquez, Philip IV in armour. 1626–8. *Prado*

Plate 48. Velázquez, Philip IV. 1626–8. *Prado*

Plate 49. Velázquez, Philip IV. 1623. *Prado*. Radiograph of portrait hidden under that reproduced on plate 48

Plate 50. Velázquez, The Infante Don Carlos. About 1626. *Prado*

Plate 51. Velázquez, Christ after the flagellation contemplated by the Christian soul.
1626–8. *London, National Gallery*

Plate 53. Velázquez, Christ on the Cross. 1631–2. *Prado*

Plate 52. Velázquez, Supper at Emmaus. 1628–9.
New York, Metropolitan Museum

Plate 55. Velázquez, Democritus. 1628–9.
Rouen, Musée des Beaux-Arts

Plate 54. Velázquez, St. Paul. About 1619–20.
Barcelona, Museo de Arte

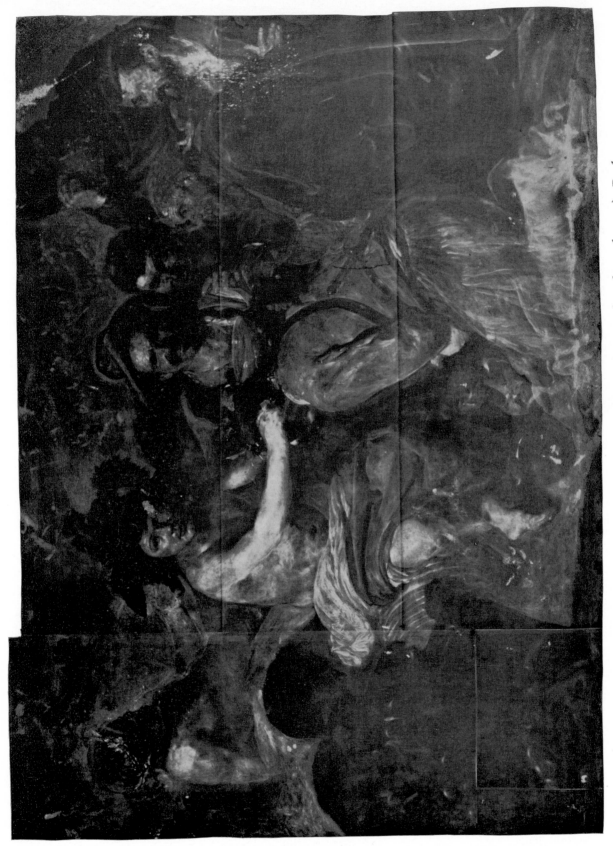

Plate 56. Velázquez, Bacchus (radiograph of painting reproduced on plate 57). *Prado*

Plate 57. Velázquez, Bacchus. 1628–9. *Prado*

Plate 58. Velázquez, Joseph's bloody coat. 1630. *El Escorial, Monasterio*

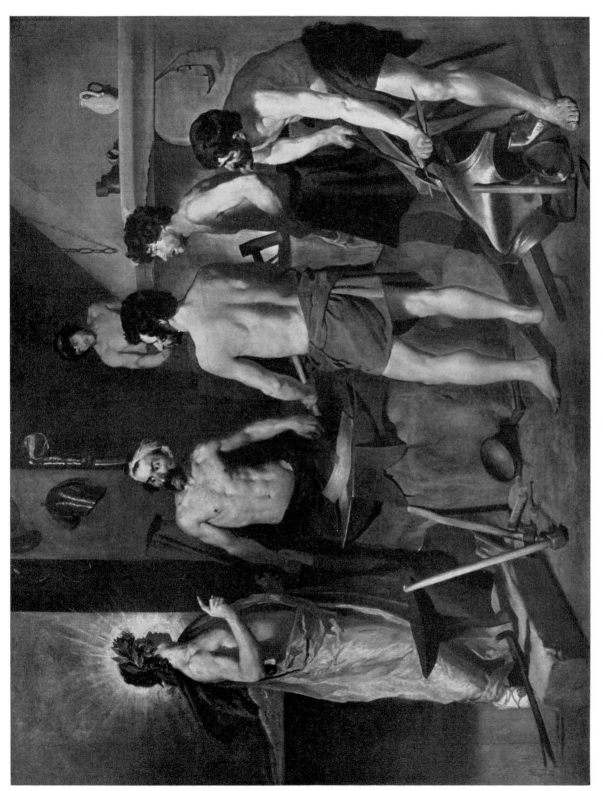

Plate 59. Velázquez, The forge of Vulcan. 1630. *Prado*

Plate 60. Velázquez, Study for the head of Apollo. 1630. *New York, art market*

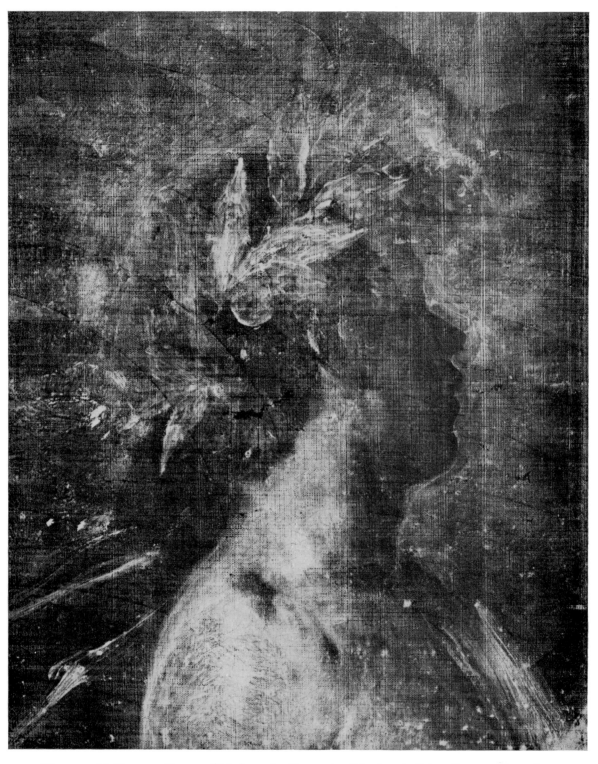

Plate 61. Velázquez, Forge of Vulcan (radiograph of the head of Apollo reproduced on plate 62). 1630. *Prado*

Plate 62. Velázquez, Forge of Vulcan (detail). 1630. *Prado*

Plate 63. Velázquez, Don Diego del Corral. 1631–2. *Prado*

Plate 65. Velázquez, Villa Medici. 1630. *Prado*

Plate 64. Velázquez, Villa Medici. 1630. *Prado*

Plate 67. Velázquez, The Infanta Doña María. 1630. *Prado*

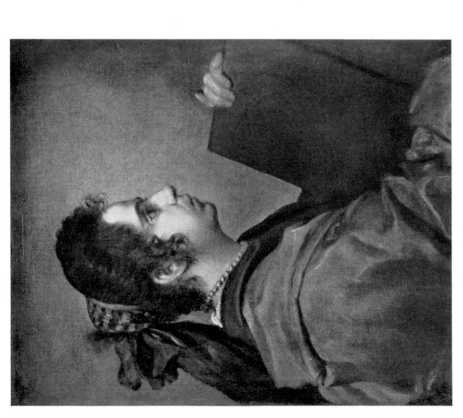

Plate 66. Velázquez, Woman as a sibyl. 1631–2. *Prado*

Plate 68. Velázquez, Prince Baltasar Carlos with a dwarf. 1631.
Boston, Museum of Fine Arts

Plate 69. Velázquez, Queen Isabel. 1631–2. *Switzerland, private collection*

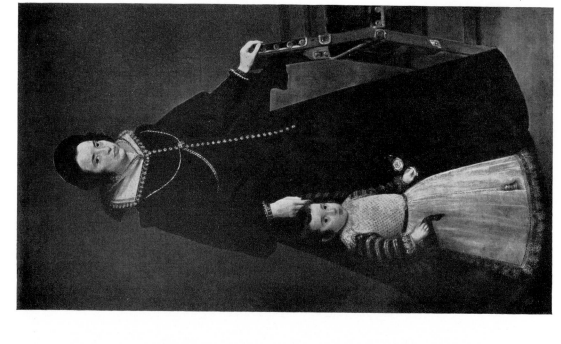

Plate 71. Velázquez, Doña Antonia de
Ipeñarrieta. 1631–2. *Prado*

Plate 70. Velázquez, Prince Baltasar Carlos. 1632.
London, Wallace Collection

Plate 73. Velázquez, Don Juan Mateos. About 1632.
Dresden, Staatliche Gemäldesammlung

Plate 72. Velázquez, Young man. About 1626.
Munich, Alte Pinakothek

Plate 74. Velázquez and other painters, Queen Isabel. 1628–35. *Prado*

Plate 75. Velázquez, Philip IV. 1634–5. *Prado*

Plate 76. Velázquez, Prince Baltasar Carlos. 1634–5. *Prado*

Plate 77. Velázquez, Olivares. 1634–5. *Prado*

Plate 79. Rubens, Philip II. 1628. *Prado*

Plate 78. Titian, Charles V at the battle of Mühlberg. 1548. *Prado*

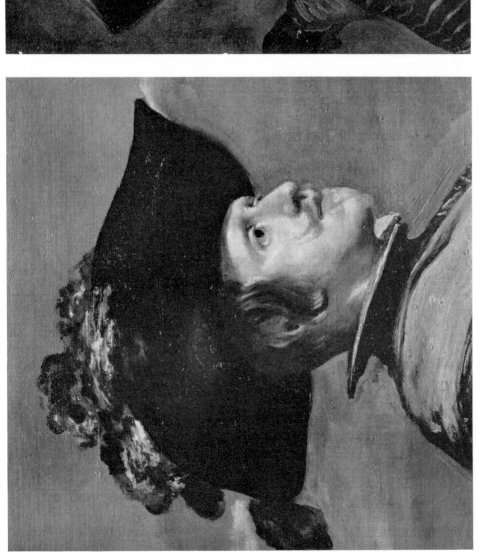

Plate 80. Velázquez, Philip IV (detail). 1634–5. *Prado*

Plate 81. Velázquez, Olivares (detail). 1634–5. *Prado*

Plate 83. Velázquez, Head of a stag. About 1628–9.
Madrid, Vizconde de Baiguer

Plate 82. Velázquez, Philip IV, equestrian (detail).
1634–5. *Prado*

Plate 85. Mazo, Olivares. Mid- or late 1630's.
New York, Metropolitan Museum of Art

Plate 84. Velázquez, A white horse. About 1634-5.
Madrid, Palacio Real

Plate 86. Velázquez, The surrender of Breda. 1635 (radiograph). *Prado*

Plate 87. Velázquez, The surrender of Breda. 1634–5. *Prado*

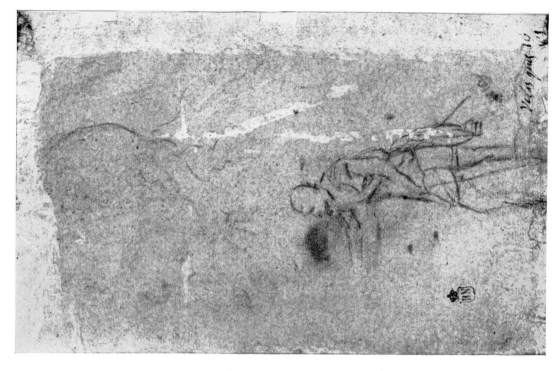

Plate 89. Velázquez, Study of Spínola. 1634–5.
Madrid, Biblioteca Nacional

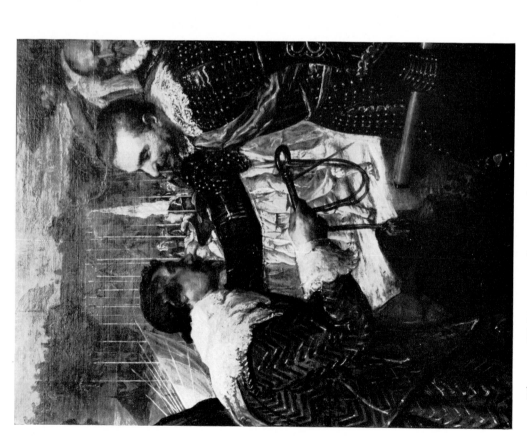

Plate 88. Velázquez, The surrender of Breda (detail).
1634–5. *Prado*

Plate 90. Maino, The Recapture of Bahia. 1635. *Prado*

Plate 92. Rubens, Spínola. 1627–8.
St. Louis (U.S.A.), City Art Museum

Plate 91. Velázquez, Figure study. 1634–5.
Madrid, Biblioteca Nacional

Plate 93. Velázquez, The surrender of Breda (detail). 1634–5. *Prado*

Plate 94. Zurbarán, The surrender of Seville. 1634.
London, Duke of Westminster

Plate 95. Jusepe Leonardo, The surrender of Jülich. 1635. *Prado*

Plate 97. Velázquez, Prince Baltasar Carlos.
1635–6. *Prado*

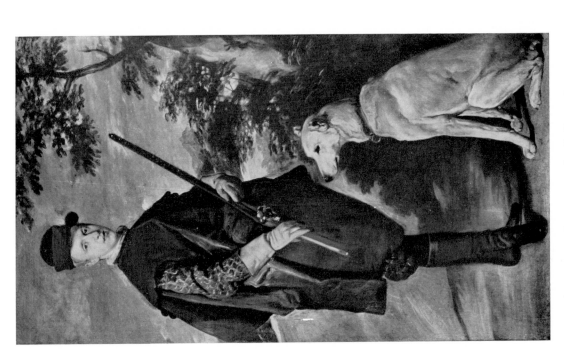

Plate 96. Velázquez, The Infante Don
Fernando. 1632–3. *Prado*

Plate 99. Velázquez's workshop copy after an early
stage of the Master's portrait of Philip IV. 1631–2.
Castres, Musée Goya

Plate 98. Velázquez, Philip IV. 1632–3. *Prado*

Plate 101. Velázquez, Aesop. 1639–42.
Prado

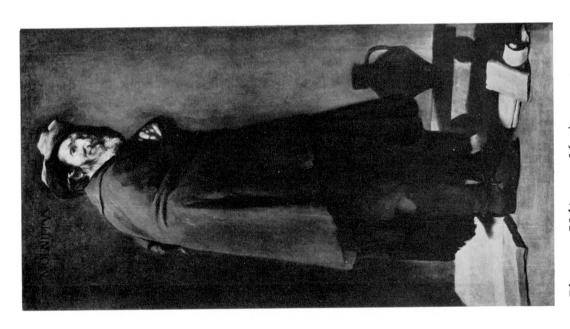

Plate 100. Velázquez, Menippus. 1639–42.
Prado

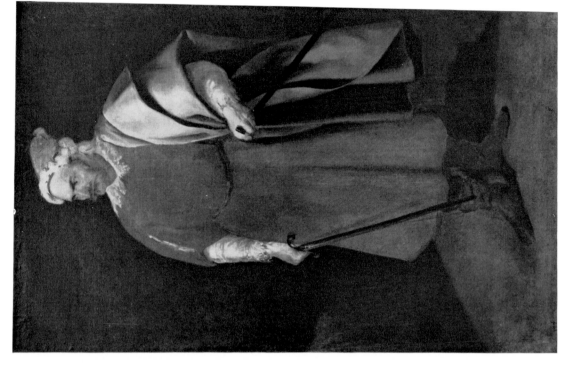

Plate 103. Velázquez and unknown painter,
Don Cristobal de Castañeda (unfinished).
1637–40. *Prado*

Plate 102. Velázquez, Mars. 1639–42. *Prado*

Plate 104. Velázquez, Calabazas. 1628–9.
Cleveland, The Cleveland Museum of Art, Leonard C. Hanna Jr. Bequest

Plate 105. Velázquez, Don Juan de Austria. 1632–3. *Prado*

Plate 106. Velázquez, Calabazas. 1637–9. *Prado*

Plate 107. Velázquez, Sebastián de Morra. Mid-1640's. *Prado*

Plate 108. Velázquez, Don Diego de Acedo. 1644. *Prado*

Plate 109. Velázquez, Philip IV in army dress. 1644. *New York, Frick Collection*

Plate 110. Velázquez, Francisco Lezcano. 1643–5. *Prado*

Plate 112. Velázquez, A bearded man. Late 1630's.
London, Wellington Museum

Plate 111. Velázquez's workshop, Philip IV. 1650's.
Prado

Plate 113. Velázquez, Young lady. Mid-1630's.
Chatsworth, Duke of Devonshire

Plate 114. Velázquez, Lady with a fan. Mid-1630's. *London, Wallace Collection*

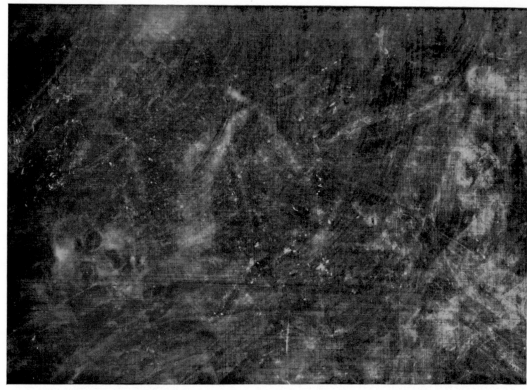

Plate 116. Velázquez, Queen Mariana. 1652–3 (partial radiograph of painting reproduced on plate 149). *Prado*

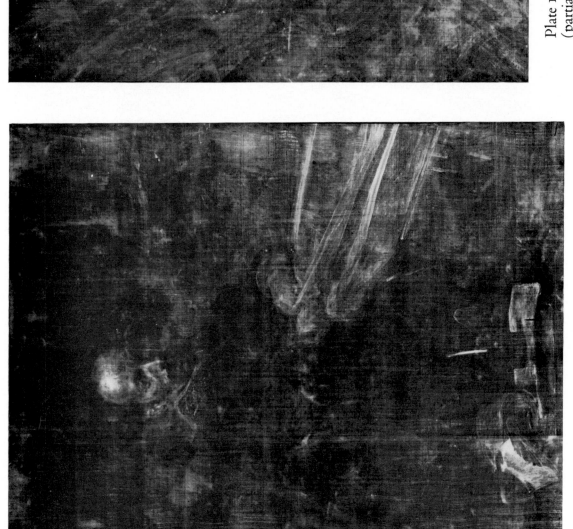

Plate 115. Velázquez, Don Diego de Acedo. 1644 (radiograph of painting reproduced on plate 108). *Prado*

Plate 118. Velázquez, Francesco II d'Este. 1638.
Modena, Pinacoteca

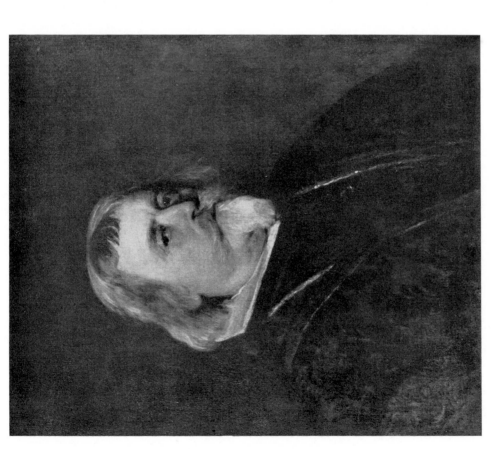

Plate 117. Velázquez, A knight of Santiago. Late 1640's.
Dresden, Staatliche Gemäldesammlung

Plate 119. Unknown painter
(and Velázquez), Philip IV, equestrian
(after a Rubens composition of 1628–9).
About 1645. *Uffizi*

Plate 120. Velázquez, Head of Philip IV in
equestrian portrait reproduced on plate 119.
About 1645. *Uffizi*

Plate 121. Velázquez, Cardinal
Borja. 1643–5.
*Madrid, Real Academia de San
Fernando*

Plate 122. Velázquez, Hand of an ecclesiastic
(fragment of a portrait). 1630's.
Madrid, Palacio Real

Plate 123. Velázquez, St. Anthony and St. Paul. Mid- or late 1630's. *Prado*

Plate 124. Velázquez, The Coronation of the Virgin. About 1644. *Prado*

Plate 125. Velázquez, The fable of Arachne (detail). 1644–8. *Prado*

Plate 126. Titian, The rape of Europa. 1562. *Boston, Gardner Museum*

Plate 127. Velázquez, The fable of Arachne (with later additions). 1644–8. *Prado*

Plate 128. Velázquez, The fable of Arachne. 1644–8. *Prado*
(The actual painting as it would approximately look without the later additions)

Plate 129. Velázquez, The fable of Arachne. 1644–8 (radiograph, leaving out the later additions). *Prado*

Plate 130. Velázquez, Venus at her mirror (after the 1965 restoration). 1644–8. *London, National Gallery*

Plate 131. Velázquez, The fable of Arachne (detail). 1644–8. *Prado*

Plate 132. Velázquez, Woman as a sibyl. 1644–8. *New York, private collection*

Plate 133. Velázquez, The Needlewoman (unfinished). Mid-1630's–early 1640's.
Washington, D.C., National Gallery

Plate 135. Velázquez, The Coronation of the Virgin (detail). About 1644. *Prado*

Plate 134. Velázquez, Venus at her mirror (detail, before the 1965 restoration). 1644–8. *London, National Gallery*

Plate 137. Velázquez, A girl. Early 1640's.
New York, The Hispanic Society of America

Plate 136. Velázquez, Self-portrait.
Late 1640's or early 1650's. *Valencia, Museo Provincial*

Plate 139. Velázquez, Monsignor Camillo Massimi. 1650.
Wimborne, Bankes Collection

Plate 138. Velázquez, Cardinal Astalli. 1650–1. *New York,*
The Hispanic Society of America

Plate 140. Velázquez, Juan de Pareja. 1649–50. *Longford Castle, Earl of Radnor*

Plate 141. Velázquez, So-called Barber to the Pope. 1650. *New York, private collection*

Plate 143. Velázquez and assistant, Innocent X. 1650.
London, Wellington Museum

Plate 142. Neri, Innocent X with a prelate.
El Escorial, Monasterio

Plate 144. Velázquez, Innocent X. 1650. *Rome, Galleria Doria-Pamphili*

Plate 146. Velázquez, The Infanta María Teresa (with strips added on all four sides). 1651. *New York, Metropolitan Museum, Bache Collection*

Plate 145. Velázquez, The Infanta María Teresa. About 1648. *New York, Robert Lehman*

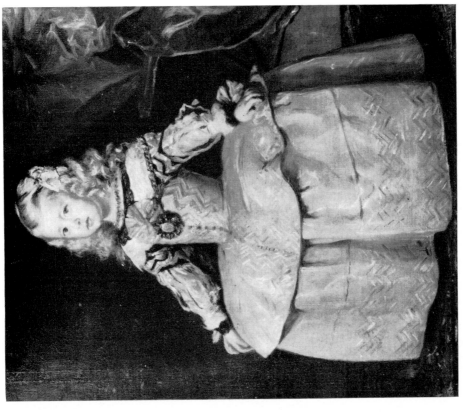

Plate 148. Velázquez, the Infanta Margarita. About 1656.
Vienna, Kunsthistorisches Museum

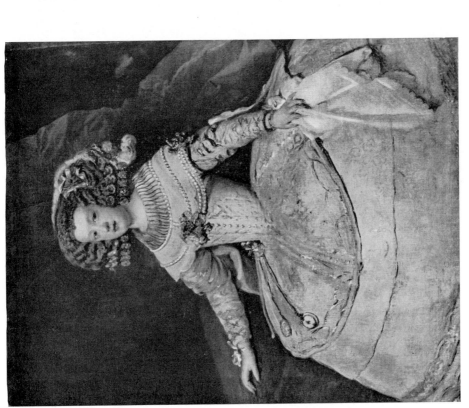

Plate 147. Velázquez, The Infanta María Teresa.
1652–3. *Vienna, Kunsthistorisches Museum*

Plate 149. Velázquez, Queen Mariana. 1652–3. *Prado*

Plate 150. Velázquez, The Infanta Margarita. 1653. *Vienna, Kunsthistorisches Museum*

Plate 151. Velázquez, Philip IV. 1652–3. *Prado*

Plate 152. Velázquez, The Royal Family. 1656. *Prado*

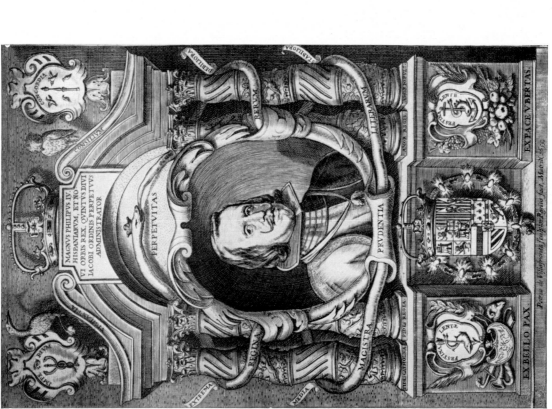

Plate 154. Villafranca, Philip IV . 1657

Plate 153. Villafranca, Philip IV . 1655

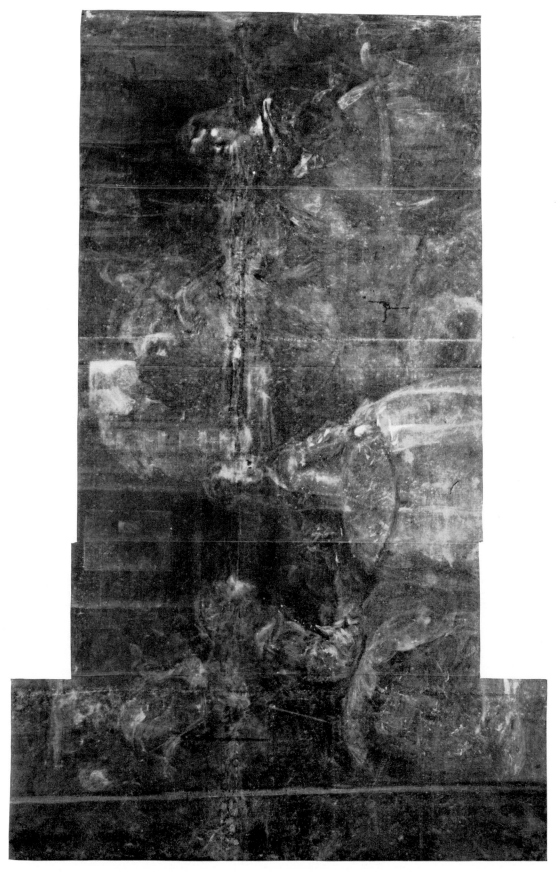

Plate 155. Velázquez, The Royal Family. 1656 (radiograph of the middle section). *Prado*

Plates 156 and 157. Details of the mirror and of Velázquez's self-portrait in The royal family. 1656. *Prado*

Plate 158. Velázquez, Mercury and Argus (with strips, amounting to about one-third of its present height, added at the top and bottom in the eighteenth century). About 1659. *Prado*

Plate 159. Velázquez, The Infanta Margarita. 1659. *Vienna. Kunsthistorisches Museum*

Plate 161. Velázquez and assistant, Queen Isabel. 1632.
Vienna, Kunsthistorisches Museum

Plate 160. Velázquez and assistant, Prince Baltasar Carlos.
About 1639. *Vienna, Kunsthistorisches Museum*

Plate 163. Mazo, Portrait of Philip IV in *The family of the artist*. About 1660–1. *Vienna, Kunsthistorisches Museum*. (The actual size of this portrait is slightly more than one-fifth of the life-size bust reproduced on Plate 162)

Plate 162. Mazo, Philip IV. Mid-1650's. *London, National Gallery*

Plate 164. Roman bust (Domitia Lucilla?).
Mid-II century. *Prado*

Plate 165. Mazo, Sketch for boy in *The
family of the artist*. 1660–1. *Dulwich College
Picture Gallery*

Plate 166. Velázquez's assistant,
Queen Isabel. 1639. *Hampton Court*

Plate 167. Neri, Cristoforo Segni.
Swiss private collection

Plate 168. Mazo, View of Saragossa. 1647. *Prado*

Plate 169. Mazo, The family of the artist. About 1660–1. *Vienna, Kunsthistorisches Museum*

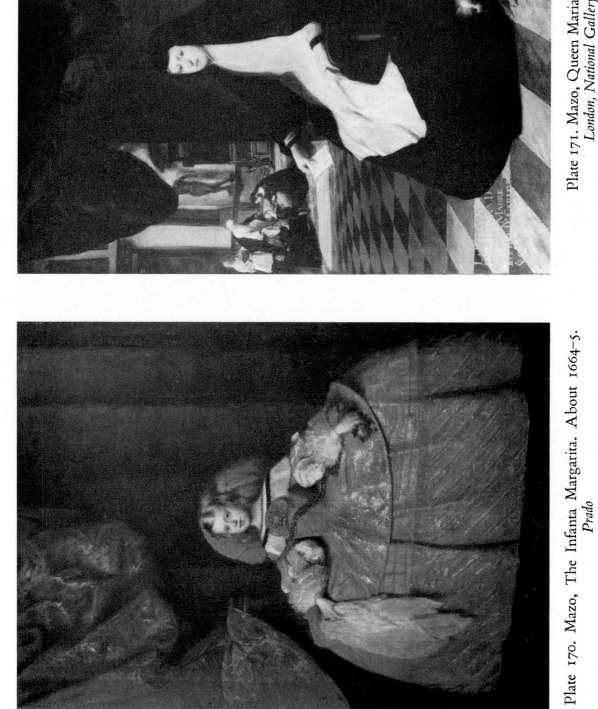

Plate 171. Mazo, Queen Mariana. 1666.
London, National Gallery

Plate 170. Mazo, The Infanta Margarita. About 1664–5.
Prado

Plate 172. Charles Lebrun (tapestry after original by him, cartoon by Mathieu père). Meeting of Philip IV and Louis XIV on the Isle of Pheasants. *Versailles Museum*

Plate 173. Mazo, The stag hunt at Aranjuez. *Prado*

Plate 174. Jusepe Leonardo, The taking of Brisach. About 1635.
Prado